Praise for *How to Fail at Life: Lessons for the Next Generation*

"Wow. I guess I gave you too much encouragement in high school. I regret that now."

> —Mark's high school English teacher

"Great draft! This book has nothing but potential."

> —Paul C. (a good friend of Mark)

"Amazing. We can't believe it. Are you sure you want to use your real name?"

> —Erik and Pat Aspelin (Mark's parents)

"… I laughed, I cried. As for your book, I haven't had a chance to read it yet."

> —A friend who saw Oprah Winfrey at the airport once

"I give it 5 stars (out of 10)!"

> —Erik Aspelin (Mark's brother)

HOW TO
FAIL
AT LIFE

LESSONS FOR THE NEXT GENERATION

GYPSY ROAD
PUBLISHING

MARK ASPELIN

For my son:

I've done some pretty stupid things in my life. Some of my blunders were so dumb and embarrassing that I couldn't even bring myself to include them in this book!

In these pages, I've shared some ideas that I recommend you try for yourself and others that I hope you'll avoid like the plague. Learn from the many people who've been there, done that, and got the t-shirt.

I've had some pretty amazing adventures in far-flung corners of the world. But, without a doubt, the brightest star in a vast array of great moments in my life is you. I'm very lucky and proud to have you as my son.

Carpe diem. Seize the day, Erik. Fail smart, keep it simple, have fun, smile, laugh, and go big. Okay, I've run out of pithy, motivational phrases, but you know what to do. Get out there and make your life extraordinary.

With love,

Dad

Table of Contents

Acknowledgments

Given that I told virtually no one I was writing a book, the number of people whom I can thank for helping me draft it is pretty small. To make matters worse, the person who provided the most input prefers to remain anonymous. You know who you are. *Thank you!*

However, when it comes to editing and publishing the book, I received plenty of much-needed help. Joanne Shwed of Backspace Ink provided outstanding design and editing assistance, and the CreateSpace team provided feedback on editing, marketing, and publishing. Thanks to the efforts of Joanne and CreateSpace, the final product is infinitely more polished and professional.

As for inspiration for the book's content, the list of people to thank is much too long to call out here. I do want to give special thanks to Darren Hardy, the late Jim Rohn, Rich Roll, Chef Jeff Henderson, Dave Ramsey, Brian C. Taylor, Rev. Michael J. Himes, and Dr. Wayne Dyer for the knowledge and stories they have shared to inspire and motivate me—and countless others—to make significant, positive changes in life. Of course, there's also a long list of legendary heavyweights, such as Mahatma Gandhi, Lao-Tzu, Dr. Martin Luther King, Jr., Thích Nhất Hạnh, Nelson Mandela, and the Dalai Lama, who were instrumental in helping me solidify my core beliefs and philosophy of life.

I would also like to thank my family and my small circle of close friends who have provided me with many fun and rewarding experiences over the years. I'm so lucky and grateful to have you in my life.

To the many new friends and acquaintances whom I've met during my travels across the globe: Meeting you has bolstered my faith that we're all connected on this amazing planet.

Finally, I would like to thank *you* for taking time out of your busy schedule to read this book! I hope you find it entertaining and thought-provoking, and I also hope you find a few ideas that you'll test drive in your own journey through life.

Introduction

"When I die, if the word 'thong' appears in the first or second sentence of my obituary, I've screwed up."
Albert Brooks

The late, great, personal development guru Jim Rohn lamented, "It's too bad failures don't give seminars. Wouldn't that be valuable? If you meet a guy who has messed up his life for forty years, you've just got to say, 'John, if I bring my journal and promise to take good notes, would you spend a day with me?'"

Well, Jim, your wish has come true. I'm here to spend time with you and share some of the best methods I've encountered for how to fail at life. I've done a fine job at implementing many of these practices over the course of my 46 years with impressively dismal results: alcoholism, divorce, debt, career uncertainty, and a lack of clarity about my purpose and direction in life ... some good stuff that I'll think you'll find entertaining and worth your time.

For the areas of life that I've managed to handle pretty well over the years, I've called in some outside experts to lend some "failure cred" to those sections.

In these pages, you'll have the opportunity to gawk at the car accidents of life that many of us have left in our wake. I'll also show you how some of these poor souls managed to emerge from the wreckage and chart a whole new course for their lives, just in case you happen to know someone in a similar situation.

I've tried to avoid a preachy tone so I don't annoy you (or me, for that matter). I'm not a "know-it-all," coming down from the mountaintop to tell you what you should and should not do. I'm not trying to sell or convince you of anything. I'm just sharing some of the best ways to fail in life—or, if you're so inclined, some of the best ways to avoid that fate.

You won't find any fancy buzzwords or "secret formulas" that are guaranteed to give you fame, fortune, enlightenment, and six-pack abs in 30 days without leaving your couch. To claw my way out of the hole I dug for myself, I read a bazillion books in the personal development space. I quickly found that the principles of success are simple and consistent and have been documented ad nauseam. Why are the same success principles used again and again? Simple. *They work.*

I've packaged these life lessons within stories of people who've learned them through the School of Hard Knocks. You'll find true, inspirational stories of failure and redemption. You'll see a few household names that you may know well, and some obscure and unknown names, such as my own.

If I've done my job well, you'll also see a bit of yourself in these stories. After all, that's one of the goals of this book: to give you a chance to pause, reflect, and say, "Hey, that's me!" Then you can decide if you need to make some changes to get back on track.

I've found that there really is a right way and a wrong way to fail in life. For the few key areas that you want to develop and master, failure is something to be actively pursued and celebrated. It may sound strange, but when you fail fast and fail big in those few vital areas, you'll be on the fast track to accomplishing your definition of success.

For the other areas of your life, the right way to fail is to let others do it for you and learn from their mistakes. Staggering amounts of time and suffering can be avoided by learning from the mistakes of others. When it comes to failure in most areas of life, it's better to watch the movie than be a character in it. Rest assured, you'll still have plenty of opportunities to fail, but you might as well narrow down the list so you'll fail "smart."

This one's for you, Jim Rohn. I'm happy to spend a day with you to show how failure is *really* done. Get ready to take some notes.

CHAPTER 1

Get addicted to alcohol and drugs

"To alcohol! The cause of, and solution to, all of life's problems."
Homer Simpson, from *The Simpsons*

Addiction = epic fail

To reach the pinnacle of failure in life, it's hard to beat the path of alcohol or drug addiction, and I'm no stranger to that world. I've bartended at Notre Dame sports bars, an Irish pub in Omaha, and a rugby pub in Bath, England. I know how to make a lot of drinks, and I'm even better at drinking them. Over the years, I've sampled an incredibly vast variety of beer, wine, and liquor from all over the world. I know alcohol. I like the taste of it, I like how it makes me feel, and I used to drink a lot of it.

I also know that it can take you down. *Hard.* Drug or alcohol addiction opens up so many fantastic opportunities for failure, and in such catastrophic proportions, that I can't help but start a book about how to fail at life with this topic.

We all know the damage that "hard-core" drugs like meth and heroin can do to someone. That's a no-brainer. As for using "softer" options like marijuana and prescription drugs, those can certainly yield tragic results too. I don't claim to be an expert in abusing any of those drugs; I just didn't have enough time. But, if you want to talk about alcohol abuse, I'm your guy. So let's focus on our friend alcohol in this chapter.

When I say that drinking alcohol is a great way to fail in life, I am not referring to sipping on three glasses of wine at a wedding reception, dancing like a fool to the Macarena, and then waking up the next day feeling a bit sluggish and dehydrated. No, no, no. That's amateur stuff and certainly not the path to failure that I'm talking about. (Then again, I suppose it depends on what you did in your version of the Macarena.)

Like most things in life, if you want to get really good at something, you need to give it your all. You must practice regularly in order to significantly improve your skills. You need to be passionate about your craft. With that in mind, let's revisit the wedding reception from the perspective of a true professional: the alcoholic.

An hour or two before the wedding reception—the time of day is irrelevant—you warm up with a few strong drinks in your hotel room. After all, you don't want to attract too much attention with frequent trips to the open bar at the reception. Of course, you already know in the back of your mind that you'll become best friends with the bartender before the night is over, but let's not worry about that for now. After your pregame prep, you make your way down to the hotel bar to meet some friends for "a drink" before the reception starts. *Game on.*

You enter the reception hall, looking good and feeling good. This is your home turf: a special occasion with an open bar. With drink surgically attached to hand, you ooze sophistication and class as you work the room. Everyone is impressed with your witty stories and intellectual knowledge about—well, just about—everything. You catch the most desirable people in the room glancing your way, clearly thinking you're fabulous. You make a mental note to steer yourself in that direction later. First priority: more wine. Suddenly, you hear the Macarena song, and you know that this is your moment to shine. You leap to the dance floor and dazzle everyone with moves that have never before or since been seen, not even by you.

Then things get a little fuzzy.

You wake up. You haven't opened your eyes yet, but you can tell that you are partially clothed and still wearing your shoes. What you can't tell is whether you are alive or dead. Given how you feel at that moment, you assume dead. Just to make sure, you open your eyes and scan the room for Charon, the ferryman of Hades. Not there. Okay. It looks like you're alive. Now it's time to assess the damage.

You turn over in bed and spot a stranger lying next to you. It doesn't look good. Your keen mind senses that this stranger could prove to be a valuable resource in helping you locate your car. You say nothing.

You check to confirm that you have no cash, and you're missing a credit card. No surprises yet. You find a crumpled credit card receipt in your pocket that displays a triple-digit drinking tab from a bar. Well, now you know where to find your credit card. You make a mental note to stop by the bar when it opens to do the walk of shame and claim your credit card.

You suddenly notice that your head is pounding. *Ouch.* You also have the vague sensation that you might throw up and recognize that it's probably for the best if you do. You glance over to the nightstand to see if there might be a leftover drink to help you readjust to the world of the living. *Nothing.*

Okay. It's time to go. You're now on a mission to get home as quickly as possible to suffer in the privacy of your own home. With labored speech and a throbbing head, you attempt to speak to the stranger lying next to you with the sole purpose of eliciting hints to narrow down the location of your car. Somehow, you manage to get through the next hour or two, locate your vehicle, and find your way home. You're alone again, and you feel very ill.

Suddenly, you get a brilliant idea: "Maybe if I have a drink, then I'll start to feel better." Hair of the dog, as they say. You try it. It works. You feel a bit better. Granted, you've set a low bar. You have another, with the justification of needing a "taper" day. After all, you don't want to shock your body with immediate sobriety. That drink goes down quickly; then another, and another. Next thing you know, you're back in action. Not quite like the night before but not bad, all things considered. It turns out to be another "fun" day and evening after all.

You wake up again. This time you hear the sound of your alarm clock. It's Monday morning. Time to go to work. *Uggh.* Can't do it. You call in sick and go back to sleep. (Alcoholics hate Mondays.)

The true professional doesn't stop here. Not even close. This scenario is repeated more frequently over time until it becomes somewhat normal. Daily drinking is the routine now. It's just a question of how many.

It's getting harder to recapture the "good ol' days" of drinking. It's not always that fun anymore. You begin to have dark, negative moods when drinking, with frequent blackouts.

One day, usually after a binge, you decide to take a break from drinking for a while. Just a little break to rest your nerves. There's just one problem: You're shocked to discover that you can't seem to quit. Your body revolts with shaking, anxiety, sweating, and heart palpitations. You quickly give in and feed your body what it wants: another drink. The physical withdrawals subside.

Over the following months and years, you play around with monitoring how many drinks you have in a day. You experiment with drinking only wine or beer—none of that hard stuff. You decide to only drink on "special occasions" for a while. Special occasions soon evolve into any day that you are wearing a blue shirt (or any shirt at all). You haven't given up though. You know that you can go back to drinking responsibly. It just takes some discipline. In other words, you continue to fail.

Around this part of the addiction journey, the true professional will move on to experience a few notable rites of passage over time:

- First car accident
- First driving-under-the-influence (DUI) citation
- First time in jail
- First time getting severe shakes after a particularly epic binge
- Repeated humiliation and regret

By now, you're regularly hiding alcohol (in different places in the house, yard, or car) where other people won't find it. Drinking in the morning feels perfectly natural from time to time. Your poor performance at work starts to become noticeable to others. You experience a few uncomfortable conversations with your boss or colleagues at work. You eventually lose your job. That's all right. You didn't like it much anyway. It wasn't a good fit.

For your next stop on the addiction journey, the most important relationships in your life start to fall apart. Usually, this has already been happening for a while, unbeknownst to you, but now it's escalated to a different level. You start hearing the "choose me or alcohol" threat from your significant other. Unfortunately, you also have the frightening realization that it's not a simple choice. You can't just turn off the drinking switch anymore. Your "off" switch is broken.

In the home stretch, you become isolated. You lose touch with your friends and family. You get divorced or separated. You may lose your kids. You may even become homeless. You start to develop more health problems with frequent visits to the hospital, if you can afford to go. You start to lose your desire to live. Life with or without alcohol seems impossible. All you can see in front of you are trips to the liquor store, jail, the hospital, or the graveyard.

You have arrived. Welcome to failure at life via addiction.

> "First realize that you are sick; then you
> can move towards health."
> Lao-Tzu

Failure quiz: addictions

Most chapters include a "failure quiz" to help you assess your progress in that particular area of life. These questions are written from an adult perspective. Younger readers may find that some of the questions don't yet apply, but they'll serve to heighten your awareness of the issues and help you understand what may be going through the mind of many of those "old" people in your life.

Simply answer "yes" or "no" for each question, tally the number of "yes" answers, and the rest is up to you. While the questions below are focused on alcohol, feel free to substitute alcohol with any other drug of choice.

1.   When you honestly want to, do you find that you cannot quit entirely?   ❑ Yes   ❑ No

2.   Once you start drinking, do you have little control over the amount you take?   ❑ Yes   ❑ No

3.   Have you ever thought that you should cut down your drinking?   ❑ Yes   ❑ No

4.   Have you ever felt annoyed when people have commented on your drinking?   ❑ Yes   ❑ No

5.   Have you ever felt guilt or regret about your drinking?   ❑ Yes   ❑ No

6.   In the past year, have you had an "eye opener" first thing in the morning to steady your nerves or get rid of a hangover?   ❑ Yes   ❑ No

7.   Do you sometimes fail to do what was normally expected of you because of your drinking?   ❑ Yes   ❑ No

Failure quiz: addictions (continued)

8. Have you or anyone else been injured as a result of your drinking?
    ❏ Yes ❏ No

9. Do you hide alcohol in the house or lie about how much you drink? ❏ Yes ❏ No

10. Has your drinking caused trouble at home or at work?
    ❏ Yes ❏ No

Count up the number of "yes" answers and refer to the chart below:

0-1 Party on, but be smart about it.

2-3 Danger, Will Robinson. Be very careful. You're on the slippery path to failure.

>3   Houston, we have a problem. Don't worry. There's a lot of support available to help you move to a better path of life. A quick Internet search will yield a mind-boggling number of resources to cover just about any addiction under the sun. Someday you'll be very glad that you decided to choose a different path. Party on, but do it clean and sober.

"There's no problem that alcohol can't make worse."
Anonymous

Oh, the stories I could tell ...

At first, it was fun—just something to do with friends and family. With one side of the family 100% Irish and the other 100% Finnish, I have excellent drinking cred. I lived up to my credentials and have many hilarious and tragic stories. But, over the years of my drinking career, the fun part of drinking faded, and the dark side of alcohol showed up. Drinking was no longer just fun and games. I struggled to recreate that sense of well-being, that state of relaxation that I used to feel. Liquid courage had turned into liquid dynamite. I just got drunk and would do crazy things that I'd never consider doing when sober.

My recollection of my misadventures resembles the voyage of Jason and the Argonauts (with better animation and without being tied to a mast to avoid the Sirens). However, I've been informed by others that the reality was really more of a kaleidoscope of scenes from *The Hangover*, *Leaving Las Vegas*, and *Barfly*.

In my late 30s, I finally came to the realization that I'd already used up my lifetime quota of drinks. So I quit.

And then I quit again.

And then I quit again, and again, and again, and again.

I probably quit 20 times over a period of several years before I *really* quit drinking. Fortunately, I quit relatively early in terms of bad things happening in my life, but I could clearly see those things coming up on the horizon in the not-so-distant future. I chose to take a different road. It was one heck of a difficult choice at the time—probably the hardest thing I've ever done—but it was clearly the right decision for me.

If you're an alcoholic, the chances of going back to being a "normal" or "social" drinker are very small—virtually nil, if the truth be told. Alcoholism gets progressively worse with time. If you know that you're already on that destructive path, it's better to change course sooner than later, unless you like the taste of gutters.

This all-important decision must come from you. Threats from your spouse, family, or employer can provide initial motivation to help wake you up, but you won't make the necessary changes until you fully embrace the decision to quit for your own good. The only catch is that you also have to come to terms with the fact that you can never go back. *Ouch.* That's a hard one to swallow if you've made alcohol an integral part of your life for many years.

Famous athletes need to know when it's time to quit their sport and move on to something new. As a famous drinker, you need to know when it's time to take yourself out of the game. I used to play soccer at a competitive level (varsity soccer at the University of Notre Dame with the possibility of playing semi-professional soccer in Europe at my peak). I declined, with some "guidance" from my parents.

Once I made the decision to quit playing competitive soccer, I never looked back. Today, I have no delusions of playing professional soccer. Similarly, I have no delusions of going back to being a social drinker. It was fun while it lasted, but that chapter of my life is over.

I can still dabble in soccer by playing with my son. He is starting to play the game, and I enjoy kicking the ball around with him. Similarly, nearly all of my friends and family drink alcohol, and I can still dabble in "drinking" by enjoying nonalcoholic beer with them, but that's as close as I get to the real thing. I don't even think twice about it anymore.

Making a drastic change like this may impact some of your relationships, particularly if the relationship is largely based upon the use of alcohol or drugs. But that's okay. True friends will stick with you, and the quality of existing relationships and new friendships may even improve.

How do you know if you have a problem with alcohol? There are all kinds of checklists and questionnaires out there, but it really boils down to the following two conditions:

1. If, when you honestly want to, you find that you cannot quit entirely; or
2. If, when drinking, you have little control over the amount you take.

If these two statements ring true, then you're probably an alcoholic. It's really that simple. You can call it a "drinking problem" instead, if that's easier to digest, but the course of action is still the same. It's time to hang up your cleats and move on to something new.

> "Avoid using cigarettes, alcohol, and drugs as
> alternatives to being an interesting person."
> **Marilyn vos Savant**

Numbing your mind and stunting your growth

An interesting variation of alcohol or drug abuse comes in a more benign form—a form that in many respects is like watching mindless, "reality" TV. Perhaps you drink to check out of your body and escape the reality of your life for a while. Of course, reality is always waiting for you once you return from your escape, and it may have grown impatient while you were gone.

By consistently relying on a drink or a drug to help relax after a stressful day at work—or to help cope with loneliness, fear, anxiety, loss, or any other emotion—you miss the opportunity to develop healthier, more productive coping mechanisms for life. It's important to be able to experience emotions fully, and then process and cope with those feelings in healthy ways. (Did I just say that? *Huh*. I guess I did. That's going to cost me quite a few "manly man" points. However, it's true, and it takes practice.)

Sometimes it's useful to throw away the "crutches" of alcohol and TV and become proficient with other tools to help you navigate through the good times and the difficult times of your life. What are some other, healthy options that you can use to cope with stress, anxiety, loneliness, fear, and loss? No surprises here. It's the typical list of "to-do" items that you see again and again:

- Exercise
- Sign up for service opportunities/volunteer work
- Spend time with family and friends
- Write in a journal
- Play a musical instrument
- Watch educational TV shows
- Take a cooking or dance class
- Meditate
- Soak in a hot tub or try a sauna or steam room
- Read educational books or magazines
- Start a new hobby

The list goes on and on. There are so many healthy alternatives to consider. Instead of having a few drinks, experiment with some options. After one rough day at work, treat yourself to a favorite meal, give meditation a try, or soak in a hot tub; on another day, find a comfortable spot to settle down and read a good book; on another day, go for a walk on a nearby trail. The goal is to find a variety of healthy options to add to your tool belt for handling challenges. In the process, you may discover that opening new doors will lead to a more interesting and fulfilling life.

CHAPTER 2

Trash your health

"My doctor told me to stop having intimate dinners
for four. Unless there are three other people."
Orson Welles

The couch potato

Trashing your health is another fantastic way to achieve failure and feelings of regret in life. But don't take it from me. Aside from the aforementioned detour in Chapter 1, my healthy diet and exercise routine would annoy many of you. Rather than bore you with stories from my own life, let me introduce you to Rich Roll. Rich is someone who knows a thing or two about trashing his health.

As a child, Rich lacked any semblance of hand-eye coordination. You know the kid. He was always the last one picked to join a team in gym class—the one who always misses the basketball hoop, whiffs every baseball pitch, and drops footballs thrown straight to his chest. My heart goes out to kids like that. But they usually become our bosses later in life, so I suppose it all works out in the end.

After some awkward trials and errors in youth sports, one day Rich jumped into a pool and discovered that he could swim. *Fast.* In high school, Rich blossomed into a nationally ranked swimmer and an excellent student. This attractive combination earned him a coveted spot on the Stanford University swim team. No small feat. Rich was on the fast track to success.

Then Rich met an old friend of mine—alcohol—but it didn't take him down all at once. For Rich, it was a gradual process. First his swimming suffered, and he eventually quit the team. Rich graduated from Stanford, earned a law degree from Cornell, and enjoyed a fairly successful career as a corporate lawyer. Throughout it all, Rich was able to maintain the façade that everything was going along swimmingly (lame pun intended). But, under the surface, major cracks started to appear.

Rich began to experience some of the inevitable rites of passage associated with alcohol and drug abuse: car accidents, DUI arrests, poor work performance, and strained family relationships—the usual routine. But Rich was a fighter, and fighters tend to go down swinging. He continued to get beat up and bloodied until he finally hit bottom in 1997 and reluctantly agreed to check himself into a treatment facility.

Rich arrived at rehab in style. He took advantage of his last moments of freedom by guzzling 12 beers on his way there. *Nicely played.* (I enjoy that story way more than I should.)

My last beer was tame in comparison. Looking and feeling my best after a big night of drinking, I joined a friend to clear the cobwebs by hiking up Mt. Taylor in New Mexico. I felt like garbage but managed to make it to the summit. Once back at the car at the trailhead, we each cracked open a beer to celebrate, and I announced my intention to quit. I made a (very) small offering of my Marble Red Ale to the mountain gods, snapped a photo to commemorate the occasion, and proceeded to guzzle the rest. I vowed never to touch the stuff unless I first climb Mt. Taylor again. And that was all she wrote.

I haven't been back to Mt. Taylor—or touched alcohol—since. I still have the photo. It's pretty easy to spot among my extensive collection of drinking-related photos. It's the one where I'm deliberately dumping out a portion of my beer to the ground.

Back to Rich. After his 12-beer arrival at the treatment facility, he checked in, passed out, and woke up to harsh reality: 100 days in rehab. *Ouch.* That couldn't have been pretty. Despite the fog he was in, deep down Rich knew that this was his last hope. He made it through rehab and came out the other side with a new perspective.

Soon afterwards, Rich quit his job at the corporate law firm and began to piece together a new life. He started his own business, met his wife, and became a father. When it came to his diet and exercise routines, however, Rich was a mess. Rich's exercise routine involved watching TV with the volume on full blast until it was time to climb off the couch and lumber up the stairs to his bedroom. His typical diet consisted of cheeseburgers and junk food before capping off the evening with some nicotine gum. *Sweet.*

On the eve of his 40th birthday—eight years after his last drink of alcohol—a second drastic change took place for Rich. At 2 am, after scarfing down the usual plate of cheeseburgers and enjoying a nicotine gum buzz, Rich had the following experience during his nightly ascent of the stairs:

"With the lights already out, I had begun hauling my 208-pound frame upstairs when midway I had to pause—my legs were heavy, my breathing labored. My face felt hot and I had to bend over just to catch my breath, my belly folding over jeans that no longer fit. Nauseous, I looked down at the steps I'd climbed. There were eight. About that many remained to be mounted. *Eight steps.* I was thirty-nine years old, and I was winded by eight steps. *Man,* I thought, *is this what I've become?*"[1]

At that moment, something snapped for Rich. This seemingly innocuous event became the catalyst for radical transformation. Rich continues:

"I labored to the bathroom sink and splashed my face with cold water. As I lifted my head, I caught my reflection in the mirror. And froze. Gone was that long-held image of myself as that handsome young swimming champion I'd once been. And in that moment, denial was shattered; reality set in for the first time. I was a fat, out-of-shape, and very *unhealthy* man hurtling into middle age—a depressed, self-destructive person utterly disconnected from who I was and what I wanted to be."[2]

Rich made a decision to change. More importantly, Rich finally *wanted* to change.

The burning desire to make a change is the key that unlocks your true potential. Without a sincere desire to change, you just go through the motions.

For starters, Rich completely overhauled his diet. With the help of his wife Julie Piatt, Rich began a well-researched, seven-day, fruit-and-vegetable juice cleanse. During that week, he also tapered off his caffeine and nicotine intake. It was a tough adjustment for his body, but he stuck to the plan. After the seven-day cleanse, Rich gradually progressed to a 100% plant-based diet with no chicken, fish, dairy, or any other animal products. He also eliminated most processed foods. In other words, Rich was now a vegan. He initially had trouble with the "vegan" label. But, as Yoda would say, vegan Rich was.

The results of this experiment surprised Rich. He suddenly had a lot more energy, and he felt the need to start exercising to burn it off. "Clearly, my desire to prove this vegan thing pointless had failed. Instead, I was sold."[3]

Over time, Rich built up his exercise regimen of swimming, biking, and running, still fueled by a 100% vegan diet. He started losing weight and felt great. This pattern continued over the course of a year as he continued to increase his level of fitness, drop pounds, and keep the weight off. But Rich's success story doesn't end there. Not even close.

Two years later and 50 pounds lighter at 42 years of age, Rich competed in the Ultraman World Championship in Hawaii. Yes, that's one of those insane, three-day endurance events comprised of 6.2 miles of swimming, 260 miles of cycling, and a 52.4-mile double-marathon run. Rich placed 11th overall and was the third-fastest American. This was "after decades of reckless drug and alcohol abuse that nearly killed me and others, plus no physical exertion more strenuous than lugging groceries into the house and maybe repotting a plant."[4]

In his book, *Finding Ultra: Rejecting Middle Age, Becoming One of the World's Fittest Men, and Discovering Myself,* Rich credits his drastic switch to a vegan diet—after that out-of-breath moment on the stairs—as being instrumental in his success as an endurance athlete.

Within a few years, Rich went from a fat, out-of-shape couch potato to being named by *Men's Fitness* magazine as one of the "25 Fittest Guys in the World." As Rich said in a CNN interview in 2009, "My point is that change starts with a decision followed by baby steps along a new, consistent trajectory that, over time, can lead to dramatic results."

It all starts with a decision to change.

"True health care reform cannot happen in Washington.
It has to happen in our kitchens, in our homes, in
our communities. All health care is personal."
Dr. Mehmet Oz

Failure quiz: optimal health

Answer "yes" or "no" for each question below:

1. Do you go to sleep early enough so that you can wake up
   without an alarm and still start your day when you need to?
   ❑ Yes   ❑ No

2. Have you taken the time to understand what type of exercise
   works best for your body in terms of intensity, duration, and
   activity?   ❑ Yes   ❑ No

3. Do you exercise at least 30 minutes, five to seven days per week,
   doing something that you enjoy?   ❑ Yes   ❑ No

4. On average, do you get up and move around at least once per
   hour?   ❑ Yes   ❑ No

5. Do you generally eat seven or more servings of vegetables each
   day and approximately 20 different types of fruits and vegetables
   each week?   ❑ Yes   ❑ No

6. Do you spend time outdoors at least two days per week?
   ❑ Yes   ❑ No

7. Do you drink enough water each day? In other words, is your
   urine usually colorless or light yellow?   ❑ Yes   ❑ No

8. Do you primarily purchase whole foods rather than processed
   foods? Hint: If so, most of your purchases will be from the
   outside perimeter of the grocery store rather than the aisles.
   ❑ Yes   ❑ No

9. Have you met with an integrative holistic medicine physician or
   naturopathic provider to create a plan that will keep you healthy
   and out of the hospital?   ❑ Yes   ❑ No

Failure quiz: optimal health (continued)

10.   Do you set aside at least 10 minutes each day to meditate or have some quiet time?   ❑ Yes   ❑ No

Count up the number of "yes" answers and refer to the chart below:

0-2   Uh oh. Looks like you need to channel your inner Rich Roll and overhaul your daily habits and routines.

3-5   You've got some of this stuff down. Now pick a few more to bump yourself up to the next category.

6-8   Looking good. With a few minor tweaks, you'll be on the path to optimal physical and mental health.

9-10 You ooze health. You must be glowing. Keep it up—not that you need any encouragement from me. You've already got this stuff handled. I'll see you in the produce section, on the trails, or at the gym.

**"Anything worth doing is worth overdoing.
Moderation is for cowards."
From the movie, *Lone Survivor***

Overdoing it

After reading Rich's story in *Finding Ultra*, I was pumped up and eager to get back into the endurance event scene. I'm no stranger to that world (on a wimpier, scaled-down version). Endurance events for me included races like the Pikes Peak Ascent in Colorado Springs, Imogene Pass Run in Telluride, La Luz Trail Run in Albuquerque, and the Bataan Death March in New Mexico. I'm also an avid mountain climber, including Mt. Kilimanjaro, 13 of the 14ers in Colorado, and many other high peaks scattered across the globe.

At the time I finished reading Rich's book, I was coming off a six-month hiatus due to an injury from a failed experiment with "minimalist" running shoes. That experiment was inspired by a different book: Christopher McDougall's *Born to Run*. This book touts the benefits of barefoot running and provides colorful, inspirational stories about the ultramarathon-running exploits of the Tarahumara Indian tribe in Mexico. Books like *Born to Run* and *Finding Ultra* are kryptonite for people like me, and there should be a restraining order to prevent me from entering stores like The North Face or REI. I'm always eager to test out new exercise gear, gadgets, and routines.

As soon as I finished *Born to Run*, I predictably found myself on Amazon.com, ordering my first pair of minimalist running shoes. I opted for one of the beefier Vibram FiveFingers models. They looked and felt strange on my feet, but I immediately liked them in some quirkily, cool way.

With the FiveFingers shoes, I definitely felt it when I kicked a rock or stepped on a sharp object. It was easy to see why these shoes had the potential to change my running form. Minimalist running shoes were a very different experience compared to my regular bombproof trail-running shoes that coddled my feet.

Over the years, I've had bouts of knee tendonitis, particularly on mountain descents, so the vision of pain-free running and climbing was alluring. There was only one way to find out how my legs would respond to the strange foot gloves: It was time for an experiment.

To paraphrase a classic Jim Rohn quip regarding the limitations of motivational speaking: If you take an idiot and then you motivate that person, you end up with a motivated idiot. Knowledge is a necessary precursor to ensure that motivation is channeled in the right direction.

Knowledge, in turn, is said to be power. But knowledge is only powerful if we apply what we know. Knowledge is merely potential power. When we ignore our knowledge, we revert to being an idiot, which brings me back to my FiveFingers story.

I have a strong background in anatomy, exercise physiology, and physical therapy. But, when my new shoes arrived, I chose to ignore all of that knowledge. As a motivated idiot, I was ready to test my foot gloves with a sprint workout at a local high school track. My brain was so enchanted by the image of rekindled youth and unlimited pain-free running that I opted for a workout I did over 20 years ago when I was a sprinter on the high school track team.

This was a dumb idea on multiple levels. First, given that the minimalist running shoe concept was completely foreign to my feet, a literal walk in the park would have been more appropriate. Second, I hadn't done a sprint workout in years, in any kind of shoe. But I dismissed these trifling nits and approached the starting line in my funny-looking shoes. I even brought a stopwatch in case there were any questions about my sanity.

I started the workout with an 800-meter jog to warm up, followed by several 100-, 200-, and 400-meter sprint intervals, and ended with an 800-meter cooldown. The workout actually felt great at the time; the next morning was a different story.

When I woke up the next day, one Achilles tendon and both sets of calf muscles were so thrashed that I could barely walk, let alone run. I hobbled across the room and started to stretch but quickly realized that this was not a case of sore muscles. *This was serious damage.* In the end, it took six months for my legs to recover and feel normal again.

Of course, I'm completely to blame for the injury. I'm sure my pair of FiveFingers would've been great if I took the time to ease into them. But I didn't. Despite my failed experiment, I still believe that there is merit to the minimalist running-shoe concept, and I plan to experiment with them again—perhaps for short walks and working around the house.

With that background, I used my newfound inspiration from Rich's *Finding Ultra* book to design an ultra-cautious, cross-training program that would gradually get me to the half-marathon distance over the course of six months.

I should point out that these were mountain miles—not road-running miles—and there's a big difference between the two. For example, the Pikes Peak Ascent and Marathon website warns flatlanders to use the following rule of thumb to estimate their time to complete the 13.3-mile Pikes Peak Ascent: The estimated time to run from the starting line at 6,300 feet to the finish line at 14,115 feet will be the fastest 26.2 flatland marathon time you've ever run, PLUS add another 30 minutes. In other words, mountain miles can be slow and tough. I've done the Pikes Peak Ascent race three times and finished in 4:00:09, 4:00:33, and 4:37:47. Based on those times, my goal was pretty obvious: Break 4 hours. I can still picture the person who would not move over to let me pass on the narrow trail in the final ¼ mile of my 4:00:09 finish. (I usually picture him on my dartboard.)

Three months into my training program, I was making great progress, and my legs were holding up well. Then, one day, my vision of races and personal records came to a screeching halt. It wasn't my legs; this time, it was my heart.

I was 7 miles into a slow, comfortable, 9-mile jog when my heart rate suddenly spiked. It scared the crap out of me, to put it mildly. As a gadget geek, I was wearing a heart-rate monitor and saw the numbers suddenly leap from the high 140s to the low 180s, with no change in pace or effort. I stopped in my tracks, with the hope that some rest would cause my heart to snap out of its frenzy. About 20 seconds later, my heart rhythm was back to normal. *A weird aberration,* I tried to convince myself. No big deal. I resumed a slow jog only to feel my heart rate start to skip beats. This time, I listened to my body. I stopped, turned around, and walked slowly back to my car.

This running scenario repeated several times over the following weeks, each time with increasing anxiety about my heart. Then, one evening, I had a succession of skipped beats while lying in bed. That was enough for me. I hopped in the car and went to the emergency room to be poked, prodded, wired, and observed in typical hospital style.

Five hours later, the doctor informed me that the staff had detected an arrhythmia. This was not news to me. I had been diagnosed with a benign arrhythmia in the early 1990s, but I'd never had a problem with it. This was something different. Unfortunately, I was not able to reproduce the spiked heart rate or skipped beats in the hospital, so I was discharged from the emergency room with a clean bill of health and a bill for $2,500.

Two days later, I was back in the emergency room after another frightening episode while sitting at my desk at work. Like a fool, I decided to go to a different hospital for a second opinion. This is not a wise approach when it comes to emergency room visits. The second hospital would not accept the lab work and radiology results from the first hospital, even though I brought the printed results with me. They insisted on redoing all of the lab and radiology work, even though I only requested an electrocardiogram and stress test. Emergency room teams are reluctant to deviate from standard protocols. Physicians are worried about getting sued, so they cover their butts with duplicate tests. Several x-rays and blood vials later, I was sent home with nothing but a $3,000 bill, a referral to a cardiologist, and some extra radiation as my souvenirs.

To make a long story short, the cardiologist asked me to wear a heart monitor for several weeks, followed by several rounds of tests in a cardiology lab. Similar to the experience that many have when taking a car to a mechanic, I never had a recurrence of the spiked heart rate while I wore the monitor. I had abandoned my training program by then. In the end, the cardiologist determined that my heart's plumbing and electrical system looked good—aside from the benign arrhythmia. Her hypothesis was that long, strenuous exercise causes my heart's electrical system to go haywire.

Even though I have a curious mind and enjoy experiments, this was one hypothesis that I didn't want to test any further. The cardiologist suggested that I stick to an exercise routine that keeps my average heart rate below 150 and avoid exercising for more than an hour at a time. In other words, daily, moderate exercise would be best for me.

Darn. When it comes to drinking and exercise, moderation has never been my specialty. I have been doing strenuous endurance events ever since I quit playing competitive soccer in my early 20s. No more climbing mountains now? No more endurance trail runs? *Okay.* I was secretly happy to have such a great excuse to skip the grueling, trail-running race circuit, but the mountain-climbing part was definitely a bummer.

Whenever you face a significant change that you need to make in your life, you have two options:

1. Focus on the things you *can't* do; or
2. Focus on the things you *can* do.

It's really a simple decision when framed that way. I decided to change my attitude and focus. Since that consultation with the cardiologist, the new name of the game became "variety."

My new routine included slow jogs at a glacial 12-minute-mile pace, stationary bikes, elliptical machines, hill or stair climbs, strength training, stretches, short hikes, agility drills, and an occasional swim. This was a huge change from my former exercise routine, which was heavy on running and light on everything else. After making the switch from endurance training to a moderate routine filled with variety, I was surprised to find that I actually lost weight. I wasn't in tip-top cardiovascular shape like I used to be, but I felt happy and healthy, and my exercise routine required a much smaller time commitment each week.

My new exercise program went well for about a year until, late one evening, I woke up with a nasty bout of what I later learned were PVCs: preventricular contractions. After enduring a miserable and frightening few days where my heart skipped hundreds of beats, I decided to do two things: quit drinking caffeine and visit a naturopath. This proved to be an excellent decision on both counts. After removing caffeine and adding a few supplements to my diet, my PVCs have disappeared. On the downside, I'm running out of unhealthy vices to eliminate from my life.

I've come to disagree with the *Lone Survivor* "anything worth doing is worth overdoing—moderation is for cowards" sentiment that opened this chapter. Having said that, the last thing I want to do is turn you off from endurance sports. I have no regrets about testing my limits over the years. Endurance activities can be a great way to clear your head and get a glimpse of what your mind and body are truly capable of. Most people are nowhere near overdoing it when it comes to physically challenging their bodies.

On the flip side of the coin, it's important to listen to what your body is telling you. If things start to go awry, don't ignore the early warning signals. You may not like it, but your body changes over time. The late Sir Edmund Hillary is a great example. Hillary was the first person to climb Mt. Everest at an elevation of 29,029 feet; later in life, Hillary's body was not able to tolerate even moderately high altitudes. His body had changed. After being the first person to climb the highest mountain in the world, Hillary had to stick to lower elevations for the rest of his life.

There may come a time when it makes sense to switch to a more balanced and moderate workout routine that you can sustain for the long term. When it comes to exercise routines that optimize physical and mental health for the long haul, my money is on variety, moderation, and consistency. However, it sure is nice to have so many amazing memories to treasure from my soccer, mountain-climbing, and trail-running days.

Speaking of running, now that my heart appears to be stable again, I'm cautiously starting to train for sprint-distance triathlons. It's time for another experiment!

"I don't want any vegetables, thank you.
I paid for the cow to eat them for me."
Doug Coupland

Green sludge

There are many mysteries in life, but the ingredients of a healthy lifestyle are not among them. When I first wrote this chapter, I included 10 pages that read like an academic journal. It contained mind-numbing statistics on how much sugar, salt, and calories we eat today, along with the inevitable scary lists of diseases and ailments that are linked to the typical American diet. I even added citations for scientific studies to ensure that your eyes would glaze over. In the end, I scrapped all of it. Why? Because we already know what to do. We just choose not to do it.

If you are part of the vast majority of people who fall down in this area, the more interesting question to ask yourself is, "Why do you choose to make bad decisions when it comes to your health?"

First, health is one of those areas where it's easy to make bad decisions for a long time before you start to notice any negative effects. While the delayed consequences can be severe down the road, in the short term you feel pretty darn good about eating cake for dinner. You may even gobble down a few frosting flowers while you're at it.

There really isn't much you can do about delayed consequences. It's not as if you'll suddenly gain 10 pounds after eating a cupcake or instantly develop symptoms of cancer after smoking a cigarette. It can take years or even decades for serious issues to develop. The key is to make healthy behaviors a habit—just a normal part of your everyday life.

The second major reason you may fail is the time, inconvenience, and cost of living a healthy lifestyle. With hectic schedules filled to the brim, it's not easy to carve out time each day for sufficient exercise, healthy eating, and adequate sleep. I have to schedule these things on my calendar each day or else they often don't happen.

One strategy I use to cut down the time and effort needed for the healthy eating part of the equation is to use a VitaMix blender. Thanks to my blender, I can gulp down insane quantities of green vegetables in under a minute. My daily VitaMix concoctions are green, bitter, vegetable sludges that would make a billy goat pause and reflect before sampling. For me, this prospect is much more appealing compared to chewing my way through a monstrous pile of vegetables. Still, it takes a significant amount of time each day to prep the vegetables for my culinary travesties.

On top of that, the cost can quickly add up. However, I can either pay now in the form of fresh fruits and vegetables, or I can pay later in the form of medical bills, so I consider it money well spent. The cost also pales in comparison to what I used to spend on wine and beer, so that serves as a handy reference point as well.

Given that it takes a significant amount of time, money, and effort to create a not-so-tasty product, it's no wonder that most people avoid doing it. To help keep my mind on track, I like to recall the classic words on the basics of good nutrition from the late fitness and nutrition guru Jack LaLanne: "If man made it, don't eat it" and "If it tastes good, spit it out." I often think about these words while chugging my 16 ounces of green sludge for breakfast each morning.

Another important factor in your unhealthy decisions may be "decision fatigue." You may start your day bright-eyed and bushy-tailed with a healthy breakfast and usually make it through lunch unscathed. But, as the day wears on, you start to feel tired. The vending-machine candy bars and the break-room donuts sing their irresistible, sweet song. But, for the sake of argument, let's say you manage to hold firm.

You finish work, and then you're off to the grocery store where you're rewarded with aisle after aisle of unhealthy temptations, displayed prominently at eye level. You avert your eyes, stick your fingers in your ears, and sing *la-la-la* as you try to locate boring cans of organic black, kidney, and garbanzo beans.

Even if you finally make it back to your car with a grocery cart full of nutritious, whole foods, you're not out of the woods yet. You arrive at home and enjoy a healthy dinner. Then, at the end of a long day, a cruel member of your family (whom we'll call Beelzebub, for short) asks if anyone would like a hot fudge sundae. The other princes and princesses of hell scream "Yes!" as they shift their gaze to you: a sad figure sitting on the couch, trying to drink your eighth glass of water.

Your defenses are down. You've been saying "no" all day, and you're tired of it: "Okay. *Fine.* Give me three scoops, and don't be chintzy on the hot fudge. Add a Matterhorn of whipped cream while you're at it. I might as well go down in flames."

One effective way to avoid this depressing scenario is to incorporate a Get Out of Jail Free day each week, every other week, or every month. I call them "sugar days" since that's my weakness in the unhealthy food department. On the days when you're on the ropes, feeling down, or attending a planned event, simply declare it a "sugar day" with much fanfare, and then it's anything goes for the rest of the day.

In this way, everybody wins:

- Your friends and family are happy that you're joining the fun and not making them feel guilty, yet they're aware that you're still meeting your health goals.
- You're happy that you can cater to your weaknesses and enjoy some unhealthy treats.
- You're still on track with your overall plan to live a healthy lifestyle.

Misbehaving is part of the fun of life, especially when you have a Get Out of Jail Free card in your pocket.

Finally, let's address the argument that it's hard to know what we should do to optimize our physical and mental health because there's so much conflicting information out there. *Really?* I won't say anything about this being a lame excuse to justify your bad decisions … whoops, I just did!

Regardless, let's set the record straight. Here are some basic guidelines that hold true for just about anyone. Of course, you should first consult with your doctor before starting any new diet or exercise program. *Blah, blah, blah.* Now that I've covered my butt with that legal disclaimer, here's the CliffsNotes version of the key ingredients for a healthy lifestyle. Hint: You already know all of these (with the possible exception of #8).

1. **Don't diet.** A better option is to be honest with yourself about your bad eating habits, and then replace them with healthy eating habits that you can sustain for the long haul. Healthy eating should be a normal pattern of everyday life rather than a temporary exercise in denial in which you struggle until you meet a particular goal.

2. **Eat whole foods.** Avoid processed or refined foods whenever possible. As a bonus, this approach will also help you minimize your sugar and salt intake.

3. **Drink plenty of water.** Recommendations vary depending on criteria, such as your age and activity level. If your urine is colorless or light yellow, it's a good sign that you're drinking enough water.

4. **Eat plenty of fruits and vegetables.** Studies suggest that seven daily servings of fruits and vegetables are a good target for optimal well-being. Variety is important too. Try for about 20 different kinds each week. If that sounds insane and overwhelming, like it first did for me, you may want to try a VitaMix blender.

5. **Move around every hour and exercise at least 30 minutes each day, doing something you enjoy.** Yes, you should enjoy it! Otherwise, you probably won't be able to sustain it, and that's what we're looking for here: long-term, consistent, moderate exercise. A weekly mix of cardio, strength training, and stretching is ideal. Also ensure that you get off your chair or couch every 30-60 minutes. Studies show that people who sit for prolonged periods of time have a higher risk of dying from all causes, even for those who exercise regularly.

6. **Get ~eight hours of sleep each night.** Darren Hardy (author, speaker, and publisher of SUCCESS magazine) asked the well-known cardiothoracic surgeon and TV show host Dr. Mehmet Oz, "What's the one thing somebody can do to help with their anti-aging and wellness?" His answer? Sleep. Dr. Oz put drinking water and walking as #2 and #3. Seven to nine hours is the sweet spot for most people over the age of 18; youngsters need more sleep. Better yet, don't worry about the number of hours. Go to bed early enough so you wake up on time without the need for an alarm. Sleep is time well spent. If nothing else, you'll look and feel better, and your friends, family, and colleagues will thank you for it too.

7. **Go outside.** Studies suggest that outdoor exercise improves your mood, reduces stress, gives you a jolt of vitamin D, and contributes to your overall happiness. The fresh air, sights, and smells of nature give your mind and body a rejuvenating break. The Japanese even have a word for it—Shinrin-yoku—that translates as "forest bathing."

8. **Find a healthcare provider who focuses on prevention.** If you have crushing pain in your chest, then our healthcare system is the place to be. In the United States, our physicians are highly trained to respond to acute problems, such as heart attacks or other crises. However, when it comes to *preventing* heart attacks or managing other chronic conditions, the typical provider tool belt of prescription drugs and invasive procedures is a bad place to start. It's

far better to find an integrative medicine or naturopathic provider who will take a holistic view of your diet, lifestyle, family history, environment, lab results, and symptoms, and then work with you to develop a comprehensive, proactive plan that integrates conventional and alternative therapies designed to keep you healthy and out of the hospital. If you work with your provider to improve your diet, exercise routines, sleep patterns, lifestyle, and stress management, you'll prevent 80% of the typical ailments. As Thomas Edison put it many years ago, "The doctor of the future will no longer treat the human frame with drugs, but rather will cure and prevent disease with nutrition."

But don't take my word for any of this. Do your own research. Figure out what works well for you. Consider the ideas I've shared as hypotheses to test in your own life.

My current experiment is to spend three to four days each week eating a whole-food, plant-based diet, and three to four days eating the healthiest fish, chicken, or beef that I can find. I focus on organic vegetables and fruits to avoid pesticides, and I look for wild-caught fish, free-range chicken, and grass-fed beef that are free of extra hormones and antibiotics. I also give myself one "sugar day" each week so I can enjoy a more decadent dessert or join my son for his favorite treat: a churro. In other words, I haven't fully adopted the eating habits of people like Rich Roll and his wife Julie Piatt, but I share their belief that a diet based on a foundation of plant-based, whole foods is the way to go. As a case in point, my diet overhaul has caused my total cholesterol to steadily drop from 247 to 170 over the past three years, with no prescription drugs. Chalk up another victory for plants!

To close this section, I would like to thank Rich Roll, Julie Piatt, Jack LaLanne, Christopher McDougall, Dr. Mehmet Oz, Dr. Michael Roizen, Dr. T. Colin Campbell, Dr. Caldwell Esselstyn, Dr. Mimi Guarneri, and countless others who've challenged the status quo of food and exercise. Their stories and convictions have inspired me to experiment with many new ideas. Some of my experiments were a terrific success while others flopped in spectacular fashion. However, even the failures led to greater self-awareness and growth and have shaped my perception of what it means to live a lifestyle that optimizes physical and mental health.

One of my favorite brands—The North Face—has a tagline that's worth re-membering in all aspects of life: "Never stop exploring." Create your own experi-ments to discover what's ideal when it comes to your physical and mental well-be-ing. Then, when it comes to drinking disgusting, green vegetable smoothies, you might find that it's better to think of Nike and "Just Do It."

ENDNOTES

1.   Rich Roll, *Finding Ultra: Rejecting Middle Age, Becoming One of the World's Fittest Men, and Discovering Myself* (New York: Three Rivers Press, 2012), p. 2. Emphasis in original. Published with the written permission of Rich Roll. Thank you, Rich!

2.   Ibid., pp. 2-3. Emphasis in original.

3.   Ibid., p. 12.

4.   Ibid., p. x.

CHAPTER 3

Live paycheck to paycheck

"We buy things we don't need with money we
don't have to impress people we don't like."
Dave Ramsey

Financial hell

As a college student, things were looking good on the financial front until one fateful day towards the end of my freshman year. In my hot little hands, I held my first credit card.

No big deal. It's just a convenience thing, I told myself. *It's a lot easier and safer than carrying cash.* Then, as if reading a script, the following words actually came out of my mouth during a phone conversation with my parents: "Don't worry. I'll only use it for emergencies, and I'll pay off the balance in full each month."

Yep, I really did say it.

Over the following weeks, I decided that it made sense to use the credit card for my everyday purchases too. That way, I could accrue points and get a free airline ticket for spring break. Since I have to spend money anyway on the bare essentials of groceries, beer, and gas, I might as well get a free trip out of it. Thus began my journey as a slave to the bank.

A strange thing happened soon after I started to use my credit card for the bare essentials. Through some kind of inexplicable magic, my CD collection started to grow by leaps and bounds. I would visit music stores and walk away with 10 to 20 new CDs. Of course, these CDs could only be played on top-notch stereo equipment, so my stereo and speakers were magically upgraded too.

Next, it was time to make the transition from my electric typewriter (yes, I'm *that* old!) to my first real computer—a Macintosh Plus. I don't count the Atari 800 computer that my family had for several years. The Atari 800 was just a video game console to me, although I did play around with the BASIC computing language cartridge a few times. I didn't get very far because I was much more interested in our vast library of game cartridges. Thanks to the fact that my mom worked for Atari, we had all of the classic Atari games and most of the bad ones. (Yes, even *E. T. the Extra-Terrestrial!*)

Compared to the Atari 800's 8K of RAM and 90K floppy drive for storage, the Mac Plus was a racehorse. The Mac Plus boasted 128 KB of RAM and a built-in, 3.5-inch floppy drive. This highly coveted machine could only be acquired at the significant cost of about $2,000 back in 1987. Put in on my card.

Then there were the expenses for spring-break trips, concerts, long weekends, and a three-week summer backpacking trip in France. Put it on my card.

You may notice that I've said nothing about clothes so far. I managed to get through most of college without a care in the world when it came to my wardrobe. (Suffice it to say, I didn't have many dates.) My fanciest work clothes up to that point had been a uniform of black-and-white checkered pants, a white buttoned-down shirt, and a baseball cap that I wore as a pizza delivery guy. (At least I could play loud music while I drove around town looking like a dork.)

In my senior year of college, I finally realized that perhaps my timeless classic wardrobe of jeans, flannel shirts, t-shirts, athletic gear, and well-worn hiking boots had some room for improvement. Just put it on my credit card.

I will spare you the gory details of my path in my 20s and early 30s. Never underestimate the spending power of an alcoholic with a credit card. Instead, let's look at a more serene and typical snapshot of the financial path you may follow after finishing school:

"*Woohoo,* I'm done with school! Time for my senior trip and some work clothes for my new job. I don't have my first check yet, so I'll just put it on my credit card for now.

"What an amazing trip! I'm so glad that school is over. I can finally get a real job and start making some money. Time to wade through my stack of mail. *Huh.* What's this? My first student loan statement. *Whoa*—that's a big number! Well, no problem. With my new job, I'll pay that off in no time.

"Wow, these apartments suck. Is this cockroach-infested dump all I can get for $800 per month? There's no way I can bring a date back to *this* place. Guess I'll need to shell out some cash to get a decent place. I'd better upgrade my car too while I'm at it. No sane person will want to go for a ride with me in this junker. Plus the interest rate for a new car is amazing right now.

"I've met The One. Time to create the impression that I'm all that and a bag of chips (even though I don't even have enough cash to cover the bag of chips). I think I'll start with a nice dinner at a fancy restaurant and perhaps a weekend getaway at a quaint bed and breakfast. I'll put in on my card.

"We're engaged! Look at that ring. It's perfect! Yes, the ring was pricy, but wedding rings are forever. A wedding ring is not the place to skimp. Put it on my card.

"We're so excited about the wedding. It's going to be the best wedding ever—an event that nobody will ever forget! After the wedding is over, we're off to Tahiti where we'll stay in one of those bungalows right on top of the water (the ones where you can actually see fish swimming in the ocean through windows in the floor). It's going to be so amazing! We'll put it on our card.

"We're having a baby! We definitely need to revamp the bedroom and make this place kid-friendly. We might as well upgrade the kitchen too. Plus, we'll need some new furniture since we'll be spending a lot more time around the house. Better yet, let's just a buy a new house! That way, we can have a fresh start for our family, and we've always wanted a nice yard. We'll just get a loan. The rates are pretty decent now if we act fast.

"There's no way we can fit a stroller and a car seat in this car. Guess we'll have to buy one of those mini-vans that we've always made fun of. The convenience will be worth the embarrassment.

"I can't believe that our kids are just about to start school! Our public schools are a nightmare. I'm not putting *my* child in one of those. Let's look at some private school options. If we can't find something reasonable, then we might need to move to a better neighborhood. We'll also need to sign up our kids for sports leagues and music lessons. We need to get our kids off to a good start.

"Can you believe that our kids are starting college soon? Where does the time go! It's so amazing that our eldest child has been accepted by two Ivy League schools! Guess we'll need to look into student loans; I never expected to pay this much for tuition. But this will set up our child for life, so it's worth it. Hard to believe that we're looking at student loans for our kids, and we haven't even paid off our own student loans!

"This house is so quiet now that our kids are in college. Well, at least we can start getting our finances in order now. Speaking of which ... oh, crap! Look at these numbers! We're hundreds of thousands of dollars in debt. How did this happen? It's not like we live an extravagant life. We're so careful about how we spend money. To make matters worse, we only have $10,000 in our retirement account. We should have a few more zeros added to that number by now. This is not good. Looks like I'll need to get a second job to dig us out of this hole. At this rate, I don't see how I can *ever* retire."

Welcome to financial hell.

"Act your wage."
Dave Ramsey

Failure quiz: personal finance

1. Do you have at least three months of living expenses set aside as cash in an emergency fund? Credit cards don't count.
   ❏ Yes   ❏ No

2. Are you free of credit card debt?   ❏ Yes   ❏ No

3. Do you have a written budget that you follow each month?
   ❏ Yes   ❏ No

4. Do you earn more than you spend?   ❏ Yes   ❏ No

5. Have you and your child implemented a plan to save for your child's education?   ❏ Yes   ❏ No

6. Do you set aside a percentage of your income each month for charity, personal development, and retirement?   ❏ Yes   ❏ No

7. Do you have appropriate medical insurance, a trust or living will, a medical directive, and clear instructions for your family in the event of your incapacitation or death?   ❏ Yes   ❏ No

8. Are you debt-free, including your house?   ❏ Yes   ❏ No

9. Are you financially independent to the point where you can live off the interest of the money you've saved?   ❏ Yes   ❏ No

10. As long as you are making sound financial decisions, do you feel peaceful about money regardless of the ups and downs in net worth that you might experience?   ❏ Yes   ❏ No

Failure quiz: personal finance (continued)

Count up the number of "yes" answers and refer to the chart below:

0-2   Yikes. The name Dave Ramsey should be echoing off your walls any day now. Take a look at Financial Peace University or some other method that will encourage you to do a major overhaul of your personal finances.

3-5   Welcome to the club. I've been here awhile too. Let's create a solid financial plan that will take us to the next level.

6-8   Looking good. A few minor tweaks, and you're on the path to financial freedom.

9-10 You've arrived! Bask in the glory of financial peace.

**"If you want to be a Millionaire, start with a
billion dollars and launch a new airline."**
Richard Branson

Who wants to be a millionaire?

You say you want to be a millionaire, but are you willing to put your money where your mouth is to make that a reality? If you're one of the few who were blessed with wisdom and discipline at a young age, then you'll have it easy.

A 25-year-old only needs to invest $100 per month in a Roth IRA until the age of 65. Yes, I realize that's 40 years of contributing $100 per month, but it will be worth it when you open that envelope at age 65 and—voilà—you're a millionaire. This scenario assumes that you select a Roth IRA with a decent stock mutual fund that yields a 12% return in the long run. You'll be a millionaire at a personal cost of $100 per month. It's really that simple. That's $48,000 out of your pocket in exchange for $1,000,000. Now *that's* a bargain!

If you are 35 years old before you start saving, then you'll need to squirrel away $310 per month for 30 years in order to be a millionaire at the age of 65. That's $111,600 out of your pocket in exchange for $1,000,000 at 65. That's still a great deal.

So what about poor saps like me who are 45 years old when they finally get serious about retirement savings? Well, now it starts to sting quite a bit. We need to save $1,035 per month from age 45 to 65. That's a total of $248,400 out of your pocket over the course of 20 years in exchange for $1,000,000 at 65.

Are you 55 with zero savings? Sorry to break the news to you, but this isn't going to sting, it's going to hurt ... *a lot*. If you want to retire in 10 years, then you'll need to set aside $4,250 per month for the next 10 years. That's $510,000 out of your pocket in exchange for $1,000,000 in 10 years. Still, that doubles your money, but $4,250 is a large chunk of change to come up with each month. *Hmm*. Maybe retiring at 70 or 75 isn't all that bad as long as you're doing something you enjoy.

Also keep in mind that Roth IRAs limit you to $5,500 per year in contributions (or $6,500 per year if you are over the age of 50) with income caps. In other words, late starters to the savings game will be looking at other options in addition to the Roth IRA. Most of the other options are taxed when you cash them out, so you'll need to save even more money than the estimates provided if you want to end up with a net amount of $1,000,000 in your pocket.

Sixty-five years old with no savings? Well, I guess you already know that you won't be retiring at 65, unless you choose to live off your Social Security income or you're one of the lucky ones with a pension. It's not too late to get in the game, but the game will be a bit different for you, and it will likely involve at least a part-time job. Perhaps this is a good time to transition to a new career, doing something that you love to do and can continue to do well into the future.

Ninety-five years old with no savings? Sorry, but it's probably too late to get into the retirement savings game unless you benefit from a major breakthrough in medicine that is on the horizon.

That $100-per-month option is starting to sound pretty good about now, isn't it? That's the point: The earlier you start, the better off you are.

Here's a fact that will make many of us sigh in dismay: What if you were a precocious teen who decided to start saving money at the age of 15? That's $32 per month—just $19,200 out of our pocket—in exchange for $1,000,000 at the age of 65. I'll pause for a moment so you can join me in some self-kicking. $32 a month: How easy is that? Clearly, it's even easier *not* to do it because the vast majority don't.

This mathematical magic is made possible by the power of compound interest, and the secret ingredient of compound interest is time. To take full advantage of compound interest, you need to start young. So, on behalf of the legions of older folks who failed to save at an early age, we urge you ... beg you ... *plead* with you to start investing today! Invest now, even if you only have a small amount to invest. The results will appear slow at first, but hang in there. You'll be rewarded with a retirement balance that fills you with feelings of excitement, security, and possibility, rather than a retirement filled with Ramen and oatmeal.

Many rich retirees aren't rich because they earned a lot of money. They're rich because they saved a lot of the money they earned, starting at an early age. Thanks to compound interest, if you're in your 20s or early 30s, and you're capable of delayed gratification, it's pretty easy to become a millionaire in the United States.

"Invest three percent of your income in yourself
(self-development) in order to guarantee your future."
Brian Tracy

4-10 60 Rule

Here's a hint for another often-overlooked investment component: Invest in the person you see in the mirror each morning. Without a doubt, the best return on your investment comes from investing in yourself.

I've heard several approaches for the best way to spend each dollar that we earn. My favorite approach to building wealth is a hybrid of what Jim Rohn, Brian Tracy, and Darren Hardy recommend. I call this philosophy the 4-10 60 Rule (or 10/10/10/10/60 Rule) for how to spend a dollar. Much of this philosophy originates from George Clason's book, *The Richest Man in Babylon*. Jim Rohn regularly recommended this book to his audiences throughout his career.

Here is the breakdown of the 4-10 60 Rule:

- Give the first 10% of your income to charity or use it to help others. Use 10% of your income to make donations to a nonprofit organization, church, school, or whatever else you consider to be a worthwhile cause.

- The second 10% is what we'll refer to as "active capital," which is money you'll actively use, such as investing in real estate, renovating your house or car, publishing a book, or selling products or services. This fosters an entrepreneurial mindset, with the motivation to turn your business ideas into reality and earn profits rather than wages. As Jim Rohn's mentor, John Earl Shoaff taught Jim many years ago, "Profits are better than wages. Wages make you a living; profits make you a fortune."

- Use the third 10% for personal development to help mold you into the person you need to become to attract success. Identify the key behaviors or skills that are holding you back. Once you've identified the areas to improve, use 10% of your income to purchase books, DVDs, and magazines, or to hire a coach or attend a course or seminar on the topic. You might find it useful to tackle one personal development area each quarter, or you may want to take an entire year to focus on becoming an expert in one critical area. This can be related to work, relationships, health, communication skills, or hobbies that you want to turn into a career. Anything goes as long as it's a key behavior or skill that will advance your life in the direction you want to go. In the end, smart investments in your personal growth will yield the greatest return on investment in your life.

- Use the fourth 10% for "passive capital." Invest this money in a Roth IRA, 401k, or other long-term savings option. Make automatic contributions from your paycheck or checking account. Invest it, and then forget about it. This is money that you set aside to let compounding interest work its magic over time.

- The remaining 60% is all yours. Enjoy it! Use it to cover your living expenses and guilt-free discretionary spending. This includes your rent, bills, groceries, gas, travel, and entertainment.

The 4-10 60 Rule is a guideline to inspire some creative thinking on how you should be spending the money you earn. Depending on your current financial situation, your reality may be closer to a 4-1 96 Rule, but work towards the 4-10 60 Rule guideline as your financial situation improves.

No matter how small the numbers, get in the habit of first setting aside money for charity, active capital, personal development, and passive capital, and then spend what remains. The thought of investing first and spending what's left, rather than spending first and investing what's left, is a fundamental difference in philosophy between the rich and the poor.

"We think sometimes that poverty is only being hungry,
naked and homeless. The poverty of being unwanted,
unloved and uncared for is the greatest poverty. We must
start in our own homes to remedy this kind of poverty."
Mother Teresa

Real poverty and wealth

With all of this talk about money and investing, it's a good idea to pause and remind yourself that money is only one piece of the puzzle when it comes to your happiness. Even if you already know this, it's easy to focus too much attention on your bank account and ignore the other important aspects of life that bring you joy. What are the other important aspects of happiness that you should consider? For a fresh perspective, let's ask the Dragon King.

No, the Dragon King is not a character from *The Lord of the Rings*, although it would no doubt be an impressive-looking character if it were. This one is real. "Dragon King" is the name for the head of state of the Kingdom of Bhutan, a landlocked country at the eastern end of the Himalayas in Asia. Bhutan is translated as "The Land of Dragons," and the Bhutanese people call themselves Dragon people, so it logically follows that the leader is called the Dragon King.

Aside from having the cool title of Fourth Dragon King of Bhutan, Jigme Singye Wangchuck is known for introducing many modern reforms in his country. One day, back in 1972, the Dragon King made a casual remark that true progress should be measured by how much happier the people were rather than how much money the nation made. He used the term "Gross National Happiness" (GNH) to describe his commitment to build the economy of his country without sacrificing its Buddhist spiritual values. Thus, the concept of GNH was born.

Since 1972, the country of Bhutan has adopted GNH, rather than Gross Domestic Product, as its formal performance measure. You may have heard the term, but do you know how Bhutan defines and measures "happiness" for the country's population? After reading through "A Short Guide to Gross National Happiness Index" published in 2012 by The Centre for Bhutan Studies, I learned that Bhutan's GNH Index is composed of a whopping 33 indicators, which are grouped into nine domains. Apparently, happiness is not all that simple.

Here's the breakdown:

- **Domain 1: Psychological well-being.** This refers to an internal perception of how people evaluate their level of contentment for three indicators: life satisfaction, emotional balance, and spirituality.

- **Domain 2: Health.** In Bhutan's health system, health is viewed as a balance between the mind and the body. An individual is said to be in good health only if "heat pain" is absent from the body and sorrow is absent from the mind.

- **Domain 3: Education.** The Bhutanese government emphasizes the importance of a holistic education that includes a deep foundation in traditional knowledge, common values, and skills. In addition to the basics of reading, writing, math, science, and technology, citizens are encouraged to engage in creative learning and expression and to cultivate positive values.

- **Domain 4: Culture.** The fourth of the nine domains of the GNH Index is culture, reflecting the high importance that the Kingdom of Bhutan places on preserving and promoting its culture and identity.

- **Domain 5: Time use.** The fifth GNH Index domain assesses two indicators regarding the balance among work, leisure, and sleep. Leisure is not called out as a separate indicator, but is viewed as the time not working or sleeping.

- **Domain 6: Good governance.** The governance domain includes indicators that look at an individual's political participation and political freedom, as well as an assessment of government's efficiency and service delivery.

- **Domain 7: Community vitality.** The government of Bhutan believes that community vitality is sustained through cooperative relationships and social networks within the community. A "vital community" is described as a group of people who support and interact positively with each other. This domain includes an assessment of four indicators: social support, community relationships, family, and crime.

- **Domain 8: Ecological diversity and resilience.** Bhutan's constitution specifies that every Bhutanese citizen shall "… contribute to the protection of the natural environment, conservation of the rich biodiversity of Bhutan, and prevention of all forms of ecological degradation including noise, visual and physical pollution …" This domain looks at four indicators: pollution, environmental responsibility, impact of wildlife on agriculture, and urban issues such as traffic congestion, inadequate green spaces, lack of pedestrian streets, and urban sprawl.

- **Domain 9: Living standards.** The last of the nine domains looks at the material well-being of the citizens of Bhutan. The living domain includes three indicators that consider household income, assets, and housing quality.

Well, there you have it! If you're thinking that it must take a long time to ask these survey questions, you'd be right. When it was initially launched, the survey interview required six to seven hours to complete. I can picture how most of us would react if someone stopped us on the street to say, "Pardon me. Can you spare six hours of your time to complete a survey about your happiness?"

I realize that this is way more than you ever wanted to know about Bhutan's measure of GNH, but it's a great illustration of the wide variety of factors that influence our happiness in life.

In closing, you may be in pretty bad shape when it comes to your finances and planning for your retirement. Similar to your health, it's interesting to explore your feelings about money and analyze why you may be self-destructive when it comes to your personal finances. Most self-destructive behaviors are rooted in some kind of unresolved pain. Fixing the problem often involves changing your circumstances, becoming a better advocate for yourself, or shifting your mindset.

You may have been idealistic when you were young, refusing "the soulless path of selling out to the man" by taking a typical corporate job. Or perhaps you saw your parents work their butts off all of their lives, and you decided that you don't want to go down that path. However, once you have a family and start to edge closer to retirement, you may end up with feelings of regret and anxiety about the financial hole that you dug while you were young.

Take some time and explore your relationship to money. Develop a plan for your life that will leave you with a feeling of abundance and happiness.

Happiness may just be a mindshift away.

CHAPTER 4

Relationships:
My will be done

"How people treat you is their karma; how you react is yours."
Wayne Dyer

It's my way or the highway

For me, it started in the sixth grade. One day at recess, I received a folded piece of paper from a friend of a friend of a girl. As I opened it, my keen mind quickly deduced that she had a crush on me. I think the note was something along the lines of "I like you."

Dressed in my finest Garanimals, I bravely asked the girl if she wanted to "go around with me," which was the custom back in the day in San Jose, California. (By "brave," I mean that I wrote those words in a note and had a friend deliver it to a friend of the girl in question.) I soon received the response, delivered via the standard circuitous route: "Yes," along with a heart drawn on the note.

Next class period, we exchanged an awkward "hi" as we walked past each other. I didn't know what else to say, so I kept walking. I had no idea what was expected of me with this "going around" stuff and, given that I was painfully shy, I had no intention of following through with anything that might be expected of me.

Over the coming weeks, things started to heat up, mostly due to friends who literally dragged me along. I vaguely recall a few roller-skating outings and a slow dance at a birthday party, where we rocked back and forth on stiff, wooden legs.

A few weeks later, our torrid romance was over. There was no official declaration from either party, but it was clear that we were through. She probably figured out that the only way she would be able to spend time with me was if she happened to be on the opposing team in a soccer game. Little else interested me at the time.

That was my last relationship for a very long time—until my junior year of college, if the sad truth be told—but not for lack of interest. I was simply too shy, too clueless, and too focused on soccer. As an off-the-charts introvert, I chased after girls who were completely different than I was, with the hope that their extroversion would rub off on me. (By "chase," I mean that I said hello to the same girl several times in a single month when I walked past her on campus.) This approach yielded poor results, so I took the next logical step to meeting women: I drank a lot of alcohol.

Thanks to alcohol, I could temporarily morph into a loquacious extrovert, but only for a few hours. I was even known to bust out a few break-dancing moves in public. Alcohol gave me the courage to do the things that I would regret the next morning. I would wake up with a desire to live in a debris hut in the woods until the embarrassment of the previous evening wore off.

This was my go-to pattern throughout my 20s and early 30s. Along the way, I pursued relationships that weren't a good fit and passed up more suitable opportunities. I wasn't comfortable in my own skin, so the thought of finding someone similar to me was not an appealing prospect. Instead, I continued my alcohol-fueled forays in my quest to shed my true nature. In short, *I failed.*

That was just the beginning. I won't air my dirty laundry in the relationship department because of the impact that it might have on others. Let's just say I neglected so many of the keys to a healthy relationship that you'd think I was deliberately trying to avoid checking boxes on one of the healthy relationship questionnaires created by Dr. John Gottman.

John is world renowned for his 40+ years of work, 190 published academic articles, and 40+ books on the topics of marital stability, divorce prediction, and parenting. John and his wife Dr. Julie Schwartz Gottman cofounded the Gottman Institute and the Love Lab, where much of his couples' interactions research was conducted. In his book, *The Seven Principles for Making Marriage Work*, Dr. Gottman runs through the key characteristics of a healthy marriage. In keeping with the theme of this book, I simply turned Dr. Gottman's list on its head to explore best practices on how to fail in relationships and marriages.

Of course, the low-hanging fruit for ruining relationships can be found in the form of behaviors such as infidelity, addiction, and abuse. But let's explore more subtle approaches. Here are seven Love Lab-tested principles that you can employ to ensure that your relationships will fall apart.

Principle 1: Ignore what's important to your partner. For an added twist, you can degrade or downplay your partner's interests. There are lots of ways to do this. You can bring home some decadent Ben & Jerry's ice cream as a gift for your partner who is allergic to dairy and doesn't like sweets. Bound into the house and roughhouse your partner to the ground if she has expressed a preference for sweet cuddles. Planning an event? Just do what you want to do. I'm sure your partner will have fun tagging along!

Principle 2: Don't waste your breath on praise. Your partner already knows she is pretty. Plenty of other guys tell her. If your partner got a promotion at work, they've already received recognition and praise, so why would he or she need anything more from you? The best policy is to use your limited alone time together to talk about yourself.

Principle 3: Immerse yourself in your gadgets. Modern technology has given us so many wonderful ways to avoid true intimacy. Take advantage of them! Frequently look at your phone when conversing with your loved ones. This works for any close relationship, not just your partner. Turn on the TV during dinner. Play solitary video games during family time. And be sure to stay on top of all of your social media accounts. Seriously, what is more fun: listening to your partner talk about their day or watching videos of cats in costumes?

Principle 4: Full steam ahead! The best way to chart a course in life is to put in earplugs and barrel forward. Block out the noise from your partner and keep your eyes on the prize. Ignore their protests for now. Everyone will see the value in your direction later. Remember: You don't need help or advice. You've got this.

Principle 5: Turn molehills into mountains. You've heard the expression, "Give them an inch, and they'll take a mile." That should be your mantra in any healthy relationship. No problem is too small to dig in your heels. Transform small, solvable problems into gridlock, and don't budge on anything.

Principle 6: Locking horns is fun. Here's a cool fact about reindeer: They lock horns for sport, untangle themselves, and then do it all over again. Granted, sometimes they can't get untangled and die. But don't worry about that part. Locking horns is fun! You can apply this to your relationship. If you're having the same arguments again and again, then you'll know you're on the right track. Conflict as sport. Have at it, and have fun!

Principle 7: I did it my way. As Americans, we cherish our independence. When it comes to independence, more is better. Relentlessly pursue your own dreams, and let your partner do the same. If your plans happen to overlap, great! If not great! You take care of yourself, and let your partner take care of him or herself. You can compare notes later.

Put these seven principles into practice, and you're virtually guaranteed to fail in all of your meaningful relationships.

"If you change the way you look at things,
the things you look at change."
Wayne Dyer

Failure quiz: relationships

1. Can you describe your partner's dreams, hopes, worries, goals, and interests? Can you list the names of his or her closest friends and family members?   ❏ Yes   ❏ No

2. Do you seek out meaningful opportunities to connect with your partner each day?   ❏ Yes   ❏ No

3. Do you and your partner have a strong sense of shared meaning? Can you describe the goals, dreams, and values that you and your partner share?   ❏ Yes   ❏ No

4. When appropriate, do you find that you frequently smile when interacting with your family, friends, and colleagues?
❏ Yes   ❏ No

5. When you realize that you're partially to blame for something, are you quick to perform the four steps of a sincere apology?
❏ Yes   ❏ No

6. When you're in an argument, do you make repair attempts to prevent the conversation from spiraling out of control?
❏ Yes   ❏ No

7. In your relationships, do you communicate in a way that is honest, empathic, and with the intention to obtain a positive outcome that will enrich both of your lives?   ❏ Yes   ❏ No

8. Would you say that you truly know yourself and your partner?
❏ Yes   ❏ No

9. Do you have and express feelings of fondness and admiration for your partner?   ❏ Yes   ❏ No

10. At the end of an argument or dispute, do you choose to end on love, no matter what?   ❏ Yes   ❏ No

Failure quiz: relationships (continued)

Count up the number of "yes" answers and refer to the chart below:

0-2   Come on. You can do better than that!

3-5   Room for improvement. Consider some changes to improve the quality of your relationships.

6-8   Your relationship skills are looking good!

9-10   Impressive! You're a relationship guru whom we can all learn from.

"Know thyself? If I knew myself I would run away."
Johann Wolfgang von Goethe

Know thyself

The prerequisite to any healthy relationship is to first know yourself. One of the best tools available to help you get oriented is to take a Myers-Briggs test. There are other well-regarded tests out there, such as the Enneagram, which categories human personality into one of nine interconnected personality types (Reformer, Helper, Achiever, Individualist, Investigator, Loyalist, Enthusiast, Challenger, and Peacemaker), but I've found the Myers-Briggs test to be more useful.

In a nutshell, the Myers-Briggs test is a personality test that can help us understand our psychological preference in terms of how we make decisions and perceive the world. There is plenty of theory behind it; however, in simple terms, each of us falls into one of 16 buckets based on a combination of the following pairs of categories: extroversion (E) or introversion (I); sensing (S) or intuition (N); thinking (T) or feeling (F); and judging (J) or perceiving (P).

I've taken the test about five different times over the past 30 years and have seen a significant shift in my results as I became more aware and comfortable with ... well, me. I started off as an ISTJ (introversion + sensing + thinking + judging) in my 20s; then, over the years, I've become firmly planted in the INFJ camp (introversion + intuition + feeling + judging), reflecting my shift from being a logical, memorizing machine to embracing a much more intuitive, reflective, and empathic approach to life.

Many good resources will teach you about the Myers-Briggs test, so I won't go into the details here. I do recommend, however, that you take the Myers-Briggs and Enneagram tests, and then read about your personality profile.

Using the insight gained from your personality tests, continue your self-discovery process by writing down your answers to the following questions:

1. What is your ultimate passion and purpose in life?
2. What are your strengths?
3. What are your weaknesses?
4. Describe your ideal life and lifestyle.
5. Describe your ideal partner or spouse.

6.   In light of your answers to the previous questions, describe your ideal
     career. Rather than starting with your career and building a life around
     it, start with your ideal lifestyle and design a career around that. Many
     of us do this in the wrong order and end up regretting it later in life.

Once you've written down your answers to these questions, it's worth reread-
ing your Myers-Briggs and Enneagram profiles to help ensure that the life you are
chasing is closely aligned with your core values, beliefs, and personality.

The Myers-Briggs test is one of many tools to help you better understand
yourself, but it can also be a useful tool to better understand others.

"You can discover more about a person in an
hour of play than in a year of conversation."
Plato

Know others

I've been part of several organizations that required us to take the Myers-Briggs test and strongly encouraged us to share our personality type with our colleagues and manager. This can be a useful approach for building cohesive teams and tailoring your management style for the teammates you work with.

The same is true for your relationships. It's a good idea for you and your partner to take a personality test and discuss the results afterwards. Similarly, you can both answer the questions that we covered in the previous section and compare notes. This exercise can help you gain many valuable insights on how to improve the quality of your relationship.

Armed with these insights about your partner, you can work together to design an ideal lifestyle that excites both of you. It all goes back to the concepts of creating love maps, turning towards each other, and creating shared meaning.

> **"Effective communication is 20% what you know
> and 80% how you feel about what you know."**
> **Jim Rohn**

Communication breakdown

Once we know ourselves, and we know the other person, there's still the pesky matter of communication, and it sure is easy to blow it in this department. The goal of communication is to give and receive in a loving and compassionate manner. Instead, we often resort to our knee-jerk reactions of withdrawal, attack, or defensiveness in the face of judgment or criticism.

In Dr. Marshall Rosenberg's classic book, *Nonviolent Communication: A Language of Life: Life-Changing Tools for Healthy Relationships*, Rosenberg encourages us to develop and practice deep listening skills that reflect an awareness of what we perceive, feel, and want, rather than an impulsive reaction to a statement or event. Rosenberg's nonviolent communication process has the following four components:

1. **Observation:** Observe what is actually happening in a situation without judgment or evaluation.

2. **Feeling:** State how you feel when you observe the action. This can include positive or negative feelings. Your statement should take the form of "I feel … because I …" instead of the reactive response of "I feel … because you …" Focus on discovering the needs of each party rather than point out what's wrong with each other. By focusing on your needs, you're more likely to receive a compassionate response to your needs.

3. **Needs:** State which of your needs are connected to the feelings that you identified. When you express your needs, you have a better chance of getting them met. Communicate your needs in such a way that it's clear you're equally concerned about the other person's needs.

4. **Request:** Immediately follow Step 3 with a very specific request, indicating what you want from the other person. The goal of the nonviolent communication process is to build a relationship based on honesty and empathy and to obtain a positive outcome that will enrich both of your lives.

Each of the four pieces of information can be stated verbally or by other means, such as through physical touch. It's even possible to do each of the four components without uttering a word.

Rosenberg offers the following simple example between a mother and teenage son to illustrate how the four components are carried out in practice: "Felix, when I see two balls of soiled socks under the coffee table and another three next to the TV, I feel irritated because I am needing more order in the rooms that we share in common. Would you be willing to put your socks in your room or in the washing machine?" It's that simple. But, as we have seen throughout this book, what's easy to do is easy *not* to do.

For the inevitable situations we encounter when communication breaks down into an argument or disagreement, emotionally intelligent couples use what Dr. Gottman refers to as "repair attempts"—statements or actions that prevent negativity from escalating out of control. They can take the form of a statement, a joke, a hug, or anything else that brings feelings of love, compassion, and connection back into the room. Dr. Gottman believes that, "The success or failure of a couple's repair attempts is one of the primary factors in whether their marriage is likely to flourish of flounder … and what determines the success of their repair attempts is the strength of their marital friendship."

If you find yourself in a conversation with someone who is angry, Dr. Rosenberg offers this memorable piece of advice: "Never put your 'but' in the face of an angry person." Answering with "but …" to an angry person will usually make matters worse. Instead, take a deep breath and focus your attention on the angry person's feelings and needs, and then empathize with that person. This empathic approach will often disarm an angry person and get you both on track to find a positive outcome that will enrich both of your lives.

Obviously, we are only skimming the surface on the vast topic of communication in relationships. Fortunately, there are plenty of great resources available on the subject of effective communication, and I encourage you to read advice taken directly from the experts on this all-important topic.

> "Right actions in the future are the best
> apologies for bad actions in the past."
> **Tryon Edwards**

"I'm sorry you feel that way" (how to apologize)

Apologies are simple in theory but can end up being difficult in practice. I've certainly botched my share of apologies over the years. Usually this was due to my peacemaking nature. My desire to avoid conflict in my younger days resulted in making apologies for the weather. I would apologize even when I didn't think that I did anything wrong and had no intention of changing my behavior in the future. I had not yet internalized this lesson: When we don't really feel sorry or don't feel that we share any responsibility for what happened, then our apology will fall flat.

People are looking for sincerity in an apology, and different people have different ideas about what a "sincere apology" looks like. What follows are some key points taken from Gary Chapman and Jennifer M. Thomas's book, *The Five Languages of Apology: How to Experience Healing in All Your Relationships.*

To cover all of the bases, a good apology boils down to a few simple steps and one important caveat. We'll start with the caveat. You must truly feel sorry, and you must feel that your actions or words played a role in the situation. If these conditions are not true, then hold off on your apology. You're not ready to apologize yet. If, after some genuine reflection, you truly believe that you are innocent, then you may first need to practice your constructive confrontation and nonviolent communication skills. However, if you agree with the caveat's conditions, then follow these four simple steps:

Step 1: Express regret, accept responsibility, and initiate restitution. While that might sound tough, it's actually very simple. Say each of the following sentences to the person you hurt:

- "I am sorry."
- "It's my fault" or "I was wrong."
- "What can I do to make it better?"

Now that wasn't so bad, was it?

Step 2: Listen. It's important to listen with your ears, not your mouth. Listen to the response, and thoughtfully consider what is said. Reflect on the requested amends, determine if you are willing and able to follow through on the requested amends, and take legitimate steps to prevent it from happening again.

Step 3: Verbalize your intended amends and request forgiveness. Okay, now it's time for you to speak again. Thank the person for sharing his or her feedback with you. Verbalize what you intend to do to make amends and prevent it from happening again. Then request—not demand—forgiveness. This goes something like, "Will you please forgive me?"

Step 4: Take action. Now it's time to follow through on what you said you would do to make amends. You may not be able to address the issues right away, and you may continue to slip up. However, the important part is to make it clear that you are taking concrete steps to improve the situation, and you are serious about it. If you apologize but don't do anything to change your future behavior, then all of your efforts in Steps 1 through 3 may be wasted.

Different people place greater value on different steps of the apology. Some people really want to hear the other person ask for forgiveness before they consider an apology to be genuine and sincere; others are more interested in the "I am sorry" and "I was wrong" part of the apology. There is a large group of people who are much more interested in action, not words. Many people want to see each step take place. That's why it's best to go through all four steps to ensure that your apology will be interpreted as genuine and sincere.

That's it ... apology complete! If you make a genuine effort to go through each of these four steps, then chances are high that you'll be forgiven, although it might take a long time in some cases. In the unfortunate cases where the other person refuses to forgive you—despite your honest attempts to apologize and make amends— then you need to move on while doing your best not to repeat the offense.

With experience, you'll get better at identifying when your actions might have hurt others. You'll be able to more quickly identify and acknowledge your role in something that went wrong. This awareness shortens the gap between your action and your apology and makes it much easier to address.

In some cases, you may catch yourself as soon as the words leave your mouth. When you call it out on the spot, you may prevent it from becoming a big issue and may even be able to laugh about it with the person you offended. As the gap in time increases between your action and your apology, you give resentment and anger time to fester. It's good practice to apologize as soon as you are aware of a wrong that you have done.

In situations where there are mutual feelings of bitterness or resentment, consider the following words from Lao-Tzu: "Someone must risk returning injury with kindness, or hostility will never turn to goodwill."

In Dr. Wayne Dyer's book, *Change Your Thoughts—Change Your Life: Living the Wisdom of the Tao,* he shares the previous quote from Lao-Tzu, along with the following words to consider: "As the storm of a quarrel subsides, you must find a way to disregard your ego's need to be right. It's time to extend kindness by letting go of your anger. It's over, so offer forgiveness to yourself and the other person and encourage resentment to dissipate. Be the one seeking a way to give, rather than the one looking for something to get." At the termination of any argument or dispute, choose to end on love, no matter what.

"Be helpful. When you see a person
without a smile, give him yours."
Zig Ziglar

Smile

Did you know that it requires more muscles to make a frown than to make a smile? You may have also heard that annoying saying, "Turn that frown upside down"—usually at a time when we want to throttle the person saying it. But, like it or not, smiles and laughter are very important forms of communication for our physical and mental health.

Smiles and laughter have been shown to enhance relationships, strengthen the immune system, diminish pain, boost energy, and offer protection from stress. Like vegetables, laughter and smiles are wonder drugs. Seek out people and activities that cause you to laugh and smile. Approaching life with a sense of humor will make you more relaxed, positive, balanced, creative, and joyful. Not a bad list of traits to have at your disposal, free of charge!

Now go forth and smile.

CHAPTER 5

We don't need no education

"The great end of education is to discipline rather than to furnish the mind; to train it to the use of its own powers, rather than fill it with the accumulation of others."
Tryon Edwards

Vomit on a page

It stings a bit when I read these words by Tryon Edwards. After all, I was a master of vomiting on a page. Original thought? *Hah!* No, my aim was to memorize, word for word, what the teacher said in the classroom. Then I spewed those words on an exam paper, waited a day, and collected my "A"—much to the annoyance of my friends who truly understood the course content and could apply it in the real world.

How did I do this? Here's the foolproof strategy I used in school to make me the fool for so many years:

Step 1: Sit in the back corner of class. As a shy kid, my primary goal was to make it through each class without uttering a word, and the back corner of the classroom seemed like the best spot to make that a reality. Even if the teacher asked if anyone knew how to spell the name "Aspelin," my head would be down, eyes glued to my paper, while the words *please don't call on me* raced through my head. It was pathetic.

On the occasions when the teacher had the nerve to call on me, it always caught me off guard, as if I were shocked to have been spotted in my camouflaged perch. I would get flustered, and my face would turn bright red. This pattern was so predictable that it earned me the nickname "Monsieur Le Rouge" from my high school French teacher.

It never occurred to me that I could circumvent this unpleasant routine by simply raising my hand to give answers I knew rather than waiting for the teacher to ask me questions that might stump me. (What can I say? I was young and dumb.) Regardless, my lack of class participation rarely had a significant impact on my overall grade, so I stayed the course.

Step 2: Take excellent notes. This step was the key to my success in school. I took notes that would make a court reporter proud. Thinking was irrelevant. I would write down everything I heard verbatim. This was partly due to the fact that I majored in biology, with a heavy load of fundamental science classes that were held in large auditoriums. Not exactly the kind of topic or setting that encouraged debate or discussion, and that suited me just fine. I figured that I could start thinking and questioning in upper-level classes or in graduate school. I also knew that, if I took excellent notes, I wouldn't have to "waste" my time reading textbooks, which brings me to Step 3.

Step 3: Never read anything in an assigned textbook unless absolutely necessary. As a college freshman, I started out with a very different approach to school: Skip class or daydream in class, and then try to memorize the textbooks. During one semester, I even managed to double-book two classes because I knew that I would only attend one of them at best.

Unfortunately, my textbook memorization experiment failed miserably. I was put on academic probation after receiving an impressive 1.5 grade point average in the first semester of my sophomore year. Back then, I only took one class seriously—Advanced Partying—even though I was awkwardly shy. This usually involved getting together a few friends to crank Pink Floyd, The Doors, Neil Young, and other classic rock music; attending Grateful Dead concerts; going to off-campus parties; using fake identification to get into bars; and maintaining a prominently displayed beer checklist to ensure that my roommates and I were drinking at least one beer each day. (As if I needed a checklist for that.) And, unlike Bill Clinton, I inhaled.

After that ill-fated semester, I made some drastic changes to my study and party habits. Beer checklists and inhaling were thrown out the window. Instead, I started trail running and worked part-time jobs to escape the social scene. My class attendance became perfect, my class notes were outstanding, and memorizing textbooks became a thing of the past. I didn't even buy textbooks anymore unless it was clearly a must. I only cracked a book when the teacher informed us of a topic that we didn't have time to cover in class but would still be on the test, or if I didn't understand something I had written in my notes.

Step 4: Don't study until exam week. I took great notes, day in and day out, until exam week. Then, about two or three days before the exam, I would pull out my notes and memorize them, word for word. For me, that often meant rewriting my notes with bullet points to help me memorize the material. I would pace for countless hours in empty classrooms, reciting my notes out loud until I had them memorized.

Step 5: Test-day strategy. On the day of the test, I would wake up early to give myself enough time to rehearse my notes from start to finish. For early morning exams, this often required a 4 am alarm. I didn't drink coffee back then, so I relied on a quick shower to wake me up. As I rehearsed my notes one last time, I would make a list of tricky mnemonics and formulas that I needed to stuff in my head. I would rehearse these gems until the moment the teacher handed me the test.

As soon as the exam paper touched my hand, I would go straight to an empty page and write down all of the formulas and mnemonics that were clinging for dear life to my short-term memory. With that burden lifted, it was time to relax and simply vomit on the pages. After my regurgitation was complete, I would walk up to the front of the room, hand my exam to the teacher, walk out the door, and quickly proceed to forget everything that I had stuffed in my head. (Beer helped with that.)

This new approach yielded a dramatic change in results. Instead of seeing my name on the probation list, my name became a fixture on the dean's list. Clearly, I was still too focused on the outcome rather than actual learning and practical application of knowledge. But it was a baby step in the right direction.

> "We can't solve problems by using the same kind
> of thinking we used when we created them."
> **Albert Einstein**

Failure quiz: education and continuous learning

1. Do you try to understand and apply the things you learn rather than simply memorize facts to impress others?   ❏ Yes   ❏ No

2. Are you committed to lifelong, continuous learning?
    ❏ Yes   ❏ No

3. Do you identify and experiment with a few key takeaways from each book or class that you complete?   ❏ Yes   ❏ No

4. Are you generally prepared for meetings and presentations?
    ❏ Yes   ❏ No

5. Are you focused on doing fewer things more often, so that you can get better at them? Can you clearly articulate what those few things are?   ❏ Yes   ❏ No

6. Are you giving away your knowledge and experience to others?
    ❏ Yes   ❏ No

7. Do you plan each day based on your few key priorities for that day, and then consistently execute the plan?   ❏ Yes   ❏ No

8. Do you already do many of the things that you hope to do in retirement, just in smaller doses?   ❏ Yes   ❏ No

9. Do you set aside time each week as unstructured downtime to try new things and discover new food caches?   ❏ Yes   ❏ No

10. Is your life characterized by continuous learning, curiosity, and exploration?   ❏ Yes   ❏ No

Failure quiz: education and continuous learning (continued)

Count up the number of "yes" answers and refer to the chart below:

0-2   You can do better than this! Create a personal development plan to make some improvements.

3-5   Room for improvement. Consider some changes to bump you up to the next category.

6-8   Looking good. You're on firm ground when it comes to your personal development

9-10 Impressive, oh wise one! You are an excellent role model for the rest of us, so I hope that you're sharing your knowledge with others.

**"Education's purpose is to replace an
empty mind with an open one."
Malcolm Forbes**

Oh, the humanity

Throughout my eight years of college and graduate school, there were only a few classes that threw me off my game. Most of these curve balls came in the form of humanities classes where right and wrong answers were not black and white.

The first time I experienced this twist was in a theology class taught by Rev. Michael J. Himes—one of those brilliant communicators who can captivate an audience— at the University of Notre Dame. His classes and sermons resembled sold-out, standing-room-only performances.

Rev. Himes operated under the premise that theology is too often taught in a manner suggesting an answer key to blindly accept as the truth. Instead, Rev. Himes suggested that the focus of theology should be on experiencing god. In his view, theology should summarize what people have found to be insightful and illuminating over the thousands of years of human experience. Then, our job is to take that body of knowledge, check it against our own experiences, and draw our own conclusions. Rev. Himes emphasized that both theological teaching and our own experiences have merit, and neither should be discarded lightly.

Of course, I was not aware of Rev. Himes's philosophy at the time, and I blissfully followed my normal studying routine for his class. However, when it was time to vomit on a page for my exam, there was no page to vomit on. Instead, the exam was a one-on-one, face-to-face discussion of the course content with Rev. Himes himself. Superficial spewing of facts or visual recognition of the correct answer in a multiple choice list wasn't going to fly with him. He asked open-ended questions about particular passages and philosophies.

Unfortunately, I hadn't thought much about the passages or the philosophies I had read and memorized. All I could do was tell him about the key points. But Rev. Himes wasn't interested in hearing me rattle off bulleted lists of key points. He wanted to know my thoughts on the topic. As you can imagine, I wasn't prepared for that line of questioning during my first exam.

This experience opened a new door for me, although it took many more years before I enthusiastically embraced the opportunity to cross the threshold. Once I finally stepped through that door, I had no interest in turning back.

I finally considered data and ideas as things to evaluate against my own experiences. I started to draw my own conclusions and offer my own advice. This marked the beginning of a slow, but significant shift from being a logical, memorizing machine to embracing a much more intuitive, reflective, and empathic approach to life.

Many years later, I heard a similar lesson echoed by the late Steve Jobs of Apple fame: "When you grow up, you tend to get told that the world is the way it is…live your life inside the world, try not to bash into the walls too much…that's a very limited life. Life can be much broader, once you discover one simple fact, and that is that everything around you that you call life was made up by people that were no smarter than you. And you can change it, you can influence it, you can build your own things that other people can use. Once you learn that, you'll never be the same again."

It's hard to believe that it took me so many years to fully embrace these key concepts, but better late than never. Or, as **Geoffrey** Chaucer originally put it back in 1386, "Better than never is late."

Although I only encountered the face-to-face, think-for-yourself approach to education a few times over the span of my academic career, those experiences convinced me of the effectiveness of this approach to learning. Schools in the United Kingdom appear to share this perspective as they put a much greater emphasis on verbal communication compared to the system I navigated in the United States.

Of course this dialog approach to education doesn't work well for all subjects. At Notre Dame, I also took a class on musculoskeletal anatomy that was taught by an excellent professor, Dr. John O'Malley. Given the course content and large class size, I assumed that speaking in class was not going to be on the agenda. You either know the name of the muscle—along with its origin, insertion, innervation, and action—or you don't. No participation or discussion required. I was wrong.

Dr. O'Malley had one trick up his sleeve that forced us to keep up with the course material each week rather than wait until the week of an exam. At the beginning of each class, Dr. O'Malley called the name of one unlucky soul to make the long journey to the front of the classroom, in front of the 70+ students, and be grilled for five minutes on the course content that we had learned so far. Given my aversion to speaking in class, this prospect horrified me.

To avoid public humiliation—a mighty powerful tool—I studied each week and was prepared for most classes. My name was randomly selected to stand in front of the class on two occasions. On the first occasion, I had been warned. I woke up very early that morning with a strange feeling that I would be called to the front of the class that day. Thankfully, I acted on this premonition by jumping out of bed much earlier than normal to study for an hour before class. This was something I only did on exam days.

Sure enough, at the beginning of class, Dr. O'Malley put a slide on the projector that had a cartoon along with the words "Brachial Plexus Hotline—call Mark Aspelin!"

I was simultaneously thrilled and terrified—thrilled because I had studied the material that morning and terrified because I now had to walk to the front of a large class of my peers and speak. I got off to a rocky start. I was so petrified to be standing in front of the large class that I couldn't answer the easiest questions Dr. O'Malley initially lobbed my way. My mind was blank, and I could feel my body shaking. It was as if everything I had learned a few hours earlier had been erased.

Then, as if somebody flipped a switch in my brain, I got over myself and was able to ace the rest of the questions ... even the most difficult ones. After class, some students congratulated me and expressed amazement at how well I knew the material. Little did they know that I had been somehow forewarned.

This experience reinforced the importance of preparation. Preparation is vital for performing virtually anything at a high level, and it can provide a major boost in confidence for those who are anxious about public speaking. It's worth heeding the advice of the Boy Scouts' motto: "Be prepared."

However, I thought I *was* prepared for my anatomy class when I bombed the first few questions. What I failed to grasp at the time was that "being prepared" also meant that I needed to be comfortable speaking in front of a large audience. Stage fright can trump any amount of rehearsal. I missed that part of the lesson from my anatomy class experience. Rest assured, the powers that be were quick to provide me with a refresher course on this topic.

The venue was the Classical Guitar Society of Colorado Springs. My task: Perform two songs in front of a group of 20 or 30 friendly people. Not wanting to take any chances, I picked two classical pieces that I knew cold. I could play these songs blindfolded, behind my back, with my toes, so I didn't bring sheet music with me. *Big mistake.*

I walked to the stage. I put my butt in the chair, my left foot on the footstool, and my fingers on the strings. The lights dimmed, the room became silent, and I proceeded to draw a complete and total blank. I played a few notes and stopped, apologized, and repeated this uncomfortable process three or four more times. It was hideous.

Then, just like in my anatomy class, a switch flipped in my head, and I could suddenly play the songs perfectly. It was as if I first needed to play out my worst-case scenario of making a fool of myself before I could relax and play the songs well. This time, I learned the lesson. I started to seek out opportunities to speak in public and, over time, I was able to get over my fear of speaking in front of large groups.

Twenty years have passed since then, and my aversion to public speaking has long since faded. I barely think twice about it now unless I'm in front of a really large group of people. For important events, I set aside a good chunk of time beforehand to make sure that I'm well prepared, and I usually bring notes or other reference materials to the stage, just in case. Having those references nearby puts my mind at ease. Just like having an umbrella seems to ensure that it won't rain, having my notes with me seems to ensure that I won't need them.

"Life is the art of drawing without an eraser."
John W. Gardner

Drawing without an eraser

Have you ever tried drawing without an eraser? Of course you have. We all have. Metaphorically speaking, that's what we all do every day. Along our journey through life, we learn a few things that help us produce better drawings without so many scribbled-out lines in our relationships, work, health, spiritual life, finances, and hobbies.

As I've already pointed out, I was not an intellectual giant in college; I was more of a transcriptionist. I took excellent notes that I handed back to the teacher, word for word, in the form of exam answers. Using the drawing metaphor, I used paint-by-numbers templates to create prefabricated drawings rather than dare to start with a blank canvas and see what I could create on my own.

Once I entered the workforce, the flaws of my approach to learning became obvious. The "real world" isn't very interested in my ability to memorize information and parrot it back. The real world values skills such as critical thinking, analysis, leadership, decision making, and the ability to create and communicate original ideas.

Over the years, I've focused on strengthening my skills in these areas while my memorization skills have atrophied to embarrassing levels. It's a bummer that I waited so long to start thinking for myself, but that's the way life goes sometimes. As you age, you will learn many important lessons that you may wish you had internalized when you were first exposed to the idea.

When you were young, your parents sent you to school to get you up to speed on the "Three Rs" (readin', ritin', and 'rithmetic). Parents know that their kids are doomed in most careers without the ability to read, perform basic math, or speak the local language.

After high school, you may have gone on to college or trade school to acquire additional specific knowledge or skills that you believed would help you accomplish your goals in life. If nothing else, it bought you some time to figure out what you wanted to do and gave you a decent answer to the "What are you doing?" question at the annual family picnic.

When you finally popped out of the other side of your chosen education system with diploma in hand, you may have found that you were sorely lacking in the knowledge and skills needed to succeed in life. This goes well beyond the basics of hitting the ground running in your chosen profession or trade. You may have graduated without well-developed skills in personal finance, interpersonal communication, health and nutrition, and critical thinking. You may then ask the question that has no doubt been asked millions of times throughout history: "What is the purpose of education?"

The short answer is that the purpose of education is personal. There isn't one purpose of education but a variety of objectives that depend upon the person and the culture. In general, I support the idea that there are four broad purposes of education:

1. To provide us with a solid foundation in the basics
2. To provide us with the skills and knowledge to become an expert in a chosen profession or trade
3. To produce good citizens
4. To provide wisdom for success in life (referring to the ability to see what's important in the long run and to use that vision, along with sound judgment, to identify the best course of action in the present moment)

One of the more interesting definitions of education that I've come across was something I heard in a lecture from Rev. Michael J. Himes: "Education is the long process in which we become more truly and authentically human." The goal in this life is to become as human as we can possibly be, and education helps us realize our potential in terms of what it means to be truly and authentically human. But Rev. Himes doesn't want us to stop there. He adds, "What you hold on to, you lose. What you give away, you can never run out of. ... You never fully grasp the fruits of your education until you give it away to another."

This brings up an important aspect of education: sharing what you learn with others. When you give yourself away in the form of teaching—or anything else—you exist most fully and joyfully.

When you emerge from your educational system with diploma in hand, view your graduation as just one milepost in a lifelong journey of personal development and continuous learning. Test and apply the best ideas that you've come across along the way, and draw your own conclusions. Once you've learned something that you consider to be important or profound, teach it to others so they can make more beautiful drawings in their lives.

**"Live as if you were to die tomorrow. Learn
as if you were to live forever."
Mahatma Gandhi**

Continuous learning and deliberate growth

While continuous growth is certainly a good goal to have, I've found that it's better to qualify this goal with an aim to improve our ratio of deliberate growth to accidental growth.

When I was younger, most of my growth was accidental. I drifted with the wind and picked up tidbits of information and knowledge on an embarrassingly vast array of topics. I can talk semi-intelligently about the acoustic display behavior of cone-headed katydids, best practices for protecting nuclear material from theft or sabotage, methods of setting up a captive breeding facility for cranes, how to conduct a management system audit, how to successfully implement information technology (IT) projects at a hospital, or how to pour a snakebite at a pub in England compared to a bar in the United States. (In case you're wondering, it's one part lager and one part hard cider in the United Kingdom, and a shot of Yukon Jack with a splash of lime juice in the United States.)

Most of this knowledge was acquired through accidental growth. When I was young, I lacked a clear vision of what I wanted to accomplish in my life, other than to see the world.

Now that I'm in my 40s, I find that my ratio of accidental to deliberate growth has dramatically changed. The vast majority of my growth today is very deliberate and strategic rather than accidental. I no longer feel like I have the luxury of time to dabble in a bunch of random things to see what I like and don't like. I've learned that dabbling won't get me very far in anything, so I narrow my focus to just a few key things.

In Darren Hardy's words, do fewer things more often and get better at them. Become an expert in just a few things rather than mediocre in many things. That's one of the keys to success in life. If you read the stories of famous achievers, you'll find that the majority achieved fame and fortune by doing a few key things with excellence.

As Jim Rohn, put it, "Don't major in minors." Always remember the Pareto principle (the 80/20 rule) in everything you do. There are only about a half dozen things that make up 80% of the difference in any area of your life. Be smart about how you invest your limited time. Focus your attention on the few key behaviors that will enable you to accomplish your goals.

The process I use for deliberate growth is taken largely from Darren Hardy's *Living Your Best Year Ever* CD program and daily planner, which I find to be extremely helpful in keeping me on track. I usually go through this process in the last week of December each year, and it goes something like this:

1. I identify my top three goals for the year.
2. I identify the two or three most important behaviors that will enable me to accomplish each of my three goals.
3. I identify a total of two to four skills that I will develop over the course of the year to help me accomplish my goals.
4. I shift my focus away from the goals themselves and focus all of my attention on the key behaviors, routines, and skills that I've identified. I execute my plan, day in and day out, without getting tempted by distractions. It requires a lot of discipline and focus, and it's not easy. I may have a lot of discipline, but when it comes to focus—well, I think my circuitous career path speaks for itself. I have an insatiable curiosity and eagerness to learn new things. In a typical week, I may develop a sudden interest in learning how to paint, speak Spanish, or train a pet kookaburra. The only way to rein myself in from this onslaught of new ideas and interests is to write them down.
5. I write down any new interests and ideas that cross my mind and filter them against my written list of goals, behaviors, and skills for the year. (That's when training a pet kookaburra falls off my list.) Without this discipline, I get stretched too thin, and I don't make progress towards my big goals. I get stagnant and solidify my position as a jack of all trades and a master of none. Whether I like it or not, mastery is a prerequisite for success. My written list also keeps my eyes and ears attuned to new opportunities that may help me advance my personal growth agenda. To help justify my fanatical tracking, I cling to research suggesting that we feel most happy and motivated when we see measurable progress towards our goals. If that is true, then I should be a very happy and motivated person. And I am.

Work your plan, one day at a time. After the monotony of executing your weekly and daily plans, one day you'll look up and suddenly realize that you've accomplished your goals! When you focus on deliberate growth in the key areas that you've identified as most important to you, everything else will fall into place over time ... or so I'm told.

I'm still waiting for a few things to fall into place. But I'll keep the faith and continue to work the plan.

"Not all those who wander are lost."
J.R.R. Tolkien

Very early retirement

I'm a big fan of early retirement, just not in the normal way of thinking about it. In my early 20s, I made a conscious decision to switch the order of my career and my retirement. I figured there was a good chance that I would work until the day I died, hopefully doing work I enjoy, so I might as well retire for a few years at age 23, and then focus on my career after my retirement. In that way, I could do all of the crazy things I wanted to do while I was still healthy, single, and tolerant of long, uncomfortable bus rides with farm animals.

I learned this approach from a few Aussies and Kiwis whom I met when I was on my first backpacking trip in Europe. They convinced me of the wisdom of doing a long walkabout after graduating from school and before starting a family or career, for a duration of about six months to two years. (Not that I needed much convincing at the time.) It sounded like a solid plan to me. Okay, maybe it wasn't solid, but it was very appealing nonetheless. So that's what I did, although my journey ended up taking three years to complete.

As soon as I passed my comprehensive exams to earn a Master of Science degree in biology from Creighton University, I was on a plane from Omaha, Nebraska, to Geneva, Switzerland. I didn't even wait the extra few days to attend my graduation.

Why Switzerland? I wanted to be able to speak French, and I heard that people speak the language slower in Switzerland compared to France. That was a good enough reason for me. Plus, I was an avid hiker and mountain climber; in my mind, Switzerland was synonymous with mountains. So Switzerland it was.

My parents were a bit reluctant to support my idea at first, but as long as I was able to support myself financially while I traveled, they agreed. With their blessing, I was ready to start the "deliberate wandering" phase of my life.

Even during these walkabout years, I had an agenda—albeit a vague one. My goal was to visit 100 countries by the time I was 50 years old. There was no magic in those numbers; 100 sounded like an impressive number, and 50 sounded old at the time. I figured that, if I visited 100 countries, I would have some good stories to tell, and I would hopefully acquire some nuggets of wisdom about myself and the world. Most importantly, I would have an opportunity to meet foreign women and drink exotic beer.

Later in life, I heard this concept articulated by Jim Rohn from a slightly different angle. (The women and beer parts were notably absent.) Jim had a mentor, John Earl Shoaff, who suggested that Jim set a goal of becoming a millionaire. The reason? For what it will make of him to achieve it. The money part was irrelevant. The greatest value in life is what you become, not what you get. Set goals that will make something of you to achieve them. That's solid advice, and I shamelessly use that line to justify my crazy trips.

At age 23, my plan was simple: Travel until I run out of money, find a random job abroad to save up for the next trip, and then repeat the process. I had no idea where I was going, and I didn't care. I just went with the flow and capitalized on opportunities as they came up. I did that from May 1993 through August 1996.

What kind of work did I end up doing during that time? Well, here's the basic outline:

- Biology, math, and geography teacher for five months at the Gstaad International School in Gstaad, Switzerland—the most expensive school in the world at the time.
- Bartender for four months at The Boater, a rugby pub in Bath, England.
- Aviculturist at the captive breeding program at the International Crane Foundation to help raise all species of endangered cranes, including the whooping crane. This turned into an opportunity to go to Kenya and live in a tent for several months in the western highlands, where I worked on wetland conservation projects in and around Saiwa Swamp National Park.

You get the idea. These were great experiences, and I found it to be a priceless education. While I did a lot of wandering over those three years, I never felt lost. I sometimes wonder why I ever stopped living that way. (Oh, yeah. Now I remember: family and debt.)

Fortunately, you can apply the "early retirement" concept to your life, and it doesn't have to be anything extreme. Write down the things that you dream of doing or learning when you retire. Then make some changes in your schedule so you can start doing those things today, without dropping the ball on your commitments to your family, job, and so on.

Why wait until retirement to do the things you love to do? Set aside a few hours each week, and gradually increase the amount of time you spend "in retirement" throughout your life. When I reach the normal retirement age, I want to write, play music, exercise, enjoy quality time with my family, spend time in nature, and travel. And that's precisely what I do today, just in smaller doses. I hope to allocate more time to do these things as I get older.

Start your early retirement today.

**"In wisdom gathered over time I have found that
every experience is a form of exploration."
Ansel Adams**

Find new food caches

Closely aligned with the very-early-retirement concept is the concept of seeking out new food caches. Despite my belief in the power of disciplined focus on just a few key areas at any given time, I consider continuous learning, curiosity, and an open-minded interest in new people, places, and things to be life's fountain of youth. How should we reconcile this potential discrepancy? As an American Indian coyote teacher might say, "Go ask the birds."

Birds are creatures of habit. They follow predictable time schedules and routines for foraging, roosting, and so forth. They know a good thing when they see it, and they remember it. Hummingbirds, for example, keep track of the locations of good and bad food flowers. And some species of birds, like Scrub-Jays, are planners. They will stash some food in a hidden spot that they can remember, just in case they have a bad day.

Birds could choose to spend all of their time visiting known sources of food, but that's not what all birds do. Some birds set aside part of their day off the grid, searching for new food sources. On some of these exploratory forays, birds find nothing; on other days, they find a good meal. And, once in a while, a bird will hit the mother lode and strike it rich—perhaps at a new bird feeder that you've set up in your yard.

Like birds, you can focus most of your time and attention on the known behaviors and predictable routines that support your defined goals, and set aside money and other resources to draw upon when times are tough. You can also set aside time each week for exploration—to try new things and seek out novel experiences, with no particular expectation in mind. This can take the form of new hobbies, new people, new experiences, new places, new anything. Consider it part of your much-needed downtime. Give yourself permission to try something new each week or month with reckless abandon, even when it makes no sense at all in terms of your written goals.

When you do this, you often learn new, unexpected things about yourself and the world. Sometimes, the payoff will simply be a smile on your face; on other days, the experience will be a dud or a profound waste of time. But, every once in a while, you'll hit the mother lode. You'll discover that you have a natural talent for something, or you'll fall in love with a new place, a new person, or an activity that can completely change the direction of your life.

To put this idea into practice, I include unstructured downtime in my weekly schedule. Downtime is something that I tend to neglect when left to my own devices. That's where kids can really help. Kids can provide a great excuse to see and do things that you would never consider doing on your own. And, if someone from work catches you in the act of doing something embarrassing or completely out of character, all you have to do is point to your grinning kid, and it will all make sense.

After work on Fridays, I drop everything else in my life and focus solely on my son until 3 pm the next day when I drop him off at his mom's house. This predictable schedule provides me with a nice chunk of time with my son where we can be creative, spontaneous, and open to a vast world of new experiences. I have my son during certain weekdays too, but those days are largely consumed with the routine of homework, housework, and preparation for the next day. Divorce is never easy, but I've found that the fixed schedule provides me with more focused, quality time with my son than I had when everyone was living under the same roof. I wouldn't wish the experience of divorce on anyone, but even the cloud of divorce can have a silver lining.

As the Zen Buddhists like to say, "Take some time each week to adopt a beginner's mind." See the world through the eyes of a child—or a bird. Deviate from your normal routine to seek out novel experiences, try new things, and find new food caches. After all, continuous learning, curiosity, and exploration comprise life's fountain of youth.

CHAPTER 6

Lie, cheat, and steal

"If you tell the truth, you don't have to remember anything."
Mark Twain

Cooked

Chef Jeff Henderson is an expert when it comes to lying, cheating, stealing, and cooking—especially cooking. Jeff has cooked everything from crack cocaine to foie gras, a fact that inspired the title of his bestselling autobiography, *Cooked: My Journey from the Streets to the Stove.*

As a young man, Jeff earned the street name "Hard Head" and a reputation for cooking high-quality crack cocaine. Later in life, Jeff earned the name "Executive Chef" and a reputation for cooking high-quality food at the Bellagio Hotel and Caesar's Palace on the Las Vegas strip. Chef Jeff has quite a story to tell, and it's an excellent entrée into a discussion about values, associations, and moral relativism.

A child of divorced parents, Jeff grew up in tough Los Angeles and San Diego neighborhoods. He lived with his mom and sister in South Central LA, but he also spent a lot of time with his dad's parents while his mom was at work. Jeff's grandfather had his own janitorial business that focused on cleaning commercial properties, particularly laundromats. His grandfather was a stern man who taught Jeff the values of hard work and a dollar by taking him on his rounds, starting at the age of five. He also inadvertently taught Jeff how to steal.

Jeff remembers seeing his grandfather steal quarters out of laundry machines as he cleaned laundromats and installed new machines. At the time, Jeff saw his grandfather in the same light as Robin Hood, stealing from the rich and giving to the poor. Stealing from white people was viewed as acceptable as long as the money was used to help black people. Jeff didn't have any white people to steal from back then, so he stole from anyone who let their guard down. Jeff's philosophy of life at the time was, "I gotta get mine." By the age of six, Jeff was already a pretty good thief, stealing from his relatives, his neighbors, and his mother.

As a teenager, doing wrong became a way of life for Jeff. Each year he became bolder, breaking into houses to steal anything he could find. At the age of 16, Jeff was arrested for the first time, but the experience only taught him to be a more careful thief.

Jeff's mom wanted him to live a good, honest life, far away from the bad influences of the neighborhoods they lived in during his childhood. But Jeff had other plans. Surrounded by drug dealers and gangsters—living the American Dream with fancy cars, hot women, and fat wads of cash—Jeff wanted his piece. He decided to shift his focus from stealing to dealing.

Jeff learned the ropes from established drug dealers in his neighborhood. A high roller named T-Row took Jeff under his wing and taught him the art of carjacking and dope dealing. Once Jeff earned his trust, T-Row taught Jeff how to cook and sell crack cocaine.

Jeff was a quick learner and a natural leader. He had no interest in seeking out "positive" associations at that time in his life. Big-time drug dealers and other high rollers were the only associations Jeff wanted to cultivate. He wasn't in the drug business to use the product or to become a gangster. Jeff rarely drank, and he didn't do drugs other than to taste the product to check the quality when he couldn't find addicts to test it for him. For Jeff, it was all about the money, and this seemed like the best path to reach his goals.

It was easy for Jeff to justify lying, cheating, and stealing. Everyone was doing it. It was part of the job description. As the money rolled in, even Jeff's mom changed her outlook on Jeff's activities. Jeff's "career" was a way to get the family out of poverty and out of that neighborhood, so she turned a blind eye.

Jeff went on to become a major player in the drug-trafficking world, with all of the money, women, cars, and other perks that he craved while growing up. At the peak of his drug-trafficking days, he was bringing in a whopping $35,000 a week. He was well on his way to realizing his dream of moving his family to a nice part of town. Then, on one day in 1987, all of his dreaming came to an end.

Jeff was arrested by federal agents in a sting operation and was sentenced to 19 years in federal prison. Jeff didn't realize it at the time, but his arrest marked the beginning of an amazing journey that would lead to true success. From behind bars in federal prison, Jeff Henderson was unwittingly on the path to becoming an award-winning chef, a bestselling author, and a popular public speaker. He had a lot of growing up to do; however, with a 19-year prison sentence, he had plenty of time to do it.

Not surprisingly, certain pivotal moments in prison changed Jeff's perspective. In his book, Jeff shares the following experiences that played a key role in altering his view about his life as a drug dealer.

One day, while sitting in the visiting room where prisoners meet their visitors, Jeff recalled seeing an inmate passionately kissing a woman, apparently getting caught up in the moment. Later that day, after visitation was over, that same inmate started to go into convulsions. The inmate's friends stood there and watched, refusing to call the guards to get medical help.

Why did they keep silent? Because the inmate had a balloon of heroin in his intestines, and they were waiting for him to poop it out so they could remove the balloon of heroin and get high. The inmate's girlfriend had passed it to him mouth to mouth when they were kissing in the visiting room.

The woman made the mistake of putting the heroin inside a party balloon instead of a surgical glove, and the balloon sprang a leak in the inmate's stomach. His "friends" didn't call the guards because they were more worried about getting high than saving the man's life. By the time the guards came to see what was going on, it was too late. The inmate was taken to the infirmary, and he died later that night.

While in prison, Jeff also witnessed countless scenes of inmates injecting heroin with guitar strings into any vein they could find—between their toes, into their neck, through their penis … *anything*. This solidified an important lesson for Jeff. He finally recognized the harm he had caused to others through his drug dealing.

Even though Jeff never used drugs, he signed up for a nine-month Residential Drug Abuse Program to get a year taken off his sentence. This led to another pivotal experience for him, thanks to an inspirational instructor whom he refers to as Mr. H.

Mr. H didn't buy into the victim mentality in his classes and always said, "Nobody pulled a gun on you to make you commit the crime; you made the choice." That made a big impression on Jeff and helped him take accountability for his actions. As Jeff puts it in his book, "Even if the cards were stacked differently for young African American males compared to their white counterparts, I came to understand it just meant that it was my responsibility to be stronger, smarter, and sharper than the next man."

Jeff was finally able to shed the victim mentality that was limiting his growth. After that, Jeff's life started to blossom. While in federal prison, Jeff discovered a passion for cooking. He surrounded himself with people who were positive influences in prison, people who taught Jeff the art and business of cooking. After his release, Jeff worked his way up the ranks to become a nationally recognized chef.

It's an incredible story and a great example of what happens when we combine passion, talent, positive associations, and hard work. When asked in interviews about his favorite quote, Jeff responds with the following: "No matter who you are, or what your story is, it's never too late to achieve the American Dream."

"Three things cannot be long hidden:
the sun, the moon, and the truth."
Buddha

Failure quiz: truth, nonviolence, and associations

1. Do you provide complete information, rather than conceal facts, when justifying your position or actions? ❏ Yes ❏ No

2. Do you behave in a fair and ethical manner even when you're trying to gain an advantage? ❏ Yes ❏ No

3. Do you refrain from stealing anything that isn't yours?
    ❏ Yes ❏ No

4. Do you consider yourself to be a nonviolent person, defined as living in such a way that reflects compassion, love, and empathy towards all living beings? ❏ Yes ❏ No

5. Are your thoughts, words, and deeds consistently aligned?
    ❏ Yes ❏ No

6. Using the Average of Five concept, which states that we become the average of the five people whom we spend the most time with, do you consider your five closest associates to be excellent role models when it comes to displaying a positive attitude, ethical behavior, and high standards for personal development and success in life? ❏ Yes ❏ No

7. Do you have a mentor? ❏ Yes ❏ No

8. Do you serve as a mentor for others? ❏ Yes ❏ No

9. Do you carry out the work that is in front of you today with excellence, no matter what that task is? ❏ Yes ❏ No

10. Do you take responsibility for your life, rather than think of yourself as a victim? ❏ Yes ❏ No

Failure quiz: truth, nonviolence, and associations (continued)

We covered quite a variety of topics in this quiz, with some lofty standards, so consider these questions more as food for thought instead of an indication that you're a lyin', cheatin' SOB.

Count up the number of "yes" answers and refer to the chart below:

0-2   Perhaps it's time for some soul searching to identify steps you can take to improve.

3-5   Pick one or two areas that you would like improve, and then identify a few new behaviors that you will experiment with.

6-8   Well done. You've got most of this stuff handled. Pick an area to improve to take you to the next level.

9-10 I assume that you can walk on water too. Impressive! You are no doubt an excellent role model for the rest of us.

"Everything we hear is an opinion, not a fact.
Everything we see is a perspective, not the truth."
Marcus Aurelius

You say potato, I say potahto

It is a well-known fact that lying, cheating, and stealing are clear paths to failure in life. Just look at the sport of cycling. The image of the entire sport has been trashed, thanks to a blood-doping epidemic among the sport's top athletes, such as Lance Armstrong, Floyd Landis, Alberto Contador, and a long list of others. Even as I watched a few highlights from the 2015 Tour de France, I couldn't help but wonder which cyclists were competing without drugs or blood transfusions.

You tell your kids that the lesson from the cycling scandals is clear: Never lie, cheat, or steal, or you will regret it later. End of story. *Right?*

So, when you pick up your grandmother to drive to her surprise birthday party, and she asks where you are taking her, do you tell her the truth and spoil the surprise? *Well, that's different,* we tell our kids. You should "avoid the truth" in that situation because you don't want to ruin the surprise.

Ramping things up a bit, during the Holocaust in Nazi Germany in the 1930s and '40s, there were many stories of Germans who hid Jews in their home so they wouldn't be killed or taken to a concentration camp. If that were your home and the soldiers knocked on your door to ask if there were any Jews in your home, would you lie? *Well, that's different too,* you tell your kids. You would be saving a life by lying, so lying would be the right thing to do in that situation.

Your kids see examples of government officials who make it to the top by utilizing an ability to "stretch the truth." In other words, they lie. Then your kids watch professional soccer stars dive to the ground and pretend to writhe around in agony in the hope that they can sell the referee on a penalty kick or a red card to help win the game. In other words, they cheat.

Your kids learn that an estimated 30-40% of Americans are not 100% honest when it comes to doing their taxes. Is that stealing? (I think I just heard the lid pop off a can of worms with that one.) *Well, that's different,* some would say. That's just how the game is played. Really? If that's the case, then what exactly *are* the rules that you should teach your kids when it comes to lying, cheating, and stealing?

> "All that we experience is subjective.
> There is no sensation without interpretation.
> We create the world and ourselves;
> Only when we stop do we see the truth."
> Lao-Tzu

Lying, cheating, and stealing revisited

As Mark Twain points out in the quote that opened this chapter, life sure is simpler when we tell the truth. But should we really be striving to "always tell the truth" regardless of circumstances?

Mahatma Gandhi is my go-to resource for guidance on the topics of truth and nonviolence. Gandhi devoted his life to advancing the study of these topics, although he humbly assesses his contribution with these words: "I have nothing new to teach the world. Truth and Non-violence are as old as the hills. All I have done is to try experiments in both on as vast a scale as I could."

On the subject of truth, Gandhi felt that "To believe in something, and not to live it, is dishonest." Your actions should be consistent with your words and your thoughts. You should strive for truth in thought, word, and deed.

I don't know about you, but my thoughts are far from wholesome and pure at times. But that's okay, Gandhi gently adds. Just keep practicing until your thoughts become pure, and you can consistently speak and act in accordance with your thoughts without violating your moral boundaries.

Sigh. Okay, I'll work on it.

In Keshavan Nair's excellent book, *A Higher Standard of Leadership: Lessons from the Life of Gandhi*, Nair offers some additional insight on truth and the potential conflict in standards of conduct at work versus your personal life: "We have been led to believe that there is one standard for private morality and conduct and another for public morality and conduct. We have come to accept that a lower moral standard is necessary to get things done in the real world of politics and business."

Nair goes on to provide examples of politicians who ask us to judge them on their legislative accomplishments, not on their personal conduct; Social activists who claim the high moral ground yet resort to violence to obtain results; Business executives who want us to ignore their conduct and focus exclusively on the bottom line; and journalists who are committed to truth, yet end up publishing half-truths in their quest to be the first to publish.

When you watch people succeed through nefarious means, it may leave you with the belief that you may sometimes have to forsake your ideals to achieve success. You may use this flawed reasoning to justify actions inconsistent with your core values, and then end up with feelings of stress, depression, and remorse. As Gandhi warns us, "One man cannot do right in one department of life whilst he is occupied in doing wrong in any other department. Life is one indivisible whole."

Okay, smart guy Mr. Gandhi: Who defines truth? Who are we to say that people from different backgrounds, cultures, or countries are behaving inappropriately? Aren't we just imposing our moral values and cultural beliefs on others?

In Jonathan Haidt's book, *The Righteous Mind: Why Good People Are Divided by Politics and Religion*, Haidt identifies six fundamental building blocks that support moral systems: (1) care; (2) fairness; (3) liberty; (4) loyalty; (5) authority; and (6) sanctity. Different cultures place differing amounts of emphasis on some traits over others. For example, many worldviews focus on interdependence rather than autonomy. These cultures assume that people should be treated differently according to social role or status, such as honoring elders and protecting subordinates, and prize order over equality.

These systems aren't necessarily wrong or right; they are just different. So how can we say that a single point of view is the complete truth, superior to all other points of view?

Gandhi addresses the potentially convoluted pitfalls of moral relativism and truth with the following statement: "Truth is by nature self-evident. As soon as you remove the cobwebs of ignorance that surround it, it shines clear."

When your mind is free from prejudice, fear, anger, and self-interest, the truth becomes obvious. To do this, you must step into a mindset of unconditional love and compassion, and then reassess your situation. With this frame of mind, the correct course of action is easy to see, and you will be true to yourself and to others.

Of course, it requires discipline to adopt a loving and compassionate mindset before evaluating a situation. To help with this, some people pause to reflect on the phrase, "What would Jesus do?" (You can substitute "Jesus" with Buddha, Mohammed, God, or your parents.) The point is to adopt the perspective of a positive role model to help you frame an assessment of truth and identify the best path forward.

Gandhi has plenty more to say on the topics of truth and nonviolence. He believed that the pursuit of truth does not justify violence against your opponent. For Gandhi, "nonviolence" doesn't refer to holding yourself back from punching someone. That's kindergarten stuff. Gandhi defines nonviolence as a positive love for all humanity. Nair adds that Gandhi's definition includes assisting the less fortunate, protecting the environment, and putting an end to all forms of discrimination. Welcome to graduate school.

This gives you a new perspective to consider when you hear the statement, "I am not a violent person." To put it mildly, it can be a wee bit challenging to go through each day feeling positive love towards everyone and everything. On some days, you may fail before leaving the house in the morning, even if you live alone with a dog or a cat. Add some people to the mix, and things can get really challenging, really fast.

Regardless, Gandhi encourages us to commit to the ideals of truth and non-violence, even if we know that we won't be able to attain perfection. As you're starting to see, this Gandhi fellow is one tough dude to emulate. Thankfully, Nair adds that "When the ideal seems far away, you should not be discouraged. Think of the distance as a measure of your potential—not of your imperfections." In other words, focus on progress, not perfection.

Using the advice of Gandhi and Nair, here is a handy guide that you can use to evaluate your behaviors and actions in life, even in seemingly complicated situations with competing moral values:

1. **Strive for truth and consistency in your thoughts, words, and actions.** It's good to be able to quickly recognize when your thoughts are impure, so that your words and actions don't follow your destructive thoughts. These misalignments of your thoughts, words, and deeds are also an indication that you have some room for growth.

2. **The pursuit of truth does not permit unloving acts.** Gandhi wrote that the pursuit of truth does not permit violence on one's opponent, which he defines as "an action that does not reflect a positive love for all of humanity." When you act from a place of genuine love and compassion for others, you will usually do the right thing, no matter what situation you're in.

3. **Remove the cobwebs of ignorance to see the truth.** Most of us enjoy having a few cobwebs of ignorance hanging around to cover the truth. These cobwebs come in the form of prejudice, fear, anger,

and self-interest, which we use to justify actions that feel good in the short term. However, Captain Buzzkill Gandhi suggests that we do some dusting and take an objective look at every situation from a perspective of unconditional love for everyone and everything. Sometimes you won't like the answer, and you may attempt to stick the cobwebs back into place, but it's too late. The truth is clear, and you know what you should do.

**"You cannot change your destination overnight,
but you can change your direction overnight."
Jim Rohn**

The Average of Five

It's hard to overstate the importance of the associations that you have in your life to keep you on the path of truth and nonviolence. A key concept related to your associations is the "Average of Five." This rule states that you become the average of the five people whom you spend the most time with. (That means I'm the average of my dog, my son, my parents, and some ravens that I feed in the backyard.)

As a kid, Chef Jeff chose to hang around top-notch drug dealers, and that's what he became. Thankfully, like Jeff, we all have the power to change our associations, and we can do it today.

In prison, Jeff shifted his focus away from negative influences and sought out the best cooks and positive role models that he could find. Jeff studied under the guidance of inmate chefs to learn the art and business of cooking, and he became a head chef within the confines of prison. Once out of prison, Jeff approached restaurant owner and renowned chef Robert Gadsby for a job. After weeks of persistence, Jeff was finally offered a job as a dishwasher. Jeff was thrilled because he knew this would enable him to get his foot in the door to learn from the best. You can't put a price tag on having someone like Robert Gadsby as a mentor if you want to learn how to become a professional chef.

The same is true in any pursuit in life. When you spend time with negative people, you increase the odds that you'll become a negative person. When you associate with the best and brightest, you're more likely to set high standards as your baseline for success. The simple, conscious decision to hang around high achievers will greatly boost your chances of becoming a high achiever with a positive outlook on life.

Seek out mentors who have already done the things you want to do or who exhibit traits that you want to develop. For the price of a phone call, a cup of coffee, or lunch, you can change the direction of your life.

Keep in mind that positive associations and mentors don't have to be sitting in the room with you. You can spend a lot of time with the best and brightest associations—both living and dead—through books, courses, and videos.

Another effective way to change is to become a mentor yourself. We all have gifts and experiences that we can share with others. If you attempt to help others improve in an area that you too are trying to develop or master, your own progress will grow by leaps and bounds. There's no better way to learn and reinforce a behavior or skill than to teach it and model it for others.

"We must all suffer one of two things: the pain of discipline or the pain of regret or disappointment."
Jim Rohn

Attitude, patience, and discipline

Even if you spend time with inspirational, high achievers, there's still the pesky matter of doing the hard work to improve. Chef Jeff is an excellent role model for displaying patience, self-discipline, and a positive attitude, despite some pretty grim circumstances. Jeff worked hard at the task in front of him, even when that task was dishwashing or cleaning toilets instead of cooking. He always arrived early for his job to ensure that all of the necessary prep was completed. In his free time, Jeff devoured books on cooking and went to restaurants to observe how other chefs managed their kitchen. His mentors took notice of his work ethic and eventually gave him new and better opportunities in the kitchen.

When times are tough, it's easy to slip into a mindset where you lament about what could have been: "Oh, if only I had done x, y, or z, I would be president of the universe by now, with a billion dollars in my checking account, and a pet unicorn in my backyard." That line of thinking is a waste of time. After all, you *are* in the situation you're in today.

The best way to get out of your current situation—assuming that you want out—is to be very clear about the skills, behaviors, and traits you need to attract your definition of success. Then, with that image in mind, muster the self-discipline to perform your work with excellence today, with faith in the notion that, if you do a great job on the task that's in front of you right now, better opportunities will appear on the horizon. Learn from the past, be motivated by the future, and live in the present moment.

Take it one day at a time.

CHAPTER 7

The future looks bleak, and it'll only get worse

> "Americans are apocalyptic by nature. The reason why is that we've always had so much, so we live in deadly fear that people are going to take it away from us."
> Stephen King

To hell in a handbasket

"Iran: Death to America"
"Parents' Nightmare: Futile Race to Stop Killings"
"Violence Feared as Egyptians Head to the Polls"
"Slasher Attacks Members of Japanese Girl Band"

I can hear you say, "Just another typical, happy day from the perspective of the world headlines this morning." But some people like to take things a bit further. See if the following rant sounds familiar:

"Clearly, the world is falling apart. There is violence and hatred everywhere, and it's just going to get worse.

"Just look at this new generation of spoiled brats! They want everything handed to them on a silver platter without doing any of the hard work to earn it. And what's up with these sports leagues that don't keep score? No winners or losers? Ridiculous! Back when I was young, we kept score, and we knew what it felt like to win and lose. Nowadays, kids want a trophy for properly using the toilet! Kids today are fat and lazy couch potatoes, lost in a virtual world of electronic devices. And don't get me started about the sagging jeans that expose what must be their brain. If that's our future, we're doomed!

"Then there's our government. What a bunch of inept crooks! All they care about is power and padding their own bank accounts. They tell us what to do, and they proceed to do the opposite. They vote against school vouchers, pander to unions, and dumb down our public schools while they put their own kids in fancy, private schools. They want us to pay more taxes to support their agenda while they create and exploit loopholes to avoid paying taxes themselves. Politicians won't even sign up for the same healthcare options they force down our throat. They have their own special healthcare plan.

"All politicians must swear to the "do as I say, not as I do" oath before taking office. This dysfunctional group of children that we call government is destroying our country. Even our president is trying to take our country down a few pegs.

"The worst part is that I'm powerless to do anything about it. All I can do is watch our country go down the toilet while my body and mind gradually deteriorate and my family and friends die all around me. My kids will eventually stick me in some lifeless old folk's home where I'll quietly pass my time, bored and alone, until I die of some horrible disease. Life sucks, the world is going to hell in a handbasket, *and there's nothing I can do about it!*"

Welcome to failure in life via negativity and a bad attitude.

"Wonder rather than doubt is the root of all knowledge."
Abraham Joshua Heschel

Failure quiz: attitude

1. Do you spend less than 30 minutes per day consuming media that makes you feel angry, fearful, or depressed? ❑ Yes ❑ No

2. Do you spend at least 30 minutes per day consuming positive, life-affirming media? ❑ Yes ❑ No

3. Do you have an optimistic outlook on life? ❑ Yes ❑ No

4. Do you "live life on life's terms" and accept your present situation as an opportunity? ❑ Yes ❑ No

5. Do you focus most of your attention on things you can positively affect or influence? ❑ Yes ❑ No

6. Do you respond to events in a positive way, thus increasing your chances of a positive outcome per the Event + Response = Outcome formula? ❑ Yes ❑ No

7. Do you have control over your attitude rather than behave as if you have no control over your thoughts? ❑ Yes ❑ No

8. Do you notice when you are subscribing to self-limiting beliefs that impact your growth and success, and then take steps to discard these notions? ❑ Yes ❑ No

9. Do you believe that you will be healthy, happy, and active even at a very old age? ❑ Yes ❑ No

10. Are you excited about the possibilities for positive change that are on the horizon? Are you participating? ❑ Yes ❑ No

Failure quiz: attitude (continued)

Count up the number of "yes" answers and refer to the chart below:

0-2   Time for some soul searching to identify steps you can take to get back on track.

3-5   Room for improvement. Consider some changes to bump you up to the next category.

6-8   Looking good. You've got most of this attitude stuff handled.

9-10   Impressive! You're positive attitude is infectious. Keep spreading the wealth and thanks for being an excellent role model for the rest of us.

"Your attitude, not your aptitude, will determine your altitude."
Zig Ziglar

Embrace the struggle

Does that opening tirade sound familiar? Do those words remind you of someone, perhaps even the person you see in the mirror? If that's the case, then perhaps it's time for an attitude adjustment. We all know that it can be pretty miserable to hang around someone who is consistently negative and down on life, so let's consider a few ideas on how to avoid being or becoming that person.

The late personal development legend Zig Ziglar had plenty to say about the importance of attitude. Zig was a consummate optimist who liked to say, "I'm so optimistic, I'd go after Moby Dick in a rowboat and take the tartar sauce with me."

Zig was a major proponent of the idea that we should live life on life's terms. Of course, that's easier said than done when the going gets tough. At the age of 81, Zig was provided with an opportunity to walk the talk. At least that is how he viewed a tragic incident in his book, *Embrace the Struggle: Living Life on Life's Terms*. Zig fell down a flight of stairs in his home and suffered from severe memory loss, dizziness, and other symptoms that drastically changed his life.

This turn of events could have easily been the end of the career for a motivational speaker like Zig. But he accepted this new life challenge and, with help from his family, was able to continue speaking. He could no longer prowl the stage and captivate the audience in the same way that he did in the past. Instead, he adopted a new format that involved sitting in a chair across from his daughter and adopting a question-and-answer format that enabled his daughter to guide and remind Zig of what he intended to say.

This illustrates how Zig practiced one of the key takeaways that he learned from this challenging experience: Focus on the things you *can* do rather than the things you *can't* do, and maintain a positive outlook on life no matter what. Zig was a firm believer in the importance of living in the present moment. In other words, do your best with whatever is in front of you right now, and make the most of the time you have with the people you love and the causes you care about.

But, if you're in poor health—for example, with wires and tubes coming out of places they have no business being—the present moment is not always an appealing prospect. Checking out of reality starts to sound pretty darn good. Even though many of your struggles will turn you into a stronger, better person in hindsight, you often don't see it that way when you're knee deep in it. Things can seem bleak or hopeless at times, and many years of clouds may pass before you see anything that resembles a silver lining. But, eventually, silver linings invariably appear, often in forms that you never anticipated.

On the other hand, it's possible to take all of this positive attitude stuff a bit too far. When you do that, you appear fake, delusional, or annoying to others. For example, I remember "running" a half-marathon race in the mountains when I suddenly heard a voice loudly exclaim what a glorious day it was. This was followed by a few verses of song to the flowers to tell them how beautiful they are. The rest of the runners glanced at each other with the unspoken understanding that we must be dealing with a loon. After all, we were at mile 11 of a steep mountain climb. But the unfazed runner sang on.

Rest assured that most of us are far from crossing any unspoken line of excessive positivity. So we might as well go for it, even if that means singing to the flowers. I have to confess that the song created a welcome distraction from the huffs and puffs from the rest of us. Given Zig's enthusiasm and positive energy during challenges in life, my guess is that Zig would have joined along to sing to the flowers and attempt to coax the rest of us to sing as well.

Zig passed away in November 2012, but his words echo on: "It's not what happens to you that determine how far you will go in life; it is how you handle what happens to you."

"Human nature is complex. Even if we do have
inclinations toward violence, we also have inclination
to empathy, to cooperation, to self-control."
Steven Pinker

Violence: "Can we all get along?"

You may remember a day in 1992 when riots broke out in Los Angeles, and Rodney King appeared on TV and asked the question, "Can we all get along?" Well, if you form your opinion based on newspapers or TV news, then you may be excused for answering Rodney with a skeptical, "Apparently not."

The media do an excellent job in leading us to believe that the world is becoming a more violent and dangerous place. Steven Pinker disagrees, and he backs up his claim with over 800 data-filled pages in his 2011 book, *The Better Angels of Our Nature: Why Violence Has Declined.*

Steven argues that violence in the world has declined both in the short and long term, and he offers several reasons—and plenty of data—to justify his position. Steven adds the caveat that, "The decline, to be sure, has not been smooth; it has not brought violence down to zero; and it is not guaranteed to continue."

At first I was a bit skeptical about the claim that violence was declining. But, after listening to the entire 37-hour, 30-disc, unabridged audiobook, I'm now on board with Steven's premise that the present day is the most peaceful time in history.

Steven presents data related to wars, homicide, genocide, torture, criminal justice, and the treatment of women, children, and ethnic minorities to back up his premise that violence has declined over the course of history. From this data, Steven identifies four motives that enable cooperation and altruism to win out over violence: (1) empathy; (2) self-control; (3) moral sense; and (4) reason. He rejects the idea that the decline in violence is due to an evolution in human biology and instead believes that changes in our social environment have led to the decline in violence.

There is obviously a lot more to it, given the length of the book. But the takeaway message is a positive and optimistic one for our future: The world has become more peaceful with the passage of time, and the world is less violent today than it has ever been in human history.

The book would make a nice stocking stuffer for anyone who rants about how violent and dangerous the world is today. Granted, the book's weight may rip the stocking off the mantelpiece, but it's worth it. There's a good chance that the reader will emerge with a more positive and optimistic outlook on life and society. At the very least, the rants should subside for a while since it'll take some time to get through the book.

As for Rodney King, his story has a sad ending. He lost a battle with drug addiction and was found dead at the bottom of a swimming pool in June 2012 at the age of 47. Despite multiple attempts to kick his addictions, including a successful 11-month stretch of sobriety in 2009, the autopsy results found that Rodney died of an accidental drowning with alcohol, cocaine, marijuana, and PCP in his system at the time of death. The drugs and alcohol likely exacerbated a heart condition that incapacitated Rodney when he was in the pool, and he drowned.

In an interview with the *Los Angeles Times* a few months before his death, Rodney was quoted as saying the following about his legacy: "Some people feel like I'm some kind of hero. Others hate me. They say I deserved it. Other people, I can hear them mocking me for when I called for an end to the destruction, like I'm a fool for believing in peace."

Steven Pinker's research on the topic of violence should reassure us that, despite media reports to the contrary, the world really *is* becoming a more peaceful place. I hope that Rodney King is resting in peace with the knowledge that we really can "all get along."

We're getting there, slowly but surely.

"You can change the world—your world. You can rid your
world of all wars, murders, crimes, scandals, gossip, corruption
and international disasters. You have that much power …
in the palm of your hand. How? Hit the OFF button. Turn
off your TV. Turn off your radio. Cancel your newspaper
subscription. Focus your attention on ideas, information
and knowledge that can help you grow, prosper, create and
contribute to making a positive difference in your world …
and you might just do something to change the world."
Darren Hardy

Change your media, change your world

When we feed our mind with negativity, and then carry those thoughts in our head all day, it subtly influences our behavior, attitude, and outlook on life. We've already discussed the importance of our associations and how they influence our thinking, behavior, and attitude. In this section, we'll confront another biggie: the media we consume.

One of the most significant things that we can control is what we read, hear, and see on TV, in movies, on the radio, and in books. As Darren Hardy reminds us, we have the power to turn off the vast majority of crime, scandals, wars, gossip, and corruption by simply turning off negative news media and replacing them with positive, life-affirming media.

We all know that bad news sells. Our brains are wired to be on the lookout for impending danger. To keep ratings high and advertising dollars flowing, media outlets exploit our natural tendency to look for things that might harm us. The result is the daily onslaught of disasters, murders, corruption, and scandals that we can find on any news channel or in any newspaper.

During those same 24 hours, there are millions of positive, encouraging, and wonderful stories that will lift your spirits and boost your attitude, if you had the opportunity to hear them. Of course, these stories don't sell as well, so you'll need to seek them out from alternative news sources.

Darren's advice is simple: Rather than subject yourself to the negativity onslaught, turn it off and focus on things that you can do to improve your life and your circle of influence. I took Darren's advice to heart and have been on a media fast since 2011. This is in stark contrast to pre-2011 when I spent one to two hours each day reading newspapers and magazines, keeping a watchful eye on current events to make sure that everything was running smoothly. Of course, things never seemed to be running smoothly, so I had to keep checking back each day in the hope that my vigilance would somehow turn things around.

While I'm not completely clueless about current events, I'm pretty darn close at times. I am still exposed to tidbits of news from my daily routine at work and the gym, or from family, friends, coworkers, or the Internet. These tastes of doom and gloom usually reassure me that I'm better off ignoring typical headline news.

The key takeaway is to control what's controllable. I can't control the national economy, but I can control my personal finances, and I have no shortage of work to do in that area. Even though I work in healthcare IT, there isn't much I can do to influence our country's healthcare policy, but there's a lot I can do to improve my own health and the health of my family. I can't control how a president runs a country, but I can control how I run my own business, household, and life. I can't control wars in different parts of the world, but I can create an environment of peace and harmony in my own home.

You may say that there's too much information out there, but the real problem is that you may think you need to know it all. *You don't.* Alternatively, adjust your media consumption to stay informed about the things you can impact or change, and then minimize or ignore the rest. Focus your attention on positive things that you can learn and do to improve your life, and make positive contributions to your family, friends, employers, and the community.

It requires great strength to take up Zig Ziglar on his challenge to live life on life's terms; to keep a healthy, positive attitude through thick and thin; and to respond to setbacks with a sense of optimism and humor. It also requires constant vigilance. To keep motivated and on track, feed your mind each day with encouraging, life-affirming messages, and surround yourself with positive people.

As Zig put it, "People often say that motivation doesn't last. Well, neither does bathing—that's why we recommend it daily."

"The greatest discovery of all time is that a person can change his future by merely changing his attitude."
Oprah Winfrey

Event + Response = Outcome

I often think of a handy equation whenever I'm faced with a task or a situation that doesn't sound very appealing:

Event + Response = Outcome

In other words, I may not be able to do anything about the event, but I can certainly adjust my response to it, and thus change the outcome. Once I get over my initial whining and come to terms with the fact that a particular event is inevitable, I shift my mind to think of how I can make the most of the situation.

In the face of an unpleasant event, your knee-jerk reaction might be to assume that Event = Outcome. ("It's pouring rain, so I guess we'll have to stay indoors and watch reality TV shows today.") That's one possible response, albeit a lame one. When faced with the same situation, your kids might say, "Awesome, let's go outside and play mud football!" That's a very different response to the same event, and it sounds like a lot more fun. You can choose to be lame or awesome in your response to any event.

It's all about your perception. Let's take stress as an example. Stress is just a perception, not a function of an event itself. It's a response that you choose. You assume that something negative is going to happen and feel anxious as a result. Why start out with such a negative prediction? You don't know how the event is *really* going to turn out. Why not envision something positive and optimistic instead? Consider the event as an opportunity to learn or shine. You can choose to feel excited about the opportunity rather than be stressed out about it. You are responsible for what you choose to see and the feelings you experience in any situation.

Of course, there are some situations that warrant a stress response. For example, if someone throws you into a dark closet with a bunch of angry rattlesnakes and poisonous spiders, you can be forgiven for feeling a wee bit of stress. But there are plenty of other situations in which stress is something that you needlessly create in your mind. You don't have to feel stress in response to most of the things you encounter in your day-to-day life.

The same is true for the preconceived notion that you're going to feel bored or uncomfortable at an upcoming event. Let's say you receive an invitation to a party that you can't decline, and you immediately envision being stuck in endless conversations about the weather, baseball, and the Kardashians. That's one way to approach the event: with dread. Another option is to reframe the occasion as an opportunity to practice a particular skill or meet a particular person. If you're really desperate, you can frame it as an opportunity to practice making eye contact, giving a firm handshake, remembering names, or trying to find someone who has been to Mongolia. Make a game of it.

Better yet, become a detective. Recognize that everyone has an interesting, amazing story to tell, and your job is to uncover that story by asking the right questions. Whenever I'm stuck attending an event (ahem ... let's try that again.) Whenever I *have an opportunity* to attend an event, I try to think about who will be attending and a few good questions that might lead to interesting and meaningful conversations. My fate is up to me. I can either take the time to come up with a few good questions, or I can roll the dice and risk wasting an entire evening talking about something that bores me to tears.

We have complete control over our own attitude in any situation, yet we often behave as if we have no control. As Oprah points out in the opening quote of this section, you can change your future simply by changing your attitude. This timeless nugget of wisdom has been passed down through the ages, yet it's all too easy to forget.

"If you are depressed, you are living in the past. If
you are anxious, you are living in the future. If you
are at peace, you are living in the present."
Lao-Tzu

Mindfulness: living in the now

Social psychologist and Harvard University professor Ellen Langer takes the ideas
in the previous section a step further in her two books, *Mindfulness* and *Counterclockwise: Mindful Health and the Power of Possibility.* Ellen's research suggests
that you can dramatically change your body's physical performance and longevity
with a simple shift in your mindset. When you open your mind to what is possible—rather than impossible—you can measurably improve your hearing, vision,
memory, dexterity, appetite, attitude, longevity, and general well-being at any age.

This requires a shift in your thinking in terms of the expectations and outcomes that you associate with certain ages, diagnoses, and other categories created
to simplify your world. In a telling experiment, Ellen asked 75 adults a series of
questions about old age and senility. Twenty-five adults were between the ages of
25 and 40, 25 adults were between 45 and 60, and 25 adults were older than 70.
The study found that 65% of the younger group felt certain that they would not
become senile, whereas only 10% of the older group felt similarly; in other words,
90% of the older group felt there was a good chance that they would become
senile.

So what, you ask? Medical studies found that only 4% of adults over the age
of 64 actually suffer from a severe form of senility, and an additional 10% suffer
from a milder version. In other words, 90% of the study's older group felt that
they would be part of the 14% who end up with senility. Given the abundant
evidence that suggests your expectations influence your outcome, you would be
wise to adjust your expectations.

Studies also confirm the notion that we tend to look for behaviors that prove
our negative stereotypes. For example, if we encounter an older person who for-
gets something, we are quick to label it as a symptom of senility. However, if we
observe the same scenario in a 20-year-old, we are quick to dismiss it as forgetful-
ness or a lack of attention. We don't label it as senility since that word does not fit
with our preconceived stereotype of a 20-year-old.

Be mindful of the expectations that you've set for yourself in life. If you set high expectations, you will meet them; if you set low expectations, you will meet those. If you're getting up in years, don't assume that you'll soon be frail and inactive since that's "just part of old age." My dad climbed to the summit of Mt. Kilimanjaro with me when he was 68 years old, and he is still an avid hiker at the age of 74. Jack LaLanne was still doing his daily two-hour workout, complete with fingertip pushups, well into his 90s. Apparently, my dad and Jack didn't get the memo that they should be frail and using a walker. They set high expectations to operate at a high level physically and mentally, regardless of age.

Be careful not to mindlessly buy into self-limiting beliefs that are passed along by family, friends, and society. Thoughts such as "I'm too old," "I'm too young," and "I'm too inexperienced" are not laws. They are artificial, social constructs often used as excuses not to try.

I'm not suggesting that an 80-year-old should blast the *Rocky* theme song and train to be the next starting center for the Los Angeles Lakers. After all, we do need to ground our beliefs with a modicum of reality. Simply be aware when you are subscribing to societal norms or generic rules of thumb, as these may limit your thinking and prevent you from realizing your true potential.

"The best way to predict the future is to create it yourself."
Peter Diamandis

The future looks very bright

Not only is the world getting better from the perspective of violence, as we saw earlier in this chapter, data suggest that the world is also becoming a better place from the perspective of other big-picture metrics, such as hunger, child mortality, longevity, access to education, and equal rights. Yes, there are many challenging problems that we still face today, but this is nothing new. There always have been and always will be challenges for the world to face. Fortunately, there are plenty of great minds who enjoy rising to these challenges.

People like Peter Diamandis thrive on tackling the world's biggest problems and view these challenges as the world's biggest market opportunities. Peter is an engineer, a physician, and an entrepreneur who founded the XPRIZE Foundation, Singularity University, and several other organizations with lofty goals. XPRIZE, for example, is a nonprofit organization that creates prize competitions with the mission "to bring about radical breakthroughs for the benefits of humanity, thereby inspiring the formation of new industries and the revitalization of markets." The mission of Singularity University in turn is "to educate, inspire and empower leaders to apply exponential technologies to address humanity's grand challenges."

You get the idea: Peter thinks big.

In his spare time, Peter teamed up with Steven Kotler in 2012 to write the *New York Times* bestselling book, *Abundance: The Future Is Better Than You Think*. In this book, Peter and Steven give us a glimpse from the front lines where people are developing transformational technologies, such as artificial intelligence, robotics, biotechnology, bioinformatics, 3-D printing, networks, sensors, nanotechnology, human-machine interfaces, and biomedical engineering—all of which have the potential to solve the world's biggest problems.

Abundance provides us with a helpful reminder that we're living in an age of exponential technological growth, combined with financial resources, communication tools, and information abundance that we could only dream about a century ago. Peter and Steven suggest that, when we think about the world's big challenges from a scarcity-of-resources perspective, we're not framing the problem correctly. Instead, we can view it as a challenge to make inaccessible resources accessible and abundant through the appropriate use of technology.

Thankfully, there's good news to report from the front lines. The pace of change and breakthroughs is unbelievably fast and exciting. Radical transformation is happening all over the world in virtually every industry. You can soon expect to see major breakthroughs related to food, water, energy, healthcare, engineering, medicine, construction, space exploration, education, and sustainability.

Through a fortuitous series of events, I am now part of an innovative healthcare organization called DaVita HealthCare Partners. Their mission and vision, respectively, are "To be the provider, partner, and employer of choice" and "To build the greatest healthcare community the world has ever seen." Now that is a goal worthy of a Peter Diamandis organization! It's exciting to work on the front lines of an organization committed to transforming healthcare.

Get out there and dive into whatever interests you, whether it is on your own or through a like-minded organization. Immerse yourself in it. Get excited about the possibilities for change. Don't wait for the future to come to you. Start creating the future yourself.

I have heard that the size of our life is determined by the size of the problems we solve. If that is the case, then people like Peter Diamandis, who are grappling with the biggest challenges on Earth, are on track for a very big life.

Why not you?

CHAPTER 8

Strive for intolerance

"No one is born hating another person because of the color of his skin, or his background, or his religion. People must learn to hate, and if they can learn to hate, they can be taught to love, for love comes more naturally to the human heart than its opposite."
Nelson Mandela

"Touch me. I won't bleed."

A line of young children waited outside of the doorway of a mud hut with a thatched roof. With bare feet, dirty clothes, and school-issued bright-blue sweaters, the children smiled and laughed as they anxiously fidgeted. What was the occasion? These kids were lined up for the opportunity to touch a white person for the first time, and I was that white person in the hut.

The year was 1996, and I was in a remote part of the Western Highlands of Kenya, near the border with Uganda. I was working as a representative of the International Crane Foundation (as in birds, not machinery). The International Crane Foundation is a nonprofit organization dedicated to the conservation of cranes and the wetlands that cranes depend on. I had just completed an internship as an aviculturist at the organization's captive breeding facility in Baraboo, Wisconsin, when I received an unexpected phone call from George Archibald, cofounder and chief executive officer. George asked me if I would be interested in working on a project in Kenya. After picking my jaw off the floor, I thought about it for two seconds and accepted; a few weeks later, I was on a plane to Africa.

My work in rural Kenya gave me the opportunity to meet many wonderful people who live under challenging circumstances, far off the grid. One day, while walking along a dusty trail with a community leader, a woman passed by with a baby dangling from a colorful sling on her back. As soon as the baby saw me, he let out a shriek and started to cry from his perch.

I laughed and wondered aloud what *that* was all about. My colleague smiled and explained that it was very unusual to see a white person in that part of Kenya, so it was probably the first time that the young child had seen such a creature. He then went on to tell me that some of the young children in the village believed that, if they touched a white person, the white person would bleed. It certainly wasn't a widely held belief, but it was still out there.

That last bit of information explained a few of my experiences while riding in those death traps known as "matatus." A matatu is a privately owned vehicle that functions as a bus of sorts. Matatus come in a wide variety of sizes, shapes, and colors. The only things that all matatus have in common are faulty brakes, reckless drivers, full loads, and loud horns. Where I worked, most of the matatus came in the form of small, beat-up pickup trucks with shells that covered the truck bed. Aside from walking on foot or riding a bike, matatus were the most common form of transportation in the area.

The goal of the matatu owner is, of course, to make money. And the best way to make money is to pack the vehicle with as many people as possible on three long benches, which run along the three walls inside the shell. Next, the center aisle would be filled with people who had to stand with their back hunched under the low ceiling of the shell. Small animals were welcome in this area too. Luggage generally went on top of the matatu along with a few more people. Any remaining stragglers would climb up to form a row along the back bumper of the truck and hang on to the outside of the shell. The combination of faulty brakes, fast driving, and heavy loads predictably resulted in a lot of accidents and fatalities.

I was staying in a tent in the boonies. If I wanted to make a phone call or pick up mail, I had to squeeze into one of these matatus for the 30- to 60-minute drive to the nearest town called Kitale. This was before the days of widespread smart phones. To make a call, I would get in line at the post office to use one of a handful of phones—a process that could take another hour or two, depending on the line—so I didn't make many calls.

The local matatus didn't operate on a set schedule. When they were "full," they departed, and "full" was determined by an aggressive matatu director who evaluated the amount of cash collected, the number of people clinging to some part of the vehicle, and the potential for more customers to arrive anytime soon. ("Soon" is a loosely defined word in Africa.)

If you paid the matatu director enough money, he could persuade the driver to depart, despite a relatively empty load. After collecting your payment, the director and driver would still try to pick up as many people as possible along the way, but at least the payment got the vehicle rolling towards your destination. Former aviculture interns who work in rural Africa aren't high up on the salary ladder (I'm not sure the pay even qualifies you to be in the same room as the ladder), so I never paid the premium to get the vehicle rolling.

When I first arrived, the matatu directors usually tried to charge me a higher mzungu—"white-person" rate—compared to the other passengers, despite the fact that I looked anything but rich. In my dirty jeans, hiking boots, a well-worn shirt, and with a hairstyle created after eight hours in a sleeping bag, my looks didn't scream money. But I was white, and that's all that matters in many parts of Africa. White equals rich. End of story.

After a few weeks, the matatu directors and drivers figured that I must be staying awhile, and they routinely greeted me with a local handshake and abandoned further attempts at price gouging. I paid the normal rate, climbed in, and waited for the matatu to be considered full. This could take five minutes, an hour, or more. You could only predict your arrival with a margin of error of one or two hours, assuming that you are traveling a short distance; the margin of error for long journeys was measured in days, not hours.

This was quite a change from where I had been living the previous year: Switzerland. In the land of mountains, chocolate, and fancy watchmakers, I could set my watch based on the arrival and departure of trains. In Africa, time is just a suggestion. If you arrived at your destination within a few hours of the estimated time, then you were on time.

As you may have gathered, seat selection was important in the world of matatus. The worst spots were usually the two corners where the benches met. If it was a busy day, you were virtually guaranteed to be smashed on both sides by the people seated next to you. Plus there was the bonus of having a few armpits stuck in your face from the people standing in the aisle, with their arms reaching up to the ceiling for balance. Seatbelts and air conditioning did not exist. It was hot, it was crowded, and the smell of body odor was strong. If someone coughed or sneezed, you would invariably wear and inhale whatever came out. Feeling lucky?

The best strategy that I could determine, other than walking, was to find a seat where I could stick my face as close as possible to an open window. But not all matatus had windows, let alone open ones. This is why I earned the local nickname "the mzungu who walks." But, on rainy days or on journeys that were more than 6 miles roundtrip, I rolled the dice and hopped on a matatu.

Given that I was naïve, kind, and polite, I often found myself in one of the two undesirable corner spots, which should have guaranteed some serious body smashing. However, on several occasions, and particularly when children were seated next to me, I found that there was no body contact at all. It appeared as if the kids were contorting their bodies to avoid touching me. I couldn't tell if they were just being polite or if I smelled bad, or both. But, after my colleague's disclosure during that walk along the dusty trail, I now had a hunch that these kids didn't want me to start bleeding in the matatu.

So there I was, standing in a mud hut, ready to shake hands with a long line of children to put the myth to rest. Most of the kids didn't believe in the bleeding myth. They just wanted to shake hands with a mzungu for the first time.

As the children entered the hut, they became quiet. Once they were at the front of the line, they looked up at me and smiled broadly. Some eagerly said hello and extended their hand while others waited for me to act first. Many of the kids were fascinated by my blue eyes and thick blond hair, which resembled a rat's nest. I would smile and say "Jambo" or "Habari" as I reached out to shake hands. Each child's smile would widen after hearing my terrible Swahili, and then we would shake hands.

It wasn't one of those elaborate, 30-second handshakes that you encounter in many parts of Africa, which include intricate hand maneuvers that end with a finger snap produced by using the other person's finger. This was just a simple handshake. But it did the trick, and I didn't bleed.

It was a surreal, amazing experience, although I have to confess that my mind was often distracted with thoughts of where all of those little hands had been. After all, I'd seen the local toilets—think ramshackle outhouse with a hole in the ground, two well-worn spots for your feet, and a questionable bucket of water to clean your butt afterwards ... with your hand.

Before I entered one of those outhouses, I always did a quick scan of the floor, walls, and ceiling to look for snakes, spiders, and other unmentionables before committing to the journey to enter. Once my feet were in place, my goal was to not look too closely at anything at all and get out of there as quickly as possible.

Toilet paper did not exist in these remote outhouses. For that matter, neither did sinks, running water, or electricity. Your choice was to either use the perilous water bucket or skip the cleaning part altogether. The latter seemed to be a popular choice among many of the young children. Heck, many of the kids didn't even bother using the outhouse! On plenty of occasions, I had the joy of witnessing young children on the path in front of me suddenly stop, squat down to do their business, pull up their pants, and merrily carry on as if nothing had happened, leaving little landmines to dodge.

Faced with this stark reality, I always carried a stash of toilet paper in my pocket. (Well, *almost* always.) I remember two notable instances where I forgot this prized possession. One instance forced me to use the dreaded bucket. The second instance warrants a story.

I woke up one morning with some "intestinal distress," which didn't surprise me given the risky food and water that I was exposed to on a regular basis. But, on this particular day, I had plans to meet with two community leaders to get a tour of some local conservation projects. Since there were no phones, I had no easy way to reschedule.

I reluctantly put on my hiking boots, made the trek to the neighboring village, and met my colleagues as planned. As we made our way to one of the conservation project sites, I really had to go the bathroom. There were no public facilities in the area and no easy place to squat down in private, so they took me to a nearby farm and asked the owner if I could use their outhouse.

Relieved to receive the green light, I told my colleagues, "Go ahead, and I'll catch up with you."

Their response was a distressing, "No, no. We will wait for you here."

Great.

I felt like I was about to burst, so I accepted my impending humiliation and stepped inside. What followed was a classic bout of explosive diarrhea, and the community leaders enjoyed front-row seats for the fireworks. Still, I felt relieved … until I realized that I didn't have any toilet paper with me. My eyes darted to the water bucket in the corner, and my heart sank when I realized that it was empty. Not good. In desperation, I took off my underwear and used it to wipe. Unfortunately, there was no garbage can or easy place to hide or bury the evidence. I felt that it would be rude to throw it in the toilet for someone else to fish out later, while also realizing that it's generally considered uncool to emerge from an outhouse with a pair of filthy underwear in your hand. I decided that the only way to escape with a tiny shred of dignity was to hike up one of my pant legs and stuff it in my hiking sock.

I emerged with my best poker face and said, "Okay, thanks for waiting. Let's go."

While we're dwelling in the gutter with the mature topic of human waste, I might as well share the concept of GFI (Gross Factor Index)—not to be confused with the aforementioned GNH Index in Bhutan. In fact, a high GFI directly contributes to a low GNH Index. A friend of mine, who has spent several years living in remote parts of garden spots like South Sudan and Liberia, came up with the GFI concept. We still jokingly use it to rank many of the world's bathrooms on a scale of 1-10, in terms of how disgusting they are. Let's just say that the GFI was pretty high in some of the places I have visited—often in the neighborhood of 7 or 8. To give you some context, your bathroom at home is hopefully 1 or 2 at the worst. As long as your bathroom walls aren't crawling with lots of critters, and your floor is free from smelly landmines or other hazards, then you're still below 5.

Many people find it helpful to go through life with a daily mantra to guide them and keep them on track. Mantras like "Om," "Thy will be done," and "Be the change you wish to see in the world" are common examples. My mantra in rural Africa was often an inspiring "Don't touch your face." This was the lofty thought that crossed my mind while shaking the hands of children who had never touched a white person. (I know ... I'm truly an inspiration.)

The bleeding myth was one of many misconceptions that the local population had about white people, Western culture, and technology. Another myth held in some of the more remote villages was the idea that, if someone takes a photo of you, it takes away your soul or some variant of that belief.

For this *Mythbusters* episode, a community leader asked me to come to the village the following Sunday and take photos of anyone who was interested. I assumed that 10 or 20 people might show up. I was wrong. Well over 100 people showed up, dressed in their Sunday best. Entire classes of schoolchildren lined up, according to their grade or age, to take class photos. Families assembled for family photos. Someone had even set up a motorcycle as a prop for people to sit on and look cool as I took their picture. Fortunately, I brought many rolls of film.

I had an old-school camera, so I had to send in the rolls of film to get them developed. To be safe, I shipped all of the rolls to my parents back in the United States. About a month later, I received a box full of photos. As I distributed the pictures, it was clear that many of the people had never seen themselves in a photo. There was a lot of laughter, pointing, and smiles. It was a blast and well worth the effort.

Another stereotype that pervades Africa is the previously mentioned idea that, if you're white, you're rich. I once asked someone why they believed that to be true. The answer caught me by surprise: He had seen the TV show *Beverly Hills, 90210*. What more evidence do you need? Case closed.

My heart sank when I heard that people had actually seen *Beverly Hills, 90210* in rural Africa. Why did *that* show have to be the baseline for U.S. wealth? So I asked the next logical question: "How in the heck did you manage to see *that*?" Well, one of the local outdoor "cinemas" showed it on occasion.

By cinema, you should not be envisioning red velvet curtains, large buckets of popcorn, and comfy chairs with cup holders for your giant fountain drink. Instead, think of a small TV, propped up on crates and attached to what looks like a car battery, with a bunch of old patio chairs scattered in front of it. The cinema owner or renter charges admission to anyone who wants to gather around to watch whatever show or soccer game finds its way to the TV after manipulating the rabbit ears. Apparently, the stars aligned so that *Beverly Hills, 90210* found its way to rural Kenya. I also learned that *The Dukes of Hazzard* had been seen by quite a few people. (You can decide if that's good or bad.)

Of course, the long list of misconceptions and stereotypes worked both ways. When I arrived in Kenya, I was armed with an extensive arsenal of preconceived notions and stereotypes about the local population that I believed to be true, based on *Beverly Hills, 90210*-like evidence. Once I actually met people and gained firsthand experience of the local culture, many of my misconceptions were obliterated. (More on that in the next section.)

"Anger and intolerance are the enemies
of correct understanding."
Mahatma Gandhi

Failure quiz: intolerance

1. Do you feel relaxed and open to opposing viewpoints when you are engaged in discussions about politics? ❑ Yes ❑ No

2. Do you feel relaxed and open to opposing viewpoints when you are engaged in discussions about religion? ❑ Yes ❑ No

3. Do you have a clearly defined belief system? ❑ Yes ❑ No

4. Are your core beliefs aligned with your religion? ❑ Yes ❑ No

5. Are your core beliefs aligned with how you vote in political elections? ❑ Yes ❑ No

6. Do you enjoy meeting people from different cultures or who think differently than you do? ❑ Yes ❑ No

7. Do you make an effort to broaden your horizons by seeking experiences where you will interact with people from other cultures and beliefs? ❑ Yes ❑ No

8. Do you look at each person as an individual rather than make quick assumptions based on race, religion, and other stereotypes? ❑ Yes ❑ No

9. Do you study, practice, and teach the religion or belief system that you say you follow? ❑ Yes ❑ No

10. Do you make an effort to feel love, kindness, and compassion towards everyone and everything? ❑ Yes ❑ No

Failure quiz: intolerance (continued)

Count up the number of "yes" answers and refer to the chart below:

0-2   Time for some soul-searching to identify steps that you can take to get back on track in this area.

3-5   Room for improvement. Consider some changes to bump you up to the next category.

6-8   Looking good. You've got most of this intolerance stuff handled.

9-10 Impressive! You are a paragon of tolerance and self-reflection.

"Nothing in the world is more dangerous than
sincere ignorance and conscientious stupidity."
Martin Luther King, Jr.

The mzungu has arrived

When I first arrived in Kenya at the age of 27, three objectives were given to me by George Archibald of the International Crane Foundation: (1) Meet with two local conservation groups in the region around Saiwa Swamp National Park to see if their conservation work—and the location—were suitable for hosting a regional crane and wetland conservation workshop; (2) look for opportunities to promote and support crane and wetland conservation efforts in the local communities; and (3) deliver $1,000 cash to the leader of a local wetland conservation group who won a conservation grant from a U.S.-based organization.

Other than my directive from George, and 10 $100 bills folded up in a hidden pocket inside my belt, I had the names of two conservation group leaders, two pages of notes that I wrote during a phone conversation with a German scientist who had worked in the area, and a reservation to stay in a tent for a few months at Sirikwa Safaris, also known as Barnley's Guest House. Where I was going, addresses were not helpful. My only hope was to make my way to the village, and then ask around until I found the people I hoped to meet. I packed field clothes, a water filter, a sleeping bag, hiking boots, mosquito netting, a guitar, the *Lonely Planet Kenya (Travel Guide)*, and a copy of Blaine Harden's *Africa: Dispatches from a Fragile Continent*.

I also carried a lot of stereotypes and preconceived notions about Africa and Africans. Like so many Peace Corps volunteers and other aid workers before me, I arrived with the best intentions, but I was clueless. I had no idea what to expect or what the locals expected of me. During the long journey from Chicago–Miami–Johannesburg–Nairobi, I read most of Blaine's book, which provided a glimmer of insight about what to expect in Africa. Thanks in part to Blaine, I didn't arrive with the attitude of a great savior who had come to show the locals the errors of their ways. If anything, my thoughts upon touching down in Kenya were along the lines of, "How in the hell did I end up *here*?"

As I deplaned in Nairobi, I experienced the typical culture shock of any first-time visitor to Africa. After checking in at my basic hotel, I walked the streets in search of a bus terminal where I could purchase a ticket to Kitale for the next morning. The next day, I had my first taste of African roads. The 238-mile journey took over 12 hours to complete—and that was just to Kitale! Next, I had to track down the correct matatu in a chaotic sea of trucks, cars, and people. There were no signs or anything to put my mind at ease. As I climbed into the covered truck bed of an unmarked pickup truck, I had to rely on blind faith that the matatu directors understood where I was trying to go. My first matatu didn't disappoint. It was a real eye-opener.

Finally, 14 hours after leaving the bus terminal in Nairobi, I was deposited with my luggage at the end of the long driveway that enters the little oasis of Sirikwa Safaris. It was a relief—not only because I had arrived at my destination but because I had not taken the opportunity to pee since I left Nairobi. (I was too afraid to separate from my luggage.) I was feeling ill by the time I climbed off the matatu. As soon as the truck pulled away, I found a bush and gave my bladder a chance to experience the feeling of heavenly bliss.

I gathered my belongings and lumbered down the road until I was greeted by the owner Jane Barnley, along with her three Jack Russell terriers—Pip, Wig, and Dick. After a few minutes of saying hello, I staggered to my tent and was out like a light.

There are many stories I could tell about my mishaps while trying to assess and implement conservation projects in rural Africa. One of the best examples of "sincere ignorance and conscientious stupidity," as Dr. Martin Luther King, Jr., said, can be found in Blaine Harden's book.

Blaine describes a well-intentioned Norwegian project to construct a frozen-fish plant on the shores of Lake Turkana in Kenya to help the local Turkana people survive through the inevitable cycles of drought. The Turkana people primarily herd cattle, goats, sheep, and camels in an extremely hot and desolate semi-desert region. It's a tough gig, particularly during periods of drought, which are common in the region.

The Norwegian plan was to take advantage of the natural resources within Lake Turkana and build a frozen-fish plant on its shore. The assumption was that a shift towards fishing would help the stressed soil and vegetation regenerate from excessive grazing, and the Turkana people would earn an income from the abundant perch and tilapia resources in the lake. This line of thinking was bolstered by a Food and Agriculture Organization of the United Nations' study that concluded, "No solution of the Turkana problem is possible by which all the people can continue their traditional way of life." In other words, fish were the solution to the Turkana problem.

Since Norway was experienced in commercial fishing, the Kenyan government asked Norway to help the Turkana become fisherman. Norway's development agency agreed, and volunteers started to arrive in Kenya in the early 1970s.

The Norwegians brought 20 fishing boats and a team of consultants to determine the best way to maximize fish profits. The consultant team concluded that the best option was to spend $2.2 million to build a facility on Lake Turkana, which would produce frozen-fish fillets that the Turkana people could sell in Kenya and abroad. The Norwegians built the facility and helped construct a $20.8 million road that connected the frozen-fish plant with Kenya's highway system.

The project failed spectacularly for several reasons. First, the cost to chill the fish in the furnace-like heat of the region was higher than the value of the fish fillets. Second, there wasn't enough clean water in the area to support the operation. And then there's the minor detail that the Turkana don't like fishing. For the Turkana, livestock are everything. They have a deep-rooted belief that they are born to tend livestock. The Turkana live off the blood, milk, and meat of cows, goats, camels, and donkeys. They don't have a taste for fish. From the perspective of the Turkana, to become a fisherman is to become an outcast from the tribe.

Whoops. This kind of thing happens when modern Western thinking clashes with different perceptions held in remote corners of the world. Well-intentioned people from developed nations often carry an assumption that the locals in these remote areas are uneducated and don't know what's best for them. From my travels to remote parts of the world, I have learned again and again that "uneducated" does not mean "stupid."

For the Lake Turkana project, the assumption was that the Turkana people would unwittingly destroy the rangelands they depend upon since they didn't know any better. In addition, there was the incorrect assumption that, once fishing became a viable option, the locals would be eager to abandon the lowly, nomadic life of shepherding cattle. This perspective was incorrect.

After the failed fish-plant project, experts have come to recognize that livestock shepherds like the Turkana use sophisticated techniques to conserve their land. The nomadic Turkana quickly move to areas with fresh, green grass. As a result, studies found that African herdsmen can extract four times as much protein and six times as much food energy per hectare from dry rangelands compared to modern commercial ranches in places like the arid regions of Australia.

Rangeland practices aside, the most obvious failure was that the well-intentioned aid groups didn't take enough time to understand and empathize with the people they were trying to help. After the failed project, the aid workers finally asked the Turkana what they knew and what they wanted. It quickly became clear that livestock were the key to survival for the Turkana people. The aid groups accepted that reality, switched gears, and came up with a new strategy to hire a livestock adviser and an arid-land forestry expert, and invest in initiatives to prevent animal disease. This was a much better approach. The hardscrabble life of a nomadic cattle shepherd may sound unappealing to most of us, but that's the life the Turkana people wanted to pursue.

Having read this case study before I stepped off the plane in Nairobi, this lesson was firmly etched in my mind. I was ready to observe, listen, and learn from the local population before offering any suggestions about the best path forward for crane and wetland conservation in the region.

In practice, I was far from perfect in adhering to this philosophy. My experiences with myths about cameras and bleeding didn't inspire my confidence in the levels of scientific and technical knowledge of the local community. But, when it came to farming and knowledge of the local environment, the local people were the experts and I was the student.

During that time, I made a conscious decision to "lead from the back." This phrase comes from a quote from Nelson Mandela: "Lead from the back—and let others believe they are in front." There are times when it makes sense to lead from the front, and there are times when it makes sense to lead from the back. In this case, the others were already so far in front of me that leading from the back sounded like a darn good idea. I wasn't completely worthless out there, but it sure felt like it at times.

I added value by creating formal project plans and proposals that caught the eye of Western donors, and I had a few helpful conservation ideas as well. But I always did my best to ensure that any proposed solution would come from the mouth of a local Kenyan and not my own. I also did my best to avoid implementing anything that would cut into the meager salary of the local population. Many of the people I met and worked with were subsistence farmers, scraping by on a salary of around $250 ... *per year.*

Towards the end of my stay in the boonies of Kenya, I had the unusual opportunity to visit a Turkana market that forms each month in the middle of nowhere on a desolate patch of ground in northwest Kenya. Jane Barnley wanted to show me the market since it was like going to a living museum. Pip, Wig, and Dick hopped in the back, and I hopped in the passenger seat for the three-hour journey (each way) to the site of the market, somewhere between Kitale and Lodwar. We drove through some of the most spectacularly desolate landscapes that I've ever seen. There were very few signs of life other than desert plants and massive termite mounds that towered over my head.

All of a sudden, we found ourselves in the middle of hundreds of people who looked as if they had just hopped off the pages of *National Geographic* magazine. This was the Turkana market. The Turkana people were dressed in traditional clothing and animal skins with lots of colorful beads, bracelets, and ear plugs. They carried spears, knives, bows and arrows, stools, woven baskets, and staves. I desperately wanted to take photos but felt uneasy about it. I wasn't sure how the Turkana perceived photo-taking. To this day, it's the #1 moment that I regret not capturing on film. But, given all of the visible weapons that were on display, I'm okay with my decision. Jane and I were the only mzungus in sight, and we received plenty of curious glances; there was no need to attract more attention.

The market formed in an area with no buildings or infrastructure other than the road. Jane explained that the market forms for a day or two, and then vanishes as the nomadic Turkana disappear back into the desert.

It was an amazing sight that I'll never forget. As I scanned the area, I could see a lot of cattle and goats that the Turkana use for milk, blood, meat, and currency. There were no fishing poles or fish products in sight.

"Racism is still with us. But it is up to us to prepare our children for what they have to meet, and, hopefully, we shall overcome."
Rosa Parks

Racism, Africa style

One thing that continued to surprise me during my time in Africa was how these wonderful people could be so brutally racist towards each other. There was certainly an element of racism from whites towards blacks, and blacks towards whites, but the most hostile displays of racism that I perceived were blacks towards blacks. It was all about tribe.

Tribal racism can take a relatively benign but annoying form, such as the time I saw a man casually walk to the front of a long line at the bank because, I was later told, he was from a particular tribe and therefore felt entitled to do so. Then we have the horrible extreme of racism in the form of tribal genocide, like the infamous slaughter in Rwanda that was due to a tribal conflict between the Hutus and the Tutsis.

One of the first questions that I was frequently asked in rural Kenya was, "What tribe are you in?" Apparently, the answer to this question would determine how that person intended to respond and interact with me. I would answer, "I'm from America," and that usually put an end to it, although some would persist. Surely, I must be in one of the tribes. *Which one?*

In Africa, tribes cross artificial boundaries, which were established during the time of colonial rule. Many of the country borders were drawn on the basis of a geographic feature, such as a river, rather than tribal boundaries. Many of the people whom I met considered tribe to be more important than country. This was particularly true of nomadic tribe members, who wander across large areas of land without much thought or concern about country borders. They simply go where they need to go to trade goods and find food and water for themselves and their livestock.

In the big cities like Nairobi, people are much more likely to identify with their country in addition to their tribe. City dwellers whom I met were simultaneously proud to be Kenyan, proud of their home town, and proud of their tribe. But, in the boonies, national identity takes a backseat to tribe. In my day-to-day interactions, people were much more interested in knowing if I were Kikuyu, Kisii, Massai, Turkana, Luo, Samburu, or one of the other 42 tribes in Kenya. In my situation, the answer probably didn't matter much. But, for others, it could be a very big deal.

During times of conflict, if you're in the wrong tribe at the wrong place and the wrong time, you may be brutally killed. Elections in Africa can be a very dangerous time as they create an opportunity for simmering tribal conflicts to explode. It's assumed that the elected leader's hometown will prosper from a disproportionate share of money and resources for schools, airports, hospitals, and so on. Throughout most of Africa, political corruption and tribal racism are alive and well.

"We focus so much on our differences, and that is creating,
I think, a lot of chaos and negativity and bullying in
the world. And I think if everybody focused on what
we all have in common—which is—we all want to be
happy (then the world would be a happier place)."
Ellen DeGeneres

Decrease prejudice by increasing discrimination

To make sense of your world, you may tend to place people and things into categories, and then assign a series of traits, behaviors, and expectations to everyone or everything in that category. When you hear words like "old," "young," "religious," "cancer," "Russian," "Japanese," "American," "handicapped," and "vegan," you may consciously (or unconsciously) associate characteristics with those labels and hold them in your mind until proven otherwise. While this may help simplify your world, this categorization can also limit or skew your thinking and cause you to make inaccurate assumptions.

One strategy to overcome this limited thinking is to adopt the perspective that categories create a false perception of separateness, and that perception of separateness is an illusion. I've heard it said that, when we transcend the mind, diversity fades into unity. We are all connected. But, for those of us who have not yet transcended our mind to bask in the ethereal glow of unity each day, there's another, simpler approach to consider.

An interesting alternative is to strive for *more* discrimination in the world. I first heard this concept from Ellen Langer, whom you may remember from the previous chapter in the section about mindfulness. Ellen's research suggests that the labels we attach to specific categories can dramatically influence our perceptions and actions.

Ellen cites an experiment where an ordinary man, seated in an armchair, faced another man seated in an armchair, and they talked about work. Ellen videotaped the discussion, and then showed the videotape to two groups of psychotherapists. For half of the psychotherapists, the man being interviewed was called a "job applicant"; for the second group, the man was referred to as a "patient." Each group of psychotherapists considered the job applicant to be well adjusted; when he was labeled a patient, many of the psychotherapists considered the man to have some serious psychological problems. Same man. Same videotape. Very different outcome.

We all carry preconceived notions that bias our perceptions of other people based on appearance, race, sex, and so forth. It is helpful to be aware that the labels you use impact how you perceive the world.

Despite the platitudes that you sometimes hear, none of us is truly "color-blind." If you are looking for a terrific soul food restaurant, your gut instinct is to ask someone of African American descent rather than someone who is from Japan; if you're looking for sushi, then the reverse will probably be true. Now that's not very colorblind, is it? The world is a colorful, amazing place, so let's not pretend to be blind to it all. However, it is useful to shed many of the biases and stereotypes that you may carry.

One of the best ways to overcome your inherent biases is to increase your discrimination. Ellen uses the following exercise to illustrate the point:

Ellen Langer takes a group of 20 kids and divides them based on different characteristics: Males stand on one side, females stand on the other side; dark hair stands over here, light hair stands over there. Ellen continues to split up the group based on the color of clothing and other characteristics. This continues until every child is standing alone. Then the children suddenly understand the lesson that everyone is unique. When you mindlessly categorize people, you may fail to look for and recognize the individual talents and behaviors that each possesses.

Another tactic Ellen suggests is to imagine that your thoughts are totally transparent. This tends to cleanse your mind of the not-so-nice things that you sometimes think about other people, and it can help you become more compassionate and empathetic towards others.

When you move past the categories that you have created in your mind, you may tend to like people better, develop better relationships, and appreciate why people behave the way they do. You may make a greater effort to understand other perspectives and become more open to different ways of thinking. Each of us behaves a certain way, at a certain time, and for a certain reason that makes sense to us at the time. When you look at people as individuals who are going through different life events that are specific to each of them—instead of seeing a larger, stereotypical group—you may feel more connected, compassionate, and empathetic towards others.

Perhaps the next time I go to Africa and am asked the question, "What tribe are you in?" I will answer, "Mark Aspelin," and see what kind of reaction I get.

"I don't believe in afterlife, although I am
bringing a change of underwear."
Woody Allen

In the beginning

Religion is a topic that baffles me when it comes to the hostile reactions it can elicit. I can think of few topics as interesting and important to consider and discuss. I love to hear what other people believe about the meaning of life, the existence of a creator, or the prospect of an afterlife.

Yet to engage in an honest and open discussion on the topic can lead to serious trouble. We may get defensive or angry. We may raise our voice, stomp our feet, yell, scream, and fight. We may storm out of the room, vowing never to speak with the offending person or persons again, even if they happen to be members of our family. Some people feel so threatened that they kill others who don't share their ideas or subscribe to a particular religion.

In my simplistic mind, I think of the world as having three general perspectives to choose from: (1) atheists; (2) agnostics; and (3) believers. All of us fall into one of these three general categories. Atheists believe that there is no higher power; believers believe that a higher power exists; agnostics aren't sure.

When we're born, we're firmly planted in the agnostic camp. We don't know much of anything about anything. As a one-year-old, crawling around our living room floor, we may be skilled at manipulating those servants whom we call "Mom" and "Dad," but we tend to be open to the possibility of the existence of God. (We're pretty much on board with Santa Claus and the Easter Bunny too.)

By the time we've become gangly, awkward teenagers, we've had some significant life experiences that tend to push us in one direction or the other along the atheist-agnostic-believer continuum. If we're born into a religious family, there's a pretty good chance that our first religion and basic belief structure have been chosen for us. We tend to adopt the faith and beliefs of our parents, the community, and the country in which we grew up. Some of us enroll in schools that teach a particular religion or belief system, and we further modify our position along the atheist-agnostic-believer continuum. Our parents hope that we adopt their beliefs, but many rebel teens gravitate towards beliefs that contradict their parents, mostly to annoy them. In reality, at that age, many kids don't really care at all about such things.

As we head off to college or into the work force, many of us are exposed to different religions and different ways of thinking. This is all part of our spiritual journey. Some young adults have already had life experiences that seal the deal, one way or another. We may start to feel convinced that one belief or religion is The Truth; others adults don't have spiritual experiences until they are much older; some never have such experiences at all.

If this is the general path that each of us follows, at least in the U.S., why get angry, defensive, or hostile if another person doesn't believe the same thing that you do today? We're all at different stages in our spiritual journey. Rather than feel defensive and angry, you can choose to feel compassion, kindness, and joy at the opportunity to share your experience with others, and learn about their experiences.

You may be convinced that you know The Truth, and you may feel compelled to share your beliefs with others. That's great, as long as you share your beliefs in a kind, compassionate, and loving way. This approach will make a better impression on a skeptic than fire-and-brimstone lectures or threats of physical harm or death.

Share your beliefs and experiences without dismissing or negating the experiences of the other person. They've had influential experiences that have shaped their spiritual beliefs. These experiences may be drastically different from what you've experienced in your life. Since each of us follows a unique path and timeline, let's help each other along in our respective spiritual quests. We're all in this together.

When it comes to religion, many people believe that a particular text is the literal Word of God. However, the Word-of-God approach is not very helpful to someone who doesn't know which version of God's Word to believe. After all, there are many different religions that claim to have God's Word recorded in their own spiritual texts. You can choose not to get defensive or angry if questioned about the validity of your scripture, and share with others why you believe that particular version of God's Word to be The Truth.

You may be asked why believers of your chosen religion seem to pick and choose—buffet style—which pieces of God's Word to follow from a particular text. Once again, you don't have to interpret this as a personal attack. It's a legitimate question for someone who is trying to figure out things along his or her spiritual journey. You can help that person understand your position, for what it's worth, and then move on. Respect that we're all at different points in our spiritual journey.

I've studied several of the world's religions over the years and found that each has many wonderful things to teach us. All of the major religions are built upon timeless principles of love, compassion, kindness, and forgiveness. Religions can provide a solid ethical and moral foundation to build upon, along with a sense of community and opportunity for service. However, keep in mind that religions are composed of congregations of people, and people are imperfect. We all possess the full suite of positive and negative character traits. Some distort religious teachings for personal gain, resulting in terrible outcomes that harm innocent people. These tragic events usually stem from flawed people who chose to use religion to manipulate or repress others rather than use religious teaching as a way to bring out the best in themselves and others.

Whatever religion you choose, it's important to study, practice, and teach it. For atheists, I think it is important to explore that belief as well. I tend to consider atheism as a religion of sorts in that it requires just as much faith as other religious traditions. A friend of mine counters that "atheism is as much of a religion as bald is a hair color." I then try to frame baldness as a hairstyle instead. In the end, we end up laughing about it, even though we have different beliefs. We both recognize that we're still on our journey through life, figuring out things along the way.

From my perspective, the only time that a particular religious belief needs to be challenged is when that belief causes significant, real harm to others. (And no, being exposed to a Christmas carol at a school play doesn't cut it, no matter how bad the costumes or singing.)

If you aren't sure about whether or not a religious belief needs to be challenged, then I refer you back to our pal Gandhi: "Truth is by nature self-evident. As soon as you remove the cobwebs of ignorance that surround it, it shines clear." When our mind is free from prejudice, fear, anger, and self-interest, then the truth becomes obvious.

While going through the process of organizing my thoughts and solidifying my core spiritual beliefs, I had the opportunity to meet Brian C. Taylor, Episcopal priest and author of several books, including one called *Becoming Human: Core Teachings of Jesus*. I enjoyed our conversation and am grateful for the hour he spent with me to talk through some of the challenges I had with particular religious teachings. Brian encouraged me not to "throw the baby out with the bath water" when it comes to religion—a point that I think Brian summarizes nicely in the following passage from his book:

"As the Zen tradition says, the finger pointing to the moon is not the moon. The map is not the territory. Our religious practices, teaching, and traditions are only tools, and they are only one set of tools, standing alongside the tools of other traditions. The Bible is not God. The sacraments are not God. Even the doctrines and creeds of the church are not God. They are imprecise human expressions of the infinite mystery of God.

"So here's a call to use religion lightly. We may enjoy its beauty, ponder its wisdom, and apply its guidance in our lives, but we must never mistake it for the thing itself, which is God. When we make religion overly important, we fall into pietism, a kind of sentimentalized attachment to religious trappings. Or we angrily defend our position, insisting that there be no wiggle room for heretics to compromise the faith. We point the finger at others who fall short of our moral expectations. We become scrupulous about our practice, beating ourselves up for missing a time of prayer or Sunday worship, and we feel guilty for our lack of faith or failure to love.

"And the tragedy of misplacing our attachment to God for an attachment to the form of religion is that we miss the boat. We replace a liberating relationship with the living God with mere pietism, scrupulosity, moralism, theological certainty, or perfectionism."[1]

Don't be distracted from the real thing: living freely and spontaneously in God's presence. As Brian puts it: "The finger pointing to the moon is not the moon. The map is not the territory. Religion is just a form. While fingers and maps and religions may help us get oriented, once oriented we must then venture out into the territory itself."[2]

Amen to that! Brian's perspective is a refreshing one to consider as you continue to refine and practice your beliefs.

Where have I landed with religion? Well, let's just say that I'm a work in progress. In my early years, my spiritual philosophy could be summarized as "Thy will be done—unless it conflicts with my will, in which case let's do it my way." Now that I'm a bit older, I'm confident that I've made some substantial progress. I'm just not clear if my progress has been in the right direction. For what's it's worth, here's where I am today in the world of religion and spirituality.

For starters, I don't subscribe to any one religion. When cornered, I usually explain that my beliefs are most closely aligned with Taoist philosophy. After saying that, I pause for the obligatory raised eyebrow and "Huh?" accompanied by an eye roll, and then continue with the following explanation:

I believe that there is more to life than our brief time here on Earth. I believe that part of us is separate from our physical body. Once our physical body is worn out, a part of us continues on a different journey, although I have no idea what that next phase looks like. I tend to think of our time on Earth as a training ground of sorts where we learn vital lessons to prepare us for the next phase of life.

I believe there is a universal force that is everywhere, in everything and everyone, all at the same time. Some people call it God, some call it a spirit that moves through all things, and some call it the Tao. The label doesn't matter. It's a reality experienced beyond words and concepts, although it can sometimes be felt or observed when we engage in activities such as introspective meditation, silent observation of nature, or service to others.

I gravitate towards the natural world as a reminder to be authentically me in a world that is interconnected and in a state of constant flux. Each day, I try to set aside time for what I call my "Outdoor 8," where I go outside and sit down for eight minutes to bring my mind back to the present moment and just observe and appreciate the world around me. It's my daily reminder to be authentic, mindful, and aware that everything and everyone are connected and in a state of constant change. Nature shows me how to do that. The trees, flowers, and animals simply do what they were created to do, using their unique gifts to live in a harmonious way with the rest of the natural world.

In Taoist philosophy, the fabric that weaves through all things is something to be experienced and practiced, not understood in words. Taoist philosophy suggests that we should live a life characterized by traits of harmony, balance, respect, humility, generosity, compassion, kindness, simplicity, and love.

I find that water is another helpful metaphor for life. Water is everywhere and inside each of us. Even if we don't see it or feel it, it's always there. Just as a river follows the path of least resistance, we should go with the flow of our true self and the unique gifts that each of us possesses. When our thoughts, values, and behaviors are aligned with the natural order of life and our true self, life feels easy. We are in the flow.

I like the go-with-the-flow metaphor, with one important caveat: We often have to deliberately go *against* the flow when it comes to actually getting stuff done. For many of us, our inherent nature is to be lazy, so we have to go against that nature to get off the couch and accomplish our goals in life.

Another concept that I subscribe to is the idea that "wherever you are, be there." Every person or event that comes into our life has a reason, getting back to the idea of interconnectedness. A person or event may come into our life to help us, give us a chance to help someone else, or provide an opportunity to learn and grow and ultimately fulfill our life's purpose. We are precisely where we are meant to be in this moment. One of my goals each day is to be fully present in the current moment so I don't miss the lesson. Rest assured, I often fail miserably in this pursuit, but I keep trying.

Some of us end up with a spiritual belief system that is subtly or not so subtly distinct from the teachings of any one world religion. In the end, I don't think it matters which religion we follow as long as our beliefs are sincere, do not harm others, and help us focus inward to discover our true self.

The Dalai Lama likes to compare religion to food. If someone is deriving happiness and benefit from a particular tradition that is different from ours, then that is good. We can all order different dishes according to our taste. There's no need to argue about religion, just like there's no need to argue about whether spicy food is better than bland food. It's just different. Similarly, religion doesn't need to be a source of conflict. It can be a remedy that reduces conflict and suffering, and fosters compassion, kindness, harmony, and love.

Once you've identified your preferred flavor of faith, then it's time to live your life in a way that is aligned with your core beliefs. If you don't study and practice your faith, then you may not truly understand the tenets of your religion, and you may be missing out on one of the most important aspects of personal growth.

Given my lack of spirituality and leadership cred on the sticky topic of religion, I'll rely on three heavy hitters to support my position: Nelson Mandela, Gandhi, and the Dalai Lama:

Nelson Mandela: "Religion is one of the most important forces in the world. Whether you are a Christian, a Muslim, a Buddhist, a Jew, or a Hindu, religion is a great force, and it can help one have command of one's own morality, one's own behavior, and one's own attitude."

Gandhi: "Religions are different roads converging upon the same point. What does it matter that we take different roads so long as we reach the same goal?"

Dalai Lama: "The purpose of all the major religious traditions is not to construct big temples on the outside, but to create temples of goodness and compassion inside, in our hearts. All major religious traditions carry basically the same message that is love, compassion and forgiveness—the important thing is they should be part of our daily lives."

Gandhi used the following title for his autobiography: *The Story of My Experiments with Truth*. What a great perspective to adopt as we all continue to discover The Truth in the world we share. Continue to experiment, learn, and refine your spiritual beliefs until you find The Truth for yourself.

"If government were a product, selling it would be illegal."
P.J. O'Rourke

Politics 101: How sausage is made

About 10 years ago, I made the mistake of watching a video clip about how hot dogs are made. *It wasn't pretty.* Since that day, I've only eaten hot dogs when under duress. The political process, on the other hand, makes hot-dog processing look wholesome and tasty. But, like it or not, politics as we know it is unlikely to change anytime soon, so we might as well develop strategies on how to play nice with others when it comes to this potentially explosive topic.

Like religion, many of us get so attached to, or repelled by, a person or political party that all reason goes out the window, and it can be difficult to engage in open, honest discussions. We lose sight of more important goals because we're too busy trying to protect our team and win the argument, even when we don't agree with half of what our team stands for. Independent thinking gets lost in the process. Rather than throw food or insults at family and friends whenever the topic of politics rears its ugly head, here's my strategy on how to keep cool—no matter what kind of pink-slime political horrors I inadvertently encounter.

My rose-colored political glasses enable me to view politics in the following simplistic way: Politicians have a large pot of money, collected via taxes from citizens and businesses, to manage our country. Each politician has an opinion on how that money should be divided and spent. Similarly, politicians have at their disposal a mind-bogglingly complex set of laws and incentives that they use to maintain a peaceful society and a semi-free market. Some politicians feel that the government needs more money, more regulations, and more government programs to effectively run the country; other politicians feel that government should have less money, fewer regulations, and fewer government programs; the rest fall somewhere in between.

The issues that politicians tackle can be extremely complex. Most issues are not black and white but rather many shades of grey. There are significant, legitimate differences of opinion about which programs should or should not exist. Politicians use a variety of means to push their agendas. The means can be sleazy, virtuous, or somewhere in between.

The money, time, and resources spent on one issue can impact the ability to effectively address other issues. Given the complex regulatory framework that we have created for such things as taxes, healthcare, and environmental issues, it's not easy for anyone to be well informed on more than a few key issues. This means that politicians must rely on "experts" to provide them with sound advice based on available data—a mix of scientific, socioeconomic, and political—that provide a sense of what science suggests they should do and the political fallout they would suffer if they choose to do it. Some of the expert advice is based on solid, objective data; some is based on flimsy or biased data; and some is completely subjective.

Add to the mix public opinion polls, advocacy groups, lobbyists, current events, and pressure from other politicians to steer a given politician in one direction or the other. Each politician weighs the pros and cons, and then makes the final call on how he or she will vote. In some cases, the politician decides not to show up to vote at all.

Along the way, the full spectrum of human character traits will surface, and the media uses the most sensational stories to paint someone as good or bad. Each media outlet has its own biases, and most choose to focus on the bad stuff, regardless of bias. This translates to public character assassinations in print, on the traditional airwaves, or online.

Rather than offer solutions, some politicians focus their attention on trashing their opponent. Close to election time, things start to get really ugly, and the personal attacks are well below the belt. The press loves this, and apparently the public does too. We're left with a sense that all politicians are scum.

In the end, you may feel that you are faced with the option of voting for either "bad" or "worse." When your preferred candidate has a snowball's chance in hell of winning in a primary election, you may choose not to "throw away your vote" and instead vote for someone whom you don't really like because that person has a better chance of winning against the opposing party candidates, some of whom you may despise. Alternatively, you may choose to "throw away your vote" in a primary election because you want your vote to be aligned with your core values, or you really detest the other candidates. In the final election, you may decide to adopt a mindless political robot approach and simply check the box for "democrat" or "republican" across the board without the faintest idea about the candidates or issues.

Finally, it's time to vote. After a day of drama and speculation, the winners are announced. The loser makes a concession speech, the winners celebrate, and there is music and dancing in the streets. After the dust settles, and it becomes clear that it's just going to be business as usual in Washington, D.C., you may be left with a feeling that the system is broken and that all politicians are corrupt, unethical, self-absorbed manipulators of public opinion, no matter what side of the fence they're on.

Rather than get mired in the sausage-making process we call "politics," there's another approach to take. *Ignore it.* Don't waste your limited free time reading about political squabbling and scandals. If you are passionate about certain issues, great. Get involved at a local, state, or national level, and help influence change. But, if following the negative political saga just inspires you to be angry and negative without taking any positive action, then you might want to find something better to do with your time.

Despite my "media fast," I do break it for the narrow window around election time. I research candidates and issues, discuss them with other people, and submit my vote. It takes me about two weeks to do this. After that, my work is finished. I put my head back in the sand and focus on the priorities that I have set for that year. I've made the choice to be a semi-informed voter at the time of the election, cast my vote, and then move on to what I consider to be my highest priorities in life. For me, politics is very far down the list.

Regardless of what position you hear someone take on politics, try not to get too worked up about it. Be nice. We all have different priorities and different levels of understanding of the issues. Just because our political system is messed up in many ways, and politicians can be polarizing figures, don't let politics and politicians ruin your relationships with friends, family, and the community.

If you want to fight the system, get involved with creating change rather than arguing with anyone who will listen. Sometimes that means biting your tongue, perhaps even going as far as thanking others for sharing their perspective with you—even though you may be mulling over the thought of which medieval torture device you would like to use for those persons at that moment. But, if the murky world of politics makes you angry, depressed, or fearful, then choose to ignore it and focus on keeping your own house and relationships clean and healthy.

"People travel to faraway places to watch, in fascination,
the kind of people they ignore at home."
Dagobert D. Runes

The world in my backyard

To wrap up this section on racial, religious, and political intolerance, there's a lot you can do to broaden your mind on any of these topics, and you don't have to go far to do it. You don't have to take your family on an exotic trip to become exposed to different cultures and ways of thinking. Most of us can hop into our car and drive down the street to get a taste of what life is like in another part of the world. Whether your interest is food, music, art, literature, crafts, languages, animals, fashion, history, religion, politics, plants, dance, or volunteer work, you can meet people from all over the world who will be more than happy to share a glimpse of their culture, food, and hospitality.

With abounding cultural diversity in the United States, you can easily experience a different culture every week for at least a year in most cities. Even small towns can yield many surprises, although it often takes a bit more effort to find them. Grab a local newspaper or magazine, or do a quick search online, and look for opportunities to broaden your horizons in your home town. It's a cheap, easy, rewarding, and fun way to learn more about the world and meet people whom you're not likely to cross paths with in your day-to-day routine.

If you want to take this a step further, create a list of the preconceived notions and stereotypes—both good and bad—that you have about a particular culture, religion, or country you're about to experience. Then see how your real experience of the culture compares to your list of stereotypes. It can be fun, and you may learn a lot about your community and yourself in the process.

Many researchers draw the conclusion that the major issues related to race, religion, and politics are based on fear. In the words of the wise sage Yoda: "Fear is the path to the dark side. Fear leads to anger. Anger leads to hate. Hate leads to suffering."

The more you try to understand and empathize with people who are different from you, the less fear, anger, and hate you will carry. The goal is to feel love, kindness, and compassion towards everyone and everything.

May the Force be with you.

ENDNOTES

1.   Brian C. Taylor, *Becoming Human: Core Teachings of Jesus* (Cambridge, MA: Cowley Publications, 2005), pp. 91-92. Published with the written permission of Brian C. Taylor. Thank you, Brian!

2.   Ibid., p. 94.

CHAPTER 9

Fail to fail

"Remember that failure is an event, not a person."
Zig Ziglar

Fail to fail, and you'll be a failure

Bill Gates has done it. Richard Branson has done it. Thomas Edison did it a lot. Steve Jobs did it. Mother Teresa, Gandhi, and Martin Luther King, Jr., have all done it. No, I'm not talking about bungee jumping. I'm talking about failure.

Every successful figure in history has failed in some way, often in spectacular fashion. It's one of the most powerful ways that we learn, improve, and transform our lives.

Mastery of anything requires failure. And failure, in turn, requires action. The only way you can truly master anything is to get out there and *do it*. Over the course of many hours of practice, you make subtle shifts in the movement of your body that can make all the difference in terms of executing something with perfection. The more you practice, the more subtleties you uncover until, finally, you become a true master of that pursuit. Then your mastery leads to success.

As the famous golfer Arnold Palmer pointed out, "The more I practice, the luckier I get." This is true in virtually any pursuit in life, such as sports, music, art, public speaking, writing, and leadership. To experience that "luck," you must practice. *A lot.* It's said that virtually anyone can excel at a skill with over 10,000 hours of practice. That's a huge chunk of time to commit, so be very selective about what you choose to excel in.

One of the worst failures is to lie on your deathbed with feelings of profound disappointment because you know that you never tried to live up to your potential. No one wants to have that horrible feeling at the end of our life, but many of us aren't taking steps to avoid that fate. In short, if you aren't pushing your boundaries, then you may be on the path to failure and regret.

"Failure is not an option. It is a privilege
reserved only for those who try."
Albert Einstein

Failure quiz: fail to fail

Rather than take a failure quiz for this section, go through Steps 1 through 4 of the Success Cookbook and develop your preferred method of tracking your progress as you execute your plan.

Step 1: Identify your best self and your ideal life.
- Describe your perceived strengths, weaknesses, passions, and skills.
- What is your ultimate passion and purpose in life?
- Describe your ideal life and lifestyle.
- Who do you need to become to attract your definition of success?

Step 2: Translate your vision into long- and short-term goals.
- Based on what you wrote in Step 1, create a list of your short- (for this year) and long-term goals (three, five, and 10 years from now).

Step 3: Identify your three top goals for the year.
- From your list of short-term goals in Step 2, identify the top three goals that you will focus on this year.

Step 4: Identify two to three key habits or behaviors for each goal.
- Write your key habits or behaviors in such a way that they will be easy to measure and track when you execute your plan (Step 5) and track your progress along the way (Step 6).

"Do you know the difference between education and experience? Education is when you read the fine print; experience is what you get when you don't."
Pete Seeger

Are you experienced?

Some people collect stamps, some collect coins, and others collect shot glasses. Since my early 20s, I've deliberately focused my attention on the collection of experiences. I'm an experience collector ... and so are you.

We've all heard that experience is the best teacher, but I disagree. Experience is *not* the best teacher. As prolific author and speaker John C. Maxwell said in an interview, experience only becomes valuable when we take the time to evaluate and learn from it. *Evaluated experience* is the best teacher.

When it comes to evaluating my experiences, I was a slacker for many years. More to the point, I was buzzed. A good chunk of my 20s and 30s were filtered through beer, wine, Jack & Coke, and single-malt Scotch. On the plus side, alcohol gave me the courage to experience many things that I would have never done with a clear head. Not surprisingly, many of those experiences would've been better left undone, and many of the worthwhile experiences were processed with dulled senses.

To this day, people bring up experiences from my partying past: "Remember so and so's wedding?" Well, sort of ... I remember that we got wasted. "Remember that awesome concert?" Well, sort of. I remember that we got wasted in the parking lot before the concert. "Remember that amazing restaurant in Paris?" Well, sort of. I remember that we were wasted on wine and cognac. You get the idea. John C. Maxwell wouldn't be very impressed. There wasn't much evaluating and learning going on. I was a broken record, playing the same old song, again and again, without any desire to get up and change the tune.

How do you evaluate your experience? Simple. At the end of each day, week, month, and year, set aside time to reflect on your activities, and consider what you've learned about yourself, good and bad. Reread your written goals and values, and then compare how your current behaviors and experiences stack up against your definition of your best self. If everything is aligned, great! Do it again tomorrow. If you're starting to drift off track, identify what tweaks you need to make to realign yourself with the person you want to become to attract your definition of success. Then plan to make tomorrow a better day. After that, it's rinse and repeat.

"You don't learn to walk by following rules.
You learn by doing, and by falling over."
Richard Branson

Doing must follow learning

It took me many years to realize that I wasn't making progress in certain areas of my life because I was too focused on learning. I was devouring books, taking classes, and earning multiple degrees and certifications, yet I continued to stagnate. Why?

Simple. I wasn't implementing the things that I read and learned. I focused on learning, rather than doing, and failed to put those great ideas into practice. Rather than devour stacks of books to become a walking reference library, I'm much better off when I identify just a few key takeaways from each book, class, or seminar, and then put those ideas into practice to see if they work well for me.

Book knowledge and buzzwords may get you in the door. But, to be effective, you'll need practical experience to go along with them. Get your hands dirty. Do the work yourself. You'll start to understand the wisdom and limitations of concepts that you learned in class or read in books.

As Richard Branson suggests in his quote above, we learn a lot by doing and by falling over. In the process, we also come to see the wisdom in another age-old lesson: Don't judge a person until you've walked a mile in his or her shoes.

**"Resentment is like drinking poison and then
hoping it will kill your enemies."
Nelson Mandela**

Resentment is up to you

While you go through the process of doing, failing, and evaluating your experiences, you may get a few visits from an unwelcome visitor—resentment—and it doesn't like to travel alone. It usually brings its cousin—self-pity—along for the party. When you open the door to find resentment standing there with flowers and a box of chocolates, it's hard to resist. Once you let resentment enter your home, you'll find that it has no intention of leaving anytime soon.

Two wise graduates from the School of Hard Knocks—Joe and Charlie—put it like this: Everybody goes through life armed with self-will. As people pursue their wishes and goals, they sometimes say or do things that hurt us. Some of those things are no big deal, and we can brush them off quickly; others are painful and difficult to dismiss. Let's assume that someone did something to deliberately hurt you. It's clearly wrong, and it can feel devastating. You may feel pain, anger, and lots of other emotions.

However, resentment hasn't yet entered the picture. Resentment doesn't show up until you go home and replay the event in your mind, just like the TV announcers do at a football game. You relive the pain and anguish in super slo-mo, so that you can absorb the injustice in all its spectacular glory. You play this visual in your mind again and again. Each time you replay it, you tweak the story ever so slightly. You make what the other person did just a little bit worse and your role in the event just a little bit less. Eventually, you convince yourself that you were just sitting there, doing nothing, when all of a sudden that awful person leapt into the scene and did that horrible thing to you.

Rather than go down that rabbit hole, choose not to invite resentment into your house in the first place. Instead of focusing on the injustice that some ogre did to you, focus on what *your* resentment is doing to *you.* Otherwise, you're letting that ogre control your thinking, your actions, and your life. Let it go. If you need to, think of those people as sick or just having a bad day. Think of that ogre as Shrek—large, green, crude, and fearsome on the outside; warm, kind, and cuddly inside. If you really want to change the game, turn your mind around and think of how you may be able to help that person. This behavior will catch every-one off guard and could yield some pretty amazing results.

You may have a few resentments that you really don't want to release since you use them to justify your behavior. In these hard cases, one simple strategy that Joe and Charlie offer is to pray for the person or thing that you resent. (Don't worry, my atheist friends. You don't have to get religious. Just wish for health, prosperity, and happiness for that person.) Do this every day for two weeks. At first, the words may feel hollow, and you'll know that you really don't mean it. Then, miraculously and over time, your bitterness, resentment, and hatred will start to melt away, uncovering feelings of compassionate understanding and love.

As Joe and Charlie offer, "It takes two people to make a prison: the prisoner and the jailer. Let them out, and turn them loose. All those people whom I hated, I had to turn them loose. I don't want to be a victim anymore. When everything else fails, we can pray for them. They need the prayers, and we need the practice."

Change the game by wishing well for people who have done you harm, and you'll finally be free. A similar sentiment was echoed by Lao-Tzu over 2,500 years ago: "What is a good man but a bad man's teacher. What is a bad man but a good man's job."

**"Know when to tune out. If you listen to too much advice,
you may wind up making other people's mistakes."
Ann Landers**

Make your own mistakes

Throughout your life, you're bombarded with advice to "do this" and "do that." This advice comes from people we care about, people we don't care much about, and people we don't know at all. Take any of this advice with a grain of salt, including the advice in this book! One person's experience or perspective may be legitimate for him or her, but it might not be appropriate or applicable to your situation.

If you try to please everyone, you may end up feeling paralyzed by conflicting or competing requests. Yes, there are times when you're asked to do something by a parent or boss, and the request is not up for negotiation. But there are many moments in life when you're offered well-intentioned guidance merely to consider. This well-intentioned guidance may be offered for some big decisions that can impact your career, spiritual beliefs, relationships, and health.

Don't absolve yourself from the decision-making process by letting other people make decisions for you. Consider other perspectives and learn from their experience, but draw your own conclusions and make your own decisions. After all, you're the one who gets to live with the consequences of your decisions.

**"How strange to use 'You only live once'
as an excuse to throw it away."
Bill Copeland**

Choose your failures wisely

When you hear that you should take risks, fail often, and ignore advice from other people, you may translate that as a hall pass to do things that are stupid, reckless, and pointless. You only live once, so why not bungee jump from the wing of an airplane and dip your hair in the lava of an active volcano?

You may go through a phase where you choose to ignore common sense and wisdom that's been passed down through the ages and instead adopt a mindset of "If it feels good, do it." You may thumb your nose at societal conventions and laws and seek out myriad ways to go against the grain. This approach generally results in short-lived, hollow "victories" that later in life will feel as good as the aforementioned hair dip in the lava.

An "I'll try anything once" attitude can be a fantastic and exciting approach to living life. But it can also foster a mindset that leads to some very bad decisions and outcomes. A better approach may be to steer your enthusiastic "I'll try anything once" attitude towards calculated risks aligned with significant, meaningful goals that you've set for your life. For most areas of life, it's better to let others do the failing for you and learn from their mistakes. This can save you massive amounts of time and suffering. When it comes to most types of failure, it's better to watch the movie than be a character in it.

But for those few key areas of life that you want to develop and master, failure is something that you should actively pursue and celebrate. The former president of IBM Tom Watson put it like this: "The key to success is massive failure. Your goal is to out-fail your competition. Whoever can fail the most, the fastest and the biggest, wins."

Darren Hardy likes to share the following pendulum analogy that was passed on to him when he was first getting started in real estate: "Life, growth, and achievement work like a pendulum. On one side, you have failure, rejection, defeat, and sadness. On the other side, you have success, acceptance, victory, joy, and happiness. So if you just stand still in life, you won't experience either side, neither the failure and pain nor the success and happiness. The key is that you cannot experience one side without an equal proportion of the other. The only way to achieve more success is to experience more failure."

Choose your failures wisely instead of wasting a lot of time and energy chasing after things that you really don't care about in the end. And for those areas of life that are truly important, keep the pendulum effect in mind and strive to fail fast and fail big, so that you'll be rewarded with big success, joy, and happiness.

**"You can't get a suit of armour and a rubber chicken
just like that. You have to plan ahead."
Michael Palin**

Plan your failures: the Success Cookbook

In my teens, 20s, and 30s, I didn't give much thought about what I wanted to do with my life, let alone the best path to get there. My only goal was to have a wide variety of experiences and to see the world. While this led to an adventurous and exciting life for quite a few years, I lacked a greater vision. I had no purpose or destination other than the vague goal to visit 100 countries before the age of 50, as I mentioned earlier in this book.

This approach to my life led to many successes and failures, but very few were planned. I lacked clear goals, intentions, or a plan for how to realize my ideal life. To help me develop some structure to my goals and vision, I started using Darren Hardy's *Living Your Best Year Ever* journal each year since it was first published in 2011. The first two years were a bit hit and miss, but then I got into the groove and started using it religiously to keep me on track. This planning and evaluation process is one of the most important changes that I've made in my life over the past five years.

Today, I am infinitely more deliberate about how I spend my time, and I have very clear goals and priorities each week, which I protect with a vengeance. In order to protect my schedule and priorities, I had to add a new word to my vocabulary: *no*. That word rarely escaped my lips in the early days.

Armed with the word "no" and the following eight steps from what I call the Success Cookbook, you'll be amazed at what you can accomplish in a year.

Step 1: Identify your best self and your ideal life. These are the "Who am I?' and "What do I want to do with my life?" components of developing a life plan. Once a year, I put together a description of my perceived strengths, weaknesses, passions, skills, and desired lifestyle.

To get things started, write your answers to the following questions:

- What is your ultimate passion and purpose in life?
- What is your ideal life and lifestyle?
- Who is the person that you need to become to attract your definition of success?

Your answers will change in subtle but significant ways over time, so you may find it worthwhile to repeat this exercise each year.

Step 2: Translate your vision into long- and short-term goals. Once you have a clear picture of your best self and your ideal life, it's time to make a list of long- and short-term milestones to measure your progress along the way. Your long- and short-term goals will likely shift in significant ways each year, if not more frequently.

Step 3: Identify your three top goals for the year. From that long list of goals, pick your three top goals for this year. No more, no less. You will use these three goals to structure your year, so choose them wisely. Your goals should be realistic yet challenging. Aim high. Go big. Use a mantra to inspire you to set ambitious goals that will stretch and challenge you.

Step 4: Identify two to three key habits or behaviors for each goal. Now that you've identified your top three goals, it's time to make a list of key habits or behaviors that you'll need to perform, day in and day out, in order to accomplish your three goals.

Do you have your written list of habits and behaviors? Good. Narrow that list down to the two or three most important habits or behaviors for each of your three goals. The goal is to do fewer things more often to get better at them.

Rewrite each of those habits or behaviors in such a way that they will be easy to measure and track. You can't (and shouldn't) measure everything in life. But, when it comes to these few key habits and behaviors, measure and track each of them to see that you're making progress towards your definition of success for the year and for your life.

Keep in mind that many of your failures should be in these key areas as you continue to learn and stretch yourself to become better at those few things. In this way, you have planned your failures—or at least the general flavor of failures that you're likely to experience this year. Of course, you'll also fail miserably at things that aren't on your list, such as golf or updating your Facebook page, but that's a good thing. Focus your time on the key habits and behaviors that impact your top three goals.

Step 5: Execute your plan. This is where the rubber meets the road, and you have to actually do the work. (*Bummer*, I know.) To meet your ambitious goals, put in many hours of hard work, day after day, week after week. As the saying goes, "Success is a marathon, not a sprint."

To make this a reality, carve out time each day or week to deliver on the key habits and behaviors that you've identified as essential in order to meet your three goals for the year. Make it happen by blocking off the time on your calendar. I generally do this in 60- or 90-minute chunks of time, depending on the behavior. Plan your tomorrow today by blocking off time on your calendar to ensure that you'll get your highest priorities completed.

Step 6: Track your progress. Studies have found that people feel happier and more motivated when they see evidence of progress. This implies measurement and tracking. When you can see, through objective data, that you are making progress, it keeps you motivated and optimistic that you will reach your goals, slowly but surely.

In this step, track and assess your progress at the end of each day, week, month, quarter, and year. Don't worry. It's not as bad as it sounds. It can be a quick process once you get in the groove. Darren Hardy's *Living Your Best Year Ever* journal comes in handy since everything is already structured for you. You could certainly do it in Excel or another format, but there's value in actually writing it down in old-school fashion.

Step 7: Celebrate your successes and learn from your failures. As you execute the plan, you'll quickly find that you have plenty of successes and failures. Celebrate your successes with a special treat. As for the failures, well, that's all part of the process, so you might as well celebrate those too. Dust yourself off, and figure out the best way to get back on the path towards your goals.

For example, one of my three goals was to publish this book. The key behavior I selected was to write for an hour every day. Given the realities of my day job and personal life, that goal lasted about 10 days before I had to adjust it to something more suitable for my schedule. I eventually found that a weekly writing target was a better approach for me. Granted, that usually meant that I did virtually all of my writing over the weekend, but it worked. The weekly benchmark of 420 minutes of writing became a useful metric to assess my progress each week.

Step 8: Be mindful of new opportunities. As you go through this process, you may be so focused on your key behaviors that you become completely oblivious to amazing new opportunities that are all around you. It's important to be aware that things are always changing and to be on the lookout for new ideas or approaches that will help you accomplish your goals faster or with less effort. Intermediate milestones can magically dissolve as you discover a shortcut to your next destination. Don't become so attached to your key behaviors that you become blind to other, better ways to realize your dreams.

I do Steps 1 through 4 each New Year's Eve and New Year's Day. (Do I know how to party or what?) Birthdays would also be a good day for this annual routine. But don't wait for some special day. If you've never done it before, then get started today. Follow these steps each day, week, month, and year, and you will accomplish your big goals. It's just a matter of time.

Remember that the only way you can really fail is to no longer try. As author, inventor, and futurist Ray Kurzweil puts it, "Failure is success deferred." When you're deeply committed to a project or initiative, the only person who can declare your project or effort to be a failure is you. Yes, there'll be setbacks, and you'll be tempted to give up at times. But, if it's a worthwhile goal, then commit to the bumpy journey. As Napoleon Hill encourages us, "Failure cannot cope with persistence."

So get out there and fail! You'll learn a lot in the process and probably have a lot of fun too. Fail enough times, and you may become successful beyond your wildest dreams. Remember: There are no failures, only solutions that didn't work. Keep tinkering to find the right solution at the right time in the right circumstance. Financial success may or may not follow. However, as long as you give it your best shot, you'll have one heck of a ride that will inspire others and leave you with a big smile on your face. When it's all said and done, perhaps that's the best success of all.

CHAPTER 10

The wrong tombstone

"There goes the neighborhood."
From the tombstone of Rodney Dangerfield

"I blew it"

These were said to be Sam Walton's last words on his deathbed. Obviously, Sam was not referring to the Wal-Mart Empire that he helped create. Sam was referring to his realization that he had spent too much time on his business and not enough time developing and maintaining close relationships with his family. He certainly passed on an amazing financial legacy to the next generations of his family, but he clearly must have felt that he missed the boat on some key aspects of life. If we die while harboring strong feelings of regret, then we have failed in a profound aspect of our life.

By the time I was in my early 30s, I had heard plenty of stories about deathbed regrets. I had also heard the suggestions to: (1) write an obituary as if I were going to die today; (2) write my desired obituary for my life; and (3) get busy filling in the gaps. Since I was starting to get the sense that I was not immortal after all, I decided to go through the exercise. It was an eye-opening experience—in a bad way.

My first draft resembled a hybrid between a resume and a bucket list. There was no "there" there, although I did like the part about passing away peacefully at home. The exercise left me wondering, "Is that it?" I may spend 70, 80, 90, even 100+ years on this earth, and all I can come up with is a laundry list of activities as my life summary, along with a mental placeholder that I'll probably add a few more job titles and update my country tally to 100+ countries at some point. Publish it in the newspaper, and I'm ready to go. *Pathetic.*

My obituary didn't capture the essence of what life is all about. It was just a showy list that screamed, "Look at all the cool things I did!" It lacked purpose—the "What's it all about?" or "Why?" that ties the events of my life together.

To add some perspective, I decided to write down what I thought close family and friends would say about me after I died. I guessed that it would be something along the lines of, "Mark traveled all over the world. He was quiet yet friendly and polite. He had a good sense of humor. He was a really good soccer player and athlete. He loved music. He used to get trashed on Jack & Coke and do some pretty crazy stuff." *This was not exactly the dream I had envisioned for my life.*

To me, it was a red flag that I was off track, with distorted priorities and a lack of vision for what I had to offer in this life. Granted, it was just a first draft, but it was a motivational exercise nonetheless. I felt inspired to make some significant changes in the second draft of my desired obituary. More importantly, I started to change the trajectory of my life.

Now it's your turn. You have the opportunity to write your ideal obituary today, and start working backwards from there. You can start to make decisions, create opportunities, and live the rest of your days in alignment with your most important priorities. Time is ticking, so don't waste any more of it. You don't want to lie on your deathbed with intense feelings of regret. You want to lie down with a smile on your face as you say to yourself, "That was amazing! What a great ride!" and know that you're passing on a legacy of love and support to your family and friends.

"When I am dead and buried, on my tombstone I would
like to have it written, 'I have arrived.' Because when
you feel that you have arrived, you are dead."

Yul Brynner

Failure quiz: tombstone

Like the last chapter, we'll skip the quiz and go straight to the all-important tombstone exercise. It's really an obituary exercise, but "tombstone" sounds more dramatic, so the name stuck.

- Write a draft of what your obituary would look like if you were to kick the bucket today.

- Write a draft of your ideal obituary if you were to live as long as you hope to live.

- Make changes in your life to start filling in the gaps between the first version and the second version.

> **"In three words I can sum up everything**
> **I've learned about life: it goes on."**
> **Robert Frost**

What's it all about?

It's time to address that age-old question, "What the heck are we doing here on Earth?" The short answer is, "Nobody knows for sure." But there are plenty of strong opinions on the topic—over seven billion opinions, to be precise.

If you were asked what you desire for your kids, you would probably say that you want them to have a life of happiness and meaning. If asked how you define "happiness" versus "meaning," you may say that happiness is about experiencing contentment and joy in the present moment while meaning is derived from activities that enable us to express ourselves in a way that links our past, present, and future so that our lives have a larger, intelligible context. (Okay, maybe most of us would not come up with that distinction, but let's just say that we were having a good day.)

Regardless of your definition, you likely agree that you don't want your children to dedicate their entire lives to playing the Minecraft video game, even though it might appear that your children would be very happy to give that life path a try. You wouldn't characterize that as a life filled with meaning. Many people go on to conclude that meaning is what makes life worthwhile. However, plenty of other people counter that happiness is what gives life meaning.

Now that I've left your head spinning with the meaning-and-happiness conundrum, it's time to straighten things out in your own mind. In this section, your goal is to define what the meaning of life is to you and reflect on how your life is aligned with your vision of a meaningful life.

When I was a kid, I read some of those "choose your own adventure" books. These books were written in such a way that you, the reader, are in the book, making choices that determine the actions of the characters. As you continue to make choices, the book guides you to specific page numbers until you eventually come to one of several different endings. Some of the possible endings were happy, some were ambiguous, and some were unambiguously bad. In this chapter, you can choose your own adventure—although, in this case, you're merely answering the question, "What is the meaning of life to you?"

When we look at historical and present-day musings on the meaning of life, we see common themes that pop up again and again. I've included some heavy hitters in this section to give you some food for thought and jump-start your brain.

Your challenge, if you choose to accept it, is to come up with your own mean-ing-of-life statement. This is not something that you will use to impress others. Your statement should be uniquely yours, something that you closely identify with and will use as a beacon to guide you in your journey through life.

As for the ending of your adventure book, I'll leave that part up to you.

**"The best way to find yourself is to lose
yourself in the service of others."
Mahatma Gandhi**

Service: helping others

Service to others is a common "What's life all about?" theme that has been expressed by many historical heavyweights:

Leo Tolstoy: "The sole meaning of life is to serve humanity."

Nelson Mandela: "What counts in life is not the mere fact that we have lived. It is what difference we have made to the lives of others that will determine the significance of the life we lead."

Winston Churchill: "We make a living by what we get, but we make a life by what we give."

Whenever I hear this "service to others" idea, I usually conjure up images of people like Mother Teresa, who dedicate their lives to "wholehearted free service to the poorest of the poor." Such a saint thinks nothing of giving a foot rub to a poor person who is suffering from leprosy. That's usually about where my mind switches gears and thinks, "No, I don't think I want to give foot rubs to the homeless anytime soon. I haven't quite evolved to that level yet."

At best, I donate loose change to homeless people who beg at street intersections that I drive by each day. And, if the truth be told, I probably only do that about 25% of the time, often with the accompanying thought, "Okay. Now you can go get drunk or high." (As you can see, I haven't yet attained enlightenment, but I have nothing but potential.)

Still, I do believe there is merit in the goal of living a life of selfless service; we just need to personalize it. You can determine how you can best give yourself away to those in your circle of influence—family, friends, pets, backyard, neighborhood, local community, city, state, country, or the whole world. Even if your circle of influence happens to be on the smaller end of the spectrum, Mother Teresa encourages us with this reminder: "If you can't feed a hundred people, then feed just one."

You can make small, meaningful contributions through labor, teaching, writing, financial assistance, art, music, and other skills that you may possess. Service can be as simple as lending an empathetic ear to someone in need. Ask people to tell you their stories, and then listen with your full attention. That can be a very powerful act of service.

No matter what act of service you pursue, the end result is that it will make you feel good inside, and you'll often learn and grow from the experience. In some cases, you may end up giving or receiving a missing number of the combination that unlocks a long-sought-after truth. Every person you meet offers an opportunity to help and be helped. It's a nice reminder that we're all in this together. We're all connected.

Ultimately, that's what pushed me to publish this book and make it available beyond my immediate family. In my own small way, I may be able to help people ask the right questions to discover their true self and encourage others to pursue the life they were meant to live.

No matter how busy you are, there's one act of service that you can do every day, and it doesn't cost a dime: *Smile*. This simple act can change the trajectory of someone's day and can have a ripple effect that makes the world a better place.

As the venerable Vietnamese Zen Buddhist monk and author Thích Nhất Hạnh puts it, "Because of your smile, you make life more beautiful." Mother Teresa adds, "Let us always meet each other with a smile, for the smile is the beginning of love. Spread love everywhere you go. Let no one ever come to you without leaving happier."

While I don't always give money to the homeless people on my way to and from work, there's one thing I do offer on a consistent basis: *a wave and a smile*. I make eye contact, and let them know that I see them and wish them well. Hey, it's a start.

"In our life there is a single color, as on an artist's palette, which provides the meaning of life and art. It is the color of love."
Marc Chagall

Love

Love is another popular meaning-of-life theme echoed by all kinds of people, not just from crunchy-granola hippie types:

Bible (1 Corinthians 13): "Love is eternal ... Meanwhile these three things remain: faith, hope, and love; and the greatest of these is love."

Thomas Merton: "Love is our true destiny. We do not find the meaning of life by ourselves alone—we find it with another."

Dalai Lama: "Love and compassion are necessities, not luxuries. Without them, humanity cannot survive."

When we dive into the topic of love, we quickly find that the highest standard is an unconditional, altruistic love, which does not fluctuate with circumstances. In Christianity, this type of unwavering, selfless love is described with the word "agape." Jesus describes the agape concept perfectly with the following quote: "But I say to you, Love your enemies and pray for those who persecute you, so that you may be sons of your Father who is in heaven; for he makes his sun rise on the evil and on the good, and sends rain on the just and on the unjust." In other words, Jesus is saying that God just loves, unconditionally, and we would be wise to do the same.

The Bhagavad Gita echoes a similar sentiment with the following passage:

I am the same to all beings. My love
Is the same always. Nevertheless, those
Who meditate on me with devotion,
They dwell in me, and I shine forth in them.
Even the worst sinner becomes a saint
When he loves me with all his heart. This love
Will soon transform his personality
And fill his heart with peace profound.
O son of Kunti, this is my promise:
Those who love me, they shall never perish.

About now, I'm guessing that these words are raising the hackles of my non-religious friends, so I will cut myself off. It doesn't matter if you read religious texts, philosophical treatises, Greek mythology, or romance and popular novels, you will consistently find verses that proclaim the merits of a life filled with compassion, kindness, and love.

Gandhi puts it like this: "Where there is love there is life." Or, if you prefer a more contemporary figure, bestselling author Danielle Steel has this to say on the topic of love: "Lust is temporary, romance can be nice, but love is the most important thing of all. Because without love, lust and romance will always be short-lived."

**"The purpose of our lives is to be happy. Happiness is not
something ready-made. It comes from your own actions.
If you want others to be happy, practice compassion.
If you want to be happy, practice compassion."**
Dalai Lama

Happiness

We all want happiness, but many of us waste a lot of time and money before we
figure out how to get it. We're all seeking something better in life, but we often
end up chasing the wrong things. Happiness is much like success in that it eludes
us like a rainbow if we chase after it. Happiness is a mindset. As Thích Nhất Hạnh
puts it, "There is no way to happiness—happiness is the way."

In 2014, I was fortunate to be able to attend a full-day, "Eight Verses of Mind
Training" session with the Dalai Lama in Boston. It was just me and the Dalai
Lama … and I guess there were two or three thousand other attendees. There was
a heavy contingent of Vietnamese and Tibetan monks, and the rest were a bunch
of yahoos like me who were along for the ride in the nosebleed seats of the Wang
Theatre. In preparation for the class, I read through several of the Dalai Lama's
books, including *The Art of Happiness*, to get a sense of where he stands on the
topic. Here are a few tidbits that stood out from the Dalai Lama's books and training course on the subject of happiness:

From a Buddhist perspective, there are four factors of fulfillment that people
seek in their quest to achieve happiness: (1) wealth; (2) worldly satisfaction; (3)
spirituality; and (4) enlightenment. This list correlates nicely with Western studies
that offer the following components of happiness: peace of mind, good health,
financial freedom, worthy goals and ideals, self-knowledge, and a sense of self-ful-
fillment or self-actualization.

The different approaches to inner contentment can be broken down into two
paths. One path is to strive to obtain everything that we want and desire, such as
money, houses, cars, the perfect mate, and the perfect body. The problem with
this approach is that there'll eventually be something that we want but can't have.
An alternate path is to want what we already have. Care to take a wild guess which
path the Dalai Lama suggests we pursue?

Yes, the Dalai Lama shockingly chooses Answer B: Want what we already have. However, he takes this to a deeper level than you might initially consider. The Dalai Lama reminds us that we already have everything we need to experience happiness and joy, regardless of external influences. Just like any skill, happiness is something we can deliberately cultivate by training our mind. We train our mind to be calm and at peace, with the realization that how we choose to interpret, feel, and respond to external events is our choice. Yes, it's the old Event + Response = Outcome formula that we discussed earlier in this book.

The greater the calmness of your mind, the greater your ability to enjoy a happy and peaceful life. A calm, disciplined mind doesn't mean that you zone out in a cave in some apathetic, insensitive trance. To the contrary. The Dalai Lama suggests that peace of mind is rooted in affection and kindness with a high level of engagement, compassion, and feeling. External things will not bring you happiness if you lack a calm, disciplined mind. When you possess calmness of mind, then you have everything you need to experience happiness and joy.

The Dalai Lama also writes that happiness is highly contagious and spreads like a virus, which in this case is a good thing. If you want to build a better world, then it's your duty to be happy and keep the virus spreading.

So how should you respond when you come across people who are rude, aggressive, and unkind? In these cases, the Dalai Lama suggests that we should feel deep gratitude. *Huh?* Come again? Yes, gratitude. There aren't that many people like this in the world, he explains, so when we do meet these unpleasant people, we should be grateful for the rare opportunity to practice patience and tolerance. I like that approach, and I find that it really does help to keep it in mind when I meet people who are in the "not so pleasant" category.

On the topics of meaning and purpose, the Dalai Lama says that each of us is seeking something better for our life, and none of us was born to cause trouble or harm others. In order for us to consider our lives to be meaningful, we must develop the basic human qualities of warmth, compassion, and kindness. Our basic nature is to be gentle and compassionate. When we pursue these positive human qualities, our lives will become more peaceful and happier.

The Dalai Lama wrapped things up with a reminder that our present experience—positive or negative—is a consequence of our past actions. If we change our actions today, then we will change the experiences that we will encounter in the future. What happens in the future depends on the activities that we pursue today. "The secret to our own happiness is in our own hands right now. We must not miss this opportunity."

**"Human life is purely a matter of deciding
what's important to you."
Anonymous**

Meaning

Each day, you set priorities and make choices that, over time, dictate the direction of your life. French philosopher and author Albert Camus put it succinctly: "Life is the sum of all your choices." It's all about ensuring that your choices, perspective, and priorities are aligned with what you consider to be important in life. You can decide the meaning of your life each moment of every day.

American writer Joseph Campbell summarized this concept: "I don't believe people are looking for the meaning of life as much as they are looking for the experience of being alive. Life is without meaning. You bring the meaning to it. The meaning of life is whatever you ascribe it to be. Being alive is the meaning."

Austrian neurologist, psychiatrist, and Holocaust survivor Victor Frankl adds, "For the meaning of life differs from man to man, from day to day and from hour to hour. What matters, therefore, is not the meaning of life in general but rather the specific meaning of a person's life at a given moment."

French writer, poet, and aviator Antoine de Saint-Exupery wrote, "Each man must look to himself to teach him the meaning of life. It is not something discovered: it is something molded."

The beautiful thing about choices, perspective, and priorities is that you can immediately change the direction of your life if you don't like how things are going or where you're headed. The choice is up to you. At any moment, you can choose to adopt a new attitude, a new mindset, a new behavior, or a new goal for your life. You can choose to make today the same as yesterday, or you can change course and set sail for a new and different tomorrow.

Another aspect of purpose and meaning is the commonly held belief that we must find and follow our passion in order to live a meaningful life. If taken too literally, this philosophy can lead to an arrest for stalking.

Instead, I find it helpful to consider how Darren Hardy summarizes how to "find your passion." Darren believes that we can find our passion in one of four ways: (1) what we do; (2) how we do what we do (i.e., with excellence, precision, or care); (3) why we do what we do (the mission or cause); or (4) who we do it for (our family, kids, etc.).

This is an important exercise to explore. First, identify one or more of the four approaches to find a passion that resonates with you. Next, reframe your thinking to identify ways in which your current situation is aligned with your true passion in life. This can help you recognize if you're on the right track. If you're off track, then it can help you identify the next logical step to get there.

This mindset shift can transform your perception and attitude about your current "boring, dead-end job." Rather than dwell on how lame and meaningless your current widget-making job might be, you may find meaning and passion for your work by focusing on doing your job with excellence, focusing on the mission that your work supports, or focusing on how your work enables you to provide a good life for your family. Such a simple shift in thinking can be very powerful.

In reality, you may experience all four aspects of passion in your day-to-day life. For certain activities, you may find meaning in what you do; for others, it may be about how you do it, why you do it, and who you do it for. Whether you're writing a business proposal, changing a diaper, planting a garden, emptying the trash, or driving in rush-hour traffic, you can think of the what, how, why, or for whom, and instantly transform a mundane or unpleasant activity into something meaningful.

When you wake up each morning, it's up to you to make choices and set priorities to ensure that you live a life of meaning that day, whatever that means to you in each of the present moments you experience. Tomorrow, you will do it all over again. Focus your attention on experiencing contentment and joy in the present moment.

As Gandhi put it: "Each night, when I go to sleep, I die. And the next morning, when I wake up, I am reborn."

"Never underestimate the importance of having fun. I'm dying and I'm having fun. And I'm going to keep having fun every day because there's no other way to play it."
Randy Pausch

Fun

As a shout-out to the hedonistic side of your personality, plenty of wise minds have come to the conclusion that one of the most important aspects of life is to let loose and have fun. Some of us take this to an extreme, adopting the philosophy of life articulated by Derek Smalls from *This Is Spinal Tap* fame: "Have a good time, all the time." This approach to life may be accompanied by the core values of poor health, lying to yourself and to others, infidelity, and vomiting on your shirt. On the other hand, there's the adage, "All work and no play makes Jack a dull boy," and I don't think any of us want to turn out like Jack from *The Shining*.

Clearly, we should make the most of our limited time on Earth by having some fun. Heck, even stern and serious types would have to agree that it's good for our health and our relationships, although they may quickly add the following caveat from the Bible (1 Corinthians 8:9): "Be careful, however, that the exercise of your freedom does not become a stumbling block to the weak. Our freedom to relax and enjoy our lives should never cause others to stumble in their faith."

Whether your version of fun is sitting in the garden with a good book and a cup of Earl Grey tea, or stage-diving into a mosh pit at a speed metal concert, get out there and have some fun! Embrace your hedonistic side, as long as you don't harm anyone else in the process. Laugh, dance, and make a fool of yourself, if that feels like fun to you. It's all for a good cause: your health and your happiness. For many people, having fun is the meaning of life—or at least part of the equation.

As Irish playwright George Bernard Shaw put it, "We don't stop playing because we grow old; we grow old because we stop playing."

"Sir, my concern is not whether God is on our side; my greatest
concern is to be on God's side, for God is always right."
Abraham Lincoln

Thy will be done

For thousands of years, many people have drawn the conclusion that the purpose of life is to serve God and to live a life that is aligned with God's will. The only catch is figuring out what God's will is for our life. Most of us don't receive explicit instructions from God in our mailbox, so many people rely on the guidance of scripture that was written over 2,000 years ago.

As people read these sacred texts, some come to believe that it is God's literal word while others believe it is man's inspired interpretation of God's will. Many people adopt a spiritual buffet approach to scripture—ignoring many passages of smiting, animal sacrifices, and begats—until we load our plate with some of the good stuff to incorporate into our belief system. The same sacred text can inspire one person to justify killing others who don't share the same view, and inspire another to devote an entire life to meditation, prayer, and service.

Regardless of your take on God and God's will, it's a mighty powerful force in the world. And, for many people on this globe, the purpose of life is to realize God.

**"To be what we are, and to become what we are
capable of becoming, is the only end of life."
Robert Louis Stevenson**

Realizing your full potential

Another perspective to consider while you window shop for your meaning of life is the view that the purpose of life is to discover your true self and realize your full potential.

This view doesn't require an answer to the origin-of-life riddle. This philosophy of life is well suited for believers, agnostics, and atheists alike, since there's no need to discuss religion, a creator, or any of that heady stuff. Even for people with deep, religious convictions, this philosophy is often an integral part of their overall definition of the meaning of life.

Your mission is simply to discover yourself, do your best with the gifts and time that you've been given, and be a good person. You'll figure out the rest later, perhaps after you die. Until then, your job is to become a better person than you were yesterday.

As American basketball player and coach John Wooden offered, "Success is peace of mind that is a direct result of knowing that you've done your best at becoming the best you are capable of becoming."

"I love good sense above all, perhaps because I have none."
Gustave Flaubert

None of the above

If you haven't yet found anything that resonates with you, then it looks like you've opted for Answer E, which in this case can be "none of the above," "some of the above," or "all of the above." Regardless, at the end of this chapter, you'll have the opportunity to come up with your own definition of the meaning of life.

Use these ideas with reckless abandon to come up with your own personal statement about what life is all about. I don't care if you believe that the meaning of life is to wear silly hats. Create a definition that resonates with you. After all, it's your life. Make it a good one.

**"I think one of the greatest joys I have now in my career
and in my profession is to be playing at an age where
I can appreciate it more than I used to ... It's a whole
different lens you look through the older you get."**
Andre Agassi

Tombstone revisited

Now that I'm older and have a bit more evaluated experience, I can only laugh at the first drafts of my obituary and tombstone manifesto written in my younger days. It's perfectly natural for your definition of the meaning of life to shift—subtly or drastically—as your priorities and perspectives change in different stages of your life. However, the older you get, the more experiences you will have that tend to push you in a particular direction.

When you boil it down to the basics, life is pretty simple. As a result, when my time is up, the message I will share with my son, my family, and others will likely be a simple one. Perhaps something like this:

Mark Aspelin
June 08, 1969 – XX, XX, 20XX
What an awesome ride!
Now it's your turn.

CHAPTER 11

Parting thoughts

"You can hope for a miracle in your life, or you
can realize that your life is the miracle."
Robert Brault

Try, fail, change, grow, and give it away

For me, that heading pretty much summarizes the age-old wisdom in personal development that you can apply to all areas of your life. However, there's an implied first step: Identify your goals and priorities. I decided long ago not to try, fail, change, grow, and give it away as a car mechanic. As a result, I'm lucky if I can figure out how to fill up my car with gas at the gas station. Instead, I take my car to people who love doing that kind of work and pay them to do it for me. While I wait for the car, I'll do something on my list of goals, such as daily writing. In that way, everybody wins—although I may not feel that way when I get the mechanic's bill.

Another piece of timeless wisdom, believed to have been first written by medieval Persian Sufi poets, is the notion that, "This too shall pass." These four words capture the sum total of the history of life on Earth.

Putting this together, we find a few common themes about life:
- Each of us feels the need to live a life of purpose.
- Each of us has a different purpose because we're born with a unique combination of strengths, weaknesses, interests, and special gifts.

The goal is to discover your strengths, weaknesses, and special gifts, and then pursue a life that plays to your strengths and gifts. This can take a lot of trial, error, and failure. Some people figure it out young, some when they're old, and some never at all.

One reason why many of us never discover our purpose in life is because we don't look in the right places to find it. We may allow our life's purpose to get shaped by family, friends, and culture, to the point that we may live a life that's far removed from our true nature and purpose. We may forget that the real answer can only be found within each of us. Other people may recognize your gifts and point you in the right direction, but only you know your true nature and purpose in life. Nobody can answer that question for you.

While you go through the process of uncovering your true nature and purpose, you'll make choices every day that, over time, have a major impact on the direction of your life. Some of your choices may lead you into debt, unhappy marriages, or jobs that you hate; others may lead you into financial freedom, positive relationships and associations, and work that feels like play. Over time, your choices accumulate and compound until, in the end, you hopefully draw a conclusion that you have lived a good, meaningful life and realized your true potential.

As you go through life and learn key lessons, don't forget to share what you learn with others. In a lecture, Rev. Himes once said, "You never fully grasp the fruits of your education until you give it away to another. What we hold on to we lose, what we give away never runs out. What we give away becomes everlasting."

History is full of voices great and small, giving away what they have learned along their journey. This book is my tiny contribution to that body of knowledge. For the most part, it reinforces timeless truisms passed down through many generations. My advice is not right or wrong. It's simply what I've come to believe based on my own experiences, and it will no doubt evolve over time.

Your experiences may prove to be very different than mine, so ignore the stuff you didn't agree with and experiment with a few ideas that resonate with you. Craft your own story and develop your own truth to pass on to the next generation. We're all connected. We're all in this together. Each of us seeks a life filled with happiness and meaning.

If things aren't going so well, remember that change is up to you. To paraphrase Jim Rohn, if you want your life to change, then you have to change. You can't change the direction of the wind, but you can adjust your sail by changing your philosophy and attitude. You have the ability to change the direction of your life overnight and set sail for the life of your dreams.

There's a scene from one of my favorite movies, *The Fellowship of the Ring*, where the two characters Frodo Baggins and Gandalf the Gray pretty much capture the essence of life. After some not-so-pleasant things take place, Frodo says, "I wish it need not have happened in my time." The wise, old Gandalf responds, "So do I, and so do all who live to see such times. But that is not for them to decide. All we have to decide is what to do with the time that is given us."

While we're talking about movies, here's a trip down memory lane featuring the late, great Robin Williams from the movie *Dead Poets Society*. I can still picture Williams's character, English teacher John Keating, offering the following words to his new students as they gazed deeply into the faces of former students in old school photos … students who were long since dead:

"They believe they're destined for great things, just like many of you. Their eyes are full of hope, just like you. Did they wait until it was too late to make from their lives even one iota of what they were capable? Because you see, gentlemen, these boys are now fertilizing daffodils. But if you listen real close, you can hear them whisper their legacy to you. Go on, lean in. Listen. Do you hear it? [whispers] Carpe. Carpe Diem. Seize the day, boys, make your lives extraordinary."

"Learn how to be happy with what you have while you pursue all that you want. Happiness is not an accident. Nor is it something you wish for. Happiness is something you design."
Jim Rohn

Wherever you are, be there

Well, Jim Rohn, it's getting late. While our day has come to a close, I still have quite a bit more to cover on the best ways to fail at life. There were some major topics that I didn't have a chance to cover today. But, if you found this to be a valuable use of your time, perhaps we can meet again soon to cover the rest.

In the meantime, I'll follow the advice that you shared with me many years ago:

"Don't wish it was easier; wish you were better. Don't wish for less problems; wish for more skills. Don't wish for less challenges; wish for more wisdom. Success is not to be pursued; it is to be attracted by the person we become."

Bibliography

"Be kind whenever possible. It is always possible."
Dalai Lama

Al-Anon Family Groups. *How Al-Anon Works for Families & Friends of Alcoholics.* New York: Al-Anon Family Group Headquarters, 2008.

Alcoholics Anonymous. *The Big Book.* New York: Alcoholics Anonymous World Press, 2002.

___. *Joe & Charlie Tapes—AA Big Book Study* (audio recordings, 1998; available on Amazon.com).

Chapman, Gary D., and Jennifer M. Thomas. *The Five Languages of Apology: How to Experience Healing in All Your Relationships.* Chicago: Northfield Publishing, 2006.

Clason, George S. *The Richest Man in Babylon.* New York: Classic House Books, 2008; originally published in 1926, with many newer editions.

Conrad, Jessamyn. *What You Should Know About Politics ... But Don't: A Non-Partisan Guide to the Issues That Matter.* New York: Arcade Publishing, 2012.

Dalai Lama. *Beyond Religion: Ethics for a Whole World.* New York: Houghton Mifflin Harcourt Publishing, 2011.

Diamandis, Peter, and Steven Kotler. *Abundance: The Future Is Better Than You Think.* New York: Free Press, 2014.

Dyer, Dr. Wayne W. *Change Your Thoughts—Change Your Life: Living the Wisdom of the Tao.* Carlsbad, CA: Hay House, 2007.

Fulkerson, Lee, director. *Forks Over Knives.* New York: Monica Beach Media, 2011, DVD.

Gandhi, Mohandas Karamchand (Mahatma). *Gandhi: An Autobiography—The Story of My Experiments With Truth.* New York: Beacon Press Books, 1993.

Gottman John, PhD, and Nan Silver. *The Seven Principles for Making Marriage Work: A Practical Guide from the Country's Foremost Relationship Expert.* New York: Harmony Books, 2015.

Guarneri, Mimi, MD. *The Science of Natural Healing.* Chantilly, VA: The Teaching Company, 2012, CD/DVD.

Haidt, Jonathan. *The Righteous Mind: Why Good People Are Divided by Politics and Religion.* New York; First Vintage Books, 2013.

Hardy, Darren. *The Compound Effect.* Lake Dallas, TX: Success Books, 2010.

___. *Living Your Best Year Ever.* Lake Dallas, TX: Success Media, 2011, CDs and journal.

Henderson, Jeff. *Cooked: My Journey From the Streets to the Stove.* New York: Harper Collins, 2007.

___. *If You Can See It, You Can Be It: 12 Street-Smart Recipes for Success.* New York: SmileyBooks, 2013.

King, Martin Luther. *A Testament of Hope: The Essential Writings and Speeches of Martin Luther King, Jr.* New York: HarperCollins Publishers, 1986.

Langer, Ellen. *Counterclockwise: Mindful Health and the Power of Possibility.* New York: Ballantine Books, 2009.

___. *Mindfulness.* Boston: Da Capo Press, 1989.

Mandela, Nelson. *Long Walk to Freedom: The Autobiography of Nelson Mandela.* Boston: Little, Brown and Company, 1994.

McDougall, Christopher. *Born to Run: A Hidden Tribe, Superathletes, and the Greatest Race the World Has Never Seen.* New York: Alfred A. Knopf, 2009.

Nair, Keshavan. *A Higher Standard of Leadership: Lessons from the Life of Gandhi.* San Francisco: Berrett-Koehler Publishers, 1994.

Pinker, Steven. *The Better Angels of Our Nature: Why Violence Has Declined.* New York: Penguin Books, 2011.

Pulde, Alona, MD, and Matthew Lederman, MD. *The Forks Over Knives Plan: How to Transition to the Life-Saving, Whole-Food, Plant-Based Diet.* New York: Simon & Schuster, 2014.

Ramsey, Dave. Financial Peace University (www.daveramsey.com/fpu).

___. *The Total Money Makeover: A Proven Plan for Financial Fitness.* Nashville: Nelson Books, 2013.

Ramsey, Dave, and Rachel Cruze. *Smart Money Smart Kids: Raising the Next Generation to Win with Money.* Brentwood, TN: Lampo Press, 2014.

Riso, Don Richard, and Russ Hudson. *The Wisdom of the Enneagram: The Complete Guide to Psychological and Spiritual Growth for the Nine Personality Types*. New York: Bantam Books, 1999.

Rohn, Jim. *The Five Major Pieces to the Life Puzzle: A Guide to Personal Success*. Lake Dallas, TX: Jim Rohn International, 1991.

___. *The Seasons of Life*. Lake Dallas, TX: Jim Rohn International, 1981.

Roll, Rich. *Finding Ultra: Rejecting Middle Age, Becoming One of the World's Fittest Men, and Discovering Myself.* New York: Three Rivers Press, 2012.

Roll, Rich, and Julie Piatt. *The Plantpower Way: Whole Food Plant-Based Recipes and Guidance for The Whole Family.* New York: Avery, 2015.

Rosenberg, Marshall B., PhD. *Nonviolent Communication: A Language of Life: Life-Changing Tools for Healthy Relationships*. Encinitas, CA: Puddledancer Press, 2015.

Taylor, Brian C. *Becoming Human: Core Teachings of Jesus*. Cambridge, MA: Cowley Publications, 2005.

Tieger, Paul D., Barbara Barron, and Kelly Tieger. *Do What You Are: Discover the Perfect Career for You Through the Secrets of Personality Type*. New York: Little, Brown and Company, 2014.

Ziglar, Zig. *Embrace the Struggle: Living Life on Life's Terms*. New York: Howard Books, 2009.

www.ingramcontent.com/pod-product-compliance
Lightning Source LLC
Chambersburg PA
CBHW070037100426
42740CB00013B/2713

Copyright © 2025 by Frank Moore and Dennis Landrum

The Foundry Publishing®
PO Box 419527
Kansas City, MO 64141
thefoundrypublishing.com

ISBN: 978-0-8341-4333-3

Cover design: Arthur Cherry
Interior design: Sharon Page

Library of Congress Cataloging-in-Publication Data
A complete catalog record for this book is available from the Library of Congress.

The internet addresses, email addresses, and phone numbers in this book are accurate at the time of publication. They are provided as a resource. The Foundry Publishing® does not endorse them or vouch for their content or permanence.

God the Father

Frank Moore and
Dennis Landrum

f

THE FOUNDRY
PUBLISHING

Contents

The Big Picture

Close your eyes and imagine walking into what appears to be a grove of trees. One tree in particular catches your attention. You stop for a moment and take in its beauty. A gentle breeze blows through the leaves; the tops of the leaves are green while the undersides look almost silver. The colors alternate as the breeze blows softly. You make a mental note of the tree's unusual beauty.

As you continue walking, the path begins to steepen as it goes into a forest. You reach a clearing and find yourself looking down into a valley. From this perspective, you can see your special tree as part of the entire grove. The grade of the trail becomes even steeper as you continue up what you now realize is a mountain. Your curiosity has the best of you, so with great effort, you follow the path toward the top. Finally you reach an overlook, and your efforts produce an amazing reward. The sight takes your breath away. Mountains stretch across the horizons in every direction; more trees than you could ever count cover both the mountains and the valleys. You marvel at God's creative handiwork.

Think how your perspective changed from focusing your attention on a single tree, to seeing an entire grove of trees, to finally seeing an entire mountain range of trees. This type of expansion in perspective is a key objective of this book. Many Christian believers begin their understanding of God with one-word descriptors: "Creator," "almighty," "holy," "all knowing," and more. From there, they read Scripture or listen to Bible teachers and pastors tell scriptural stories of God's involvement in the lives of his children. They learn more about who God is based on the way he interacted with various biblical characters like Abraham, Moses, King David, Isaiah, and others. Through this process, they may add a few more descriptors to their understanding of God.

However, our understanding of God can stall at that level without significant effort to expand our perspective. In order to accomplish this objective, we need to learn more about God's biblical names, his character traits and attributes, and his incredible work in our world and in the lives of his children. Beyond that, we should dig deeply into Scripture to see the big picture of God's indescribable love for us, along with his original desire for creation. Then we must study, as well as personally experience, God's work to restore our hearts and lives to his original desire for humanity. That exploration has the potential to expand our understanding of God and our relationship with him for the rest of our lives on earth.

Our Privileged Vantage Point

You might be saying to yourself, "That sounds like a lot of work." You might also be wondering why you should put so much effort into climbing the mountain, figuratively speaking. The answer is simple: it is the greatest commandment found in Scripture. "Jesus replied: '"Love the Lord your God with all your heart and with all your soul and with all your mind." This is the first and greatest commandment'" (Matt. 22:37–38).

It is impossible to love someone unless you know who they are. Furthermore, the more you love them, the more you want to know about who they are. Hence, we cannot love God unless we know who God is. From there, it follows that if we want to love God more, we must learn more about him. The Bible draws us into a deeper hunger to know God better. "Be still, and know that I am God" (Ps. 46:10). Paul said, "I keep asking that the God of our Lord Jesus Christ, the glorious Father, may give you the Spirit of wisdom and revelation, so that you may know [God] better" (Eph. 1:17). According to Jesus, we will learn more about God and love him better throughout eternity: "Now this is eternal life: that they may know you, the only true God, and Jesus Christ, whom you have sent" (John 17:3).

Fortunately, we have all of the advantages of living in the church age of Christian history. We can learn from the insights and experiences of those who came before us. The millions of Christian believers, scholars, pastors, and mentors over the past two thousand years whom we call the "great cloud of witnesses" (Heb. 12:1) have blazed a trail for us to travel in this world. We have the precious presence of the Holy Spirit living in the world and in our hearts working in our individual lives and in the corporate community of faith. Many Christians alive today are privileged enough to own a Bible in their preferred language and translation, containing both the Old and New Testaments. The written Word of the New Testament witnesses to the Living Word, who is Jesus Christ, our Lord and Savior. We are indeed blessed beyond measure with the Christian heritage and resources we possess living in the twenty-first century.

So what are we to do with the Greatest Commandment and all of the advantages we have been given? Some believers say we should only concern ourselves with the New Testament, Jesus Christ, and the Holy Spirit. We strongly disagree. Scripture teaches us about a triune God, and Jesus makes more than twenty specific references to an active, involved God the Father. The first Article of Faith for the Church of the Nazarene states, "We believe in one eternally existent, infinite God, Sovereign Creator and Sustainer of the universe; that he only is God, holy in nature, attributes, and purpose. The God who is holy love and light is triune in essential being, revealed as Father, Son, and Holy Spirit."[1]

We can only expand our understanding of the triune God by giving careful study and attention to God the Father, God the Son, and God the Holy Spirit. We cannot understand the self-revelation of God in Scripture without carefully studying all three members of the Trinity. This book positions itself in *The Wesleyan Theology Series*, which has also published individual volumes featuring and exploring, among other theo-

---

1. Church of the Nazarene, "Article of Faith I: The Triune God," *Manual: 2023* (Kansas City, MO: Nazarene Publishing House, 2023), 26.

logical topics, the Trinity, the Holy Spirit, and Jesus Christ.[2] This volume intends to send you on a scriptural search with the purpose of opening new windows of understanding about God the Father. Christian books abound on studies of Jesus and the Holy Spirit. Not nearly as many focus attention on God the Father. We pray this book will not only deepen your understanding of our heavenly Father but also draw you closer to his heart.

However, information about God for information's sake alone is unlikely to translate into deeper devotion to God. Rachelle Miller, a missionary on the continent of Africa, reminds us, "Reading about God in other kinds of books is not the best way to get to know God. If I want to get to know another human being I need to spend time with them, observing them and talking to them, not relying on secondhand information or opinion from someone else."[3] We completely endorse these sentiments and encourage you to follow Rachelle's advice. We intend for this book to be a reference and supplement to: spending time with God, observing him through the recorded Word of God, experiencing him through the natural world he created, noticing his activity and movement in contemporary events, and talking with him continually while listening for his still, small voice.

God's Ultimate Goal

God gave us the Bible for an important reason: "The Holy Scripture offers us a unified understanding of God's self-revelation to humanity."[4] God revealed himself to us, not so we would know *about* him, but so we would *know* him. In order to love God, we must get to know him and gain at least a limited understanding of who he is. Loving God completely is

---

2. See https://www.thefoundrypublishing.com/the-wesleyan-theology-series .html.

3. Rachelle "Shelly" Miller, "To Know," *Reflecting God*, April 5, 2024, https:// reflectinggod.com/2024/04/05/to-know/.

4. "One Lord, One Faith, One Baptism: Essential Teaching for Faith Formation in the Church of the Nazarene," *Holiness Today* (July/August 2017, Vol. 19, No. 4): Question 20, https://holinesstoday.org/one-lord-one-faith-one-baptism.

God revealed himself to us,

not so we would know *about* him,

but so we would *know* him.

his ultimate goal for us, and we learn how to do that through careful Bible study.

God wants us to know who he is, why he created our world and placed us in it, how he planned to redeem us from our self-inflicted fall into sin, how he gives us eternal life as he teaches us to live in this world with other believers and non-believers, and how he will transition us to live in his home forever. He wants us to recognize his mission to the world and the ways he goes about fulfilling that mission. Finally, he invites believers to join him in his mission to our world, both as examples of new life and ambassadors of his gospel message. In all of these ways, we learn more about who God is, how much he loves us, and how much we should love him and others in return.

God as Father

We wish you could get into a time machine and turn the dial back to the days when God walked with Adam and Eve in the garden of Eden. Unfortunately, time machines do not exist except in fiction. So, as we begin our study in the book of Genesis, you will need to use your imagination to visualize yourself in biblical settings. Once you begin to think that way, you will participate, in a manner of speaking, in the biblical narrative. Christian writers down through the ages have imagined children crawling through closets or getting sucked into the pages of magical books. Once they stand up and dust themselves off from their time travel, they realize they are watching Moses lead the Hebrew people through the Red Sea, or young David slaying Goliath the giant with a single stone flung from his sling. Why let children have all the fun? Adults can imagine too!

Your imaginative journey through the pages of the Old Testament offers a unique perspective. You become a citizen of the time. That means you do not yet know about Jesus Christ or the Holy Spirit, so everything you learn about our Creator on this journey will be attributed just to "God." Eventually, our analysis of the progressive self-revelation of God through Scripture will open our spiritual eyes to the coming of the other two parts of the Trinity, Jesus Christ and the Holy

Spirit. At that point, we will realize that we were initially observing and learning about God *the Father*.

Many books have analyzed divine interactions in the Old Testament by saying, "This story pictures Jesus Christ appearing in ancient times." Or, "This Bible verse shows the Holy Spirit working in the event." It is impossible for humans, with our inherently limited perspective and understanding, to determine how our triune God—Father, Son, and Spirit—works in a particular divine encounter. We obviously have limited ability to truly understand all that can be known about God. Rather than trying to discern the hand of Jesus in this situation or the influence of the Holy Spirit in that event, what if we simply acknowledge that all members of our triune God work together in our world and in our lives in ways that exceed our ability to fully comprehend? Samuel M. Powell presents detailed insights in the cooperative work of God the Father, God the Son, and God the Holy Spirit in his volume of The Wesleyan Theology Series called *The Trinity*.[5]

An attempt to comprehend all aspects of our triune God, individually and in total, would be like attempting to pour all of the oceans into one drinking glass. The words of Scripture, in both the Old and New Testaments, can guide us even in this endeavor:

> The secret things belong to the LORD our God, but the things revealed belong to us and to our children forever, that we may follow all the words of this law.
> (Deut. 29:29)

> No one has ever seen God, but the one and only Son, who is himself God and is in closest relationship with the Father, has made him known.
> (John 1:18)

Therefore, we can know enough about God to live into his plan for us even if we do not understand all of the mysteries surrounding him. Creator God is infinitely beyond our limited ability to grasp in this life. We will learn more about God

---

5. Samuel M. Powell, *The Trinity*, The Wesleyan Theology Series (Kansas City, MO: The Foundry Publishing, 2020).

when we live with him in heaven; our hunger to worship him and live in his loving presence will consume us for eternity. So, for the purposes of this book, we will limit our scriptural study of God the Father to the Old Testament and New Testament insights about him, especially the words of Jesus.

Old Testament writers referred to God as "Father" about 15 times. New Testament writers, on the other hand, referred to him as "Father" about 250 times. Believers often ask why the Old Testament so infrequently refers to God as Father. The simple answer is that, in most cases, it would be anachronistic, assuming that people in the Old Testament understood the idea of God as triune and knew about Jesus Christ and the Holy Spirit, who were not fully revealed until the New Testament. We cannot impose New Testament and church history understandings on Old Testament doctrines. That is a reminder of our privileged vantage point as inheritors of our rich faith tradition.

God referred to the Hebrew people collectively as his son, implying that he is their father. We see this in God's instruction to Moses in dealing with Pharaoh in Egypt: "Then say to Pharaoh, 'This is what the LORD says: Israel is my firstborn son, and I told you, "Let my son go, so he may worship me." But you refused to let him go; so I will kill your firstborn son'" (Exod. 4:22–23). Later, toward the end of Moses's leadership of the Hebrew people out of Egypt and into the promised land, Moses referred to the covenant people of Israel as the son and the Lord as their father: "Is this the way you repay the LORD, you foolish and unwise people? Is he not your Father, your Creator, who made you and formed you?" (Deut. 32:6). In the larger context of this Deuteronomy 32 passage, Moses describes God as the father of the Hebrew nation—not through procreation but through redemptive deliverance. God is their father not in terms of hierarchy, authority, or power, but through unconditional love that supplied their every need during the forty years of wilderness wandering from Egypt to the land God promised to Abraham, Isaac, and Jacob.

When King David made plans to build the temple in Jerusalem, the Lord spoke a message to Nathan to give to the king explaining that God would make David's name great but not through the construction of the temple. God said that, rather than David building God a house, God would build a "house" for David. That is, God would use David's lineage to bring the Messiah to his people: "He is the one who will build a house for my Name, and I will establish the throne of his kingdom forever. I will be his father, and he will be my son" (2 Sam. 7:13–14a). One of the psalmists also referred to God as Father: "He will call out to me, 'You are my Father, my God, the Rock my Savior'" (Ps. 89:26).

The prophet Isaiah referred to God as our Father: "But you are our Father, though Abraham does not know us or Israel acknowledge us; you, LORD, are our Father, our Redeemer from of old is your name" (Isa. 63:16). Again Isaiah affirmed, "Yet you, LORD, are our Father. We are the clay, you are the potter; we are all the work of your hand" (64:8).

God spoke through the prophet Jeremiah with a heartfelt message for the Hebrew people: "I myself said, 'How gladly would I treat you like my children and give you a pleasant land, the most beautiful inheritance of any nation.' I thought you would call me 'Father' and not turn away from following me" (Jer. 3:19). Later, God spoke again through Jeremiah of a divine desire to bring his exiled children back to the promised land: "They will come with weeping; they will pray as I bring them back. I will lead them beside streams of water on a level path where they will not stumble, because I am Israel's father, and Ephraim is my firstborn son" (31:9).

The prophet Malachi used parental imagery for God's relationship with his wayward people: "Do we not all have one Father? Did not one God create us? Why do we profane the covenant of our ancestors by being unfaithful to one another?" (Mal. 2:10). From the day God created Adam (Gen. 2:7) until the last book of the Old Testament, we occasionally read references to God as our heavenly Father. We will see this concept explode with new meaning in the New Testament, when we hear Jesus Christ describe God the Father in more detail than was ever understood by believers who lived in faithful relationship with God in Old Testament days.

Words of Caution

We must be careful about the way we understand God when we refer to him as Father. When the Bible describes God as Father throughout Scripture, does it mean to imply that God is male, with all the masculine qualities and faults of a human man? Do we apply our earthly, biological understanding of father to our Creator? Absolutely not! God is the Spirit who fills his entire creation with his presence. Gender is an earthly reality that in no way can be imposed on God. Nothing in Scripture says or implies that God exists as a particular gender in the same way that humans do. Even so, since our language is not up to the task of referring to God in a genderless way, we do tend to default to male pronouns when talking about God, and that is the pattern in this book. Yet it's important to remember that, even as we acknowledge the linguistic shortcomings, biblical imagery rarely, if ever, intends a literal, earthly interpretation. The term "father" refers to the way God interacts in a relational, parental manner with humanity, rather than indicating a gendered divine identity.

Human language is inadequate in this discussion. We use figurative language often in our daily lives, and understand that it is not meant literally. When children perform unexpected acts of kindness, adults might respond, "Thank you; you are an angel." It is doubtful that anyone ever means that they think a child is a literal angelic being. Or, when a colleague exhibits a consistently diligent and efficient work ethic, we might call them a "workhorse." This remark in no way indicates that the colleague is imagined as a large four-legged animal with a mane and tail. Likewise, God provides for us and relates to us *like* an earthly father might care for his children. But is God *only* like a father? No! Indeed, Scripture uses imagery that describes God like a mother as well—like any parent who lovingly guards, guides, and cares for their children. God used maternal imagery to communicate his care for Israel through the prophet Isaiah: "Can a mother forget the baby at her breast and have no compassion on the child she has borne? Though she may forget, I will not forget

The Bible presents the fatherhood of God in relational terms bathed in unconditional love for his children.

you! See, I have engraved you on the palms of my hands; your walls are ever before me" (Isa. 49:15–16).

A biblical understanding of God as Father does not imply a patriarchal despot who rules with an iron hand of authority. The Bible presents the fatherhood of God in relational terms bathed in unconditional love for his children rather than in traditional hierarchical terms that treat humanity as slaves under the command of a cosmic master. Certainly, Creator God deserves our recognition that he alone is worthy of our praise, honor, and worship. Jesus, the divine Son, demonstrates the attitude of the Trinity and gives us a full-color picture of how God positions himself in his relationship with his children: "Who, being in very nature God, did not consider equality with God something to be used to his own advantage; rather, he made himself nothing by taking the very nature of a servant, being made in human likeness. And being found in appearance as a man, he humbled himself by becoming obedient to death—even death on a cross!" (Phil. 2:6–8). This description of the humility of our triune God sounds nothing like the patriarchal, despotic characterizations of those who refuse to acknowledge God as Father.

We do not avoid using fatherly language when speaking of God simply because we live in a fallen world where earthly fathers often do not live into God's divine plan for parents. When God established the family, he gave children fathers and mothers to love, support, and nurture them from birth until the day they leave home to start a life of independence on their own. We know all too painfully how parents can become trapped in their own battles with self-identity and self-worth, and neglect their parental responsibilities. Should we refuse to acknowledge the biblical references to God as our heavenly Father because of human failures? Certainly not. Anyone who escapes the tyranny of a neglectful or abusive parent has the divine opportunity to meet the One who loves, supports, and nurtures them as a true Father, the kind of father God desired earthly fathers to be. Those who need to fall into the arms of a loving father can develop a strong familial bond with the heavenly Father and live into the relationship God planned for children to have with their parents. Psychologically or emotionally neglected children can flourish in their new identity as children of the one true divine Father.

Paul referred to our heavenly Father using the Aramaic word "Abba," which is a term of deep intimacy, respect, and affection (see Rom. 8:15). Paul also said the Holy Spirit speaks this name from within us: "Because you are his sons, God sent the Spirit of his Son into our hearts, the Spirit who calls out, '*Abba*, Father'" (Gal. 4:6). It does not get any more intimate than that! We must remember that God planned a family setting where fathers and mothers provide a nurturing environment for their children. God our heavenly Father models true parenthood for us in the numerous ways he nurtures us. We must never shy away from nor deny this biblical imagery. Tom Noble summarized it best:

> There is redemption even from the deep scars we have within us from the sinful human relationships which have shaped us. By the Spirit of Love, we are embraced by the Son who *is* self-sacrificial Love. He brings us within that circle where, with him, we may pray 'Our Father'. And this God, 'the God and Father of our Lord Jesus' (II Cor. 11:31), is source of all true love. This is the God, our heavenly Father, who wants to sanctify us fully by filling us with his Spirit, the one who *is* 'perfect love'.[6]

Religion in our World

Modern technology has quickly shrunk our world. Only a few decades ago, information from another part of the world took weeks to reach us. Now we watch videos of global events in real time. The availability to access soundbites and images from every continent of the world has expanded our understanding of world religions. Contemporary culture tends to present all of the religions of the world on level ground, with each offering spiritual perspectives from various traditions. One is considered as valid as the next, with none holding

---

6. Tom Noble, "God the Father," *Holiness Today*, (May/June 2020, Vol. 22, No. 3): 8–11.

unique positions. For Christian believers, nothing could be further from the truth.

A common definition of religion is often presented as "humanity's search for God." Practically speaking, that means that worshipers' prayers, rituals, and practices intend to garner the favor of their chosen deity or deities. Human participation in religion like this becomes somewhat transactional. The Cultural Heritage Sites & Museums in Chiclayo, Peru, feature a display that highlights a horrific illustration of how attempts to appease a local deity can go wrong. Archaeologists believe that the area north of Chan Chan sometime prior to AD 1470 experienced an extended period of drought. Farmers desperately needed rain for their crops and gardens. The local priest suggested a religious ritual to appease the anger of the rain gods. The farmers did what they thought was necessary to bring the needed rain. The museum display shows the findings of a burial site known as Huanchaquito-Las Llamas. In the ritual, residents sacrificed to the rain gods more than 140 children, ages 5 through 14, along with more than 200 llamas. Scholars call it the "largest single incident of mass child sacrifice in the Americas—and likely in world history."[7]

Christianity does not subscribe to the common definition of religion as humanity searching for God. Instead, Christianity asserts that our faith is about God reaching out to humanity. We are not required to search for God or perform perfect rituals to gain God's favor. God has proactively revealed himself to us in many different ways, and desires to have a relationship with us. In John 6:44, Jesus said, "No one can come to me unless the Father who sent me draws them." Remember John 3:16 too, where Jesus tells us that God loves everyone in the entire world and wants everyone to have eternal life with him. God seeks us out so we might be saved. Christians, therefore, do not need to trust in our prayers, rituals, and practices to win God's favor. We accept the free gift God offers in love, grace, and mercy. Scripture does not

---

7. Kristin Romey, "Ancient Mass Child Sacrifice May Be World's Largest," *National Geographic*, April 26, 2018, https://www.nationalgeographic.com/science/article/mass-child-human-animal-sacrifice-peru-chimu-science.

tell us everything we might like to know about God. However, it tells us everything we need to know in order to live rightly with him, with one another, and with ourselves, now and into eternity.

Acres of Diamonds

Somewhere in the corners of our mind, we know we ought to spend more time exploring God's self-revelation. Yet we seem to be always so busy. What we know we ought to do often does not make its way to the top of our priority list. Jesus shared a profound truth about our priorities with the parable of the hidden treasure: "The kingdom of heaven is like treasure hidden in a field. When a man found it, he hid it again, and then in his joy went and sold all he had and bought that field" (Matt. 13:44). I vividly remember joining a group of my friends in the elementary school dining room and talking about someday going on treasure hunts. We imagined one of those future adventures occurring at a diamond mine in the southern part of our state. We talked about how we would find a large diamond and sell it for enough money to make us all rich. Eventually, we decided that stories about finding diamonds were childhood myths, and we moved on to planning our next get-rich-quick adventure. Decades later, a story in recent news feeds caught my eye and returned me to my childhood. Someone had walked out of that diamond mine in my state with a large and valuable diamond. Those stories we'd heard as kids apparently were not myths after all!

God has placed vital information about himself through the entire Bible. We are not talking about a few nuggets of truth scattered sparingly; we are talking about acres of diamonds spread generously throughout the pages of the Bible. We are challenged with the task of reading the Bible carefully and discovering God's progressive self-revelation for ourselves. Again, God's purpose in sending us on this adventure is not to fill our heads with information about him but to draw our hearts and minds closer to him to enliven a deeper relationship with him. Taking the Bible seriously is a matter of priority.

Conclusion

The journey of life offers us a world of options to bring purpose and meaning to our lives. As we go through the different stages of life, we fall into routines and schedules that propel us through each day. We can always find plenty of activities to keep us busy. Some of them, like school and work, have mandatory obligations. Others, like leisure time and vacations, give us the freedom to relax, rest, and rejuvenate ourselves. Somewhere between all the routines and schedules of our lives, we must take the time to stop and reflect on our eternal soul. We realize as soon as we begin to contemplate the spiritual component of ourselves that this is not a solitary exercise. God's Spirit begins to speak to us about the big questions rolling around in our heads, like:

"Who am I?"

"Why am I here?"

"What is the meaning of my life?"

The search for answers to these and dozens of other questions leads us on a journey to find the only One who satisfies our heart's needs. This chapter has offered insights for this quest. We quickly realize that our seeking heart does not long merely for academic or factual information about this One; it desires a personal relationship. The following chapters will guide you through ways in which you can begin or deepen that relationship with God our faithful Father.

Reflection Questions

1. What new information about God did you learn in this chapter?

2. How has reading the Bible helped you learn to know God better?

3. Since God is beyond our limited ability to fully understand, why make an effort to know him?

4. What evidence do you see in Old Testament stories of God interacting with people in parental ways?

5. How are critics mistaken when they impose negative stereotypes created and perpetuated by flawed earthly fathers onto our heavenly Father?

6. How should someone who grew up in a home with a poor fatherly example be encouraged to put their trust fully in our heavenly Father?

7. How is our heavenly parent like both a father and a mother?

8. What are three ways the Christian God differs from deities of other world religions?

9. How are the biblical truths about God more valuable than the treasures of this world?

10. Why is it important to stop daily and reflect on our eternal soul?

TWO

Who God Is

We live every day of our lives taking for granted what we believe about our surroundings. We assume things will be as we expect them to be. Whatever routines have come to fill our daily lives, we expect to be able to follow those routines without much trouble or deviation. We cannot always prove these assumptions about our expectations, and sometimes life throws us off course and we have to adjust, yet in general, we tend to operate as if what we expect to be true, is true, and thus we go about our daily activities. Therefore, it makes perfect sense for the Bible to begin with the important assumption that God *exists*. "In the beginning God . . ." (Gen. 1:1). Without offering any proof or taking us through a series of logical or philosophical exercises, the Bible takes God's existence for granted.

Scholars in ancient times and down through the centuries of church history have offered a variety of proofs for the existence of God.[1] Unfortunately, rational proofs for God's existence fall short for a variety of reasons. Even the limited details of God's character and attributes discussed in this chapter make it obvious that human reason could never fully comprehend the God of the Bible. None of the analytical

---

1. Thomas Aquinas offered five logical arguments for the existence of God: (1) first mover—somebody started all motion in our world; (2) universal causation—everything in our world is the effect of a cause; (3) contingency—creation did not happen without a creator, (4) degree—human reason categorizes things in this world such as good, better, best; the very best is God; (5) final cause/ends—our world has intelligent design aimed toward a final goal for all things.

proofs for the existence of God can erase every doubt from skeptical minds. Those who choose to doubt or deny God have the free will, given by God, to do so.

I had an interesting conversation with an atheist a few years ago that helped me understand part of the mindset necessary for denying God's existence. I asked my friend a simple question: "How do you look into the night sky with its vast array of stars, planets, other heavenly bodies stretched across billions of miles of space that move about the universe with exact precision—and deny a Creator?"

He thought for a moment and answered me with words that sent chills down my spine. He said, "I choose not to think about such things."

Much like a child closing his or her eyes in order to shut out something that frightens them, those who doubt or deny God's existence simply turn a blind eye to the evidence. The Bible provides an important analysis of those who deny God's existence. "The fool says in his heart, 'There is no God.' They are corrupt, their deeds are vile; there is no one who does good" (Ps. 14:1).

Throughout my life I have heard Christians say, "I don't have enough faith to be an atheist." I agree. It takes more assumptions and leaps of faith to deny God's existence than to acknowledge it and lean into it as a starting point for encountering God personally.[2] The apostle Paul believed that God placed enough evidence of his existence in nature, in our hearts, and in our lives to erase all doubt:

> The wrath of God is being revealed from heaven against all the godlessness and wickedness of people, who suppress the truth by their wickedness, since what may be known about God is plain to them, because God has made it plain to them. For since the creation of the world God's invisible qualities—his eternal power and divine nature—have been clearly seen, being understood from what has been made, so that people are without excuse. (Romans 1:18–20)

---

2. See Norman L. Geisler and Frank Turek, *I Don't Have Enough Faith to Be an Atheist* (Wheaton, IL: Crossway Books, 2004).

According to Paul, skeptics do not doubt or deny God for lack of *evidence*. Rather, they are too preoccupied with their own sinful interests to concern themselves with God. The most frightening phrase in this passage of Scripture comes at its conclusion: "people are without excuse." The absence of excuse applies not only to this life but also to where we will spend eternity.

The Bible teaches us more about the self-revelation of God than we will ever master during our earthly lives. That sets the stage, then, for deeper study throughout eternity. In this chapter, we will offer scriptural insights into who God is, especially from the pages of the Old Testament. Starting with the book of Genesis, we will unpack God's self-revelation in an expanding fashion just as the Bible presents it. Along with quoting specific scriptures, we will also suggest in the footnotes additional verses to look up for further study.

Four Simple Words

We should not move into the biblical narrative of creation from Genesis until we ponder those first four words of Genesis 1:1: "In the beginning God." Who is this God? How do we describe him? How are we to understand him? The Old Testament uses many words and concepts to introduce God to us. However, human language and reason remain too limited to grasp the full reality of God. We can, nonetheless, explore the many ways God reveals himself to us through the pages of Scripture. With intentional effort, we will realize how profoundly amazing our God is.

The Genesis introduction indicates that the Judeo-Christian God is one. "Hear, O Israel: The LORD our God, the LORD is one" (Deut. 6:4).[3] This declaration places Judaism and Christianity in stark contrast to some religions of the world that call upon multiple deities. For example, Hinduism offers a variety of gods for worshipers, or no god if so desired. The religion of humanism offers the gods of fame, fortune, power, prosperity, and even benevolence.

---

3. See also Deut. 4:35; 2 Sam. 7:22; Ps. 86:10; Isa. 45:6; Hosea 13:4.

God always finds ways to
make himself known to
every searching heart.

Names for God

As humans, we often attach significance to the meaning of the name that a parent gives to a child. For example, the name Elijah means "Yahweh is my God," while the name Isabella means "God is my oath." Books and websites abound with tens of thousands of names and their meanings in various languages. It comes as no surprise that the Bible is filled with names to describe our God. Contemporary Christian songs often feature some of these biblical names for God.

One of my favorite memories of growing up in the country, away from city lights, was lying on the ground and studying the stars that exploded across the night sky. Moving attention from one location of the sky to another brought a completely different perspective to the beauty of God's creation. After lying in one position for a while, I realized that the entire panoramic display moved from east to west as the evening progressed, like an ever-changing kaleidoscope. One photograph from a single angle would be of little value. You need every view from every angle to grasp the magnitude of the scene. The same is true as we identify biblical names for God. We watch God's self-revelation to humanity as the names of God unfold across the pages of Scripture. Each name adds a new dimension to our understanding of just how grand our God truly is. The following list of the various names the Bible gives to God expands our perspective. Take time to meditate on the names that are the least familiar to you. Read the suggested scriptures that locate them within the context of the biblical narrative. Think of the variety of ways you can apply these descriptors of God to your relationship with him.

El or Elohim: God (Gen. 1:1). Scripture first introduces us to God with a word that declares his deity, which distinguishes him from created humanity. One aspect of this name points to the power that created everything in the natural world. This name occurs hundreds of times in the Old Testament. El is the singular form; Elohim is the plural. It most often appears in plural form to remind us of God's greatness, but it is followed by a singular verb, indicating a single being. The God of the

Bible is greater than all of the so-called deities of the surrounding nations.[4]

El Shaddai: Lord God Almighty (Gen. 17:1). First revealed to Abraham, this name for God also reveals to us more about who God is. He is not only the God of great power, but he also gives both spiritual and temporal blessings. He is the nourisher, strength giver, and satisfier. He is the God of "never failing love which freely gives itself for those whom he has redeemed."[5]

Jehovah or *Yahweh* (Exod. 3:14). God's self-revelation continues when he introduces himself with a name that invites a personal relationship. Elohim is a generic name that tells us about God; Yahweh is a proper name that connects us to him spiritually. Translations into English include "I am," "I am that I am," "He who is what he is," and "He has cause to be."[6] These translations are not definitions, however, because no one knows the correct definition. Our God is greater than human language can define. That makes this the perfect proper name for God! The Hebrew people displayed their reverence for God by never pronouncing this name aloud. Instead, they used Adonai when they were speaking.

Adonai: Lord, Master (Josh. 3:11). This name for God conveys the notion of possession and sovereign dominion. We read this name throughout Scripture, such as in the exaltation "Lord my God" (Ps. 38:15).[7]

Many other names offer insight into the being and activity of God in our world and our spiritual lives. Here is a partial list in biblical order.

- Most High (Gen. 14:22)
- El Roi, "the God who sees me" (Gen. 16:13)
- Judge (Gen. 18:2)
- Yahweh Jireh, "the LORD will provide" (Gen. 22:14)
- Our Strength (Exod. 15:2)

4. H. Orton Wiley, *Christian Theology*, Vol. 1. (Kansas City, MO: Beacon Hill Press, 1940), 243.

5. Wiley, *Christian Theology*, 247.

6. Wiley, *Christian Theology*, 244–46.

7. Wiley, *Christian Theology*, 247–48.

- Yahweh Rapha, "the LORD who heals you" (Exod. 15:26)
- Yahweh Nissi, "the LORD my banner" (Exod. 17:15)
- El Qanna, "jealous God" (Exod. 20:5)
- Yahweh Mekoddishkem, "the LORD who sanctifies me" (Lev. 20:8; Ezek. 37:28)[8]
- Lord of Lords (Deut. 10:17)
- Living God (Josh. 3:10)
- Yahweh Shalom, "the LORD is peace" (Judg. 6:24)
- LORD of Hosts [another translation of Yahweh Tsebaoth] (1 Sam. 1:11)
- LORD of Heaven's Armies [another translation of Yahweh Tsebaoth] (1 Sam. 17:45)
- Fortress (2 Sam. 22:2)
- Yahweh Rohi, "the LORD is my Shepherd (Ps. 23:1)
- King Over All the Earth (Ps. 47:7)
- Holy One of Israel (Ps. 71:22)
- El Olam, "the everlasting God" (Ps. 90:1–3)
- Yahweh Tsebaoth, "the LORD of hosts" (Isa. 1:24)
- Everlasting Father (Isa. 9:6)
- LORD God of Hosts (Jer. 5:14)
- Yahweh Tsidkenu, "the LORD our righteousness" (Jer. 23:6, 33:16)
- Yahweh Shammah, "the LORD is there [in the New Jerusalem]" (Ezek. 48:35)
- Heavenly Father (Matt. 6:9, 26)
- Lord of the Sabbath (Matt. 12:8)
- King of kings (1 Tim. 6:15)
- Father of Lights (James 1:17)

---

8. English translations usually use the spelling LORD when signifying Yahweh and Lord for Adonai or Kurios.

What We Learn about God from These Names

1. God *is.*

God introduced himself to Moses as "I am" or "I am that I am." God does not change with time as we do. He is completely self-determining. He is Creator of all other beings and Sustainer of all that lives in his creation. He causes everything to be.[9] God does not say, "I was, I am, and I will be," as we might say about ourselves living in the context of earthly time. God exists beyond the limitations of time and space. This name invites us to pause and consider what God wants to communicate about himself to us.

2. God is holy.

The Bible often refers to God's holiness in triplicate: *holy, holy, holy.* "And they were calling to one another: 'Holy, holy, holy is the LORD Almighty; the whole earth is full of his glory'" (Isa. 6:3). God's holiness is the only identifier that is repeated three times, indicating strong emphasis. This repetition describes not only the significance but also the essential quality of who God is. He does not have holiness as an attribute but defines the meaning of the word by his very being.[10] God alone is holy in this way. "There is no one holy like the LORD; there is no one besides you; there is no Rock like our God" (1 Sam. 2:2). The Hebrew word for "holiness," *qodesh,* is one of the most frequently found words in the Old Testament. Even though God's holiness is singular in nature, God yet desires to share that nature with his children, as evidenced by the often repeated command of God, "Be holy because I, the LORD your God, am holy" (Lev. 19:2b).

---

9. This chapter focuses most of its attention on the way God reveals himself to us in Genesis 1. However, in order to unpack the depth of understanding the Bible shares with us about God, we need to jump ahead and consider the entire biblical narrative.

10. See Exod. 15:11; Lev. 19:2; Ps. 22:3; 30:4; 71:22; Isa. 5:16; Ezek. 39:7.

3. God is love.

"And he passed in front of Moses, proclaiming, 'The LORD, the LORD, the compassionate and gracious God, slow to anger, abounding in love and faithfulness, maintaining love to thousands, and forgiving wickedness, rebellion and sin.'" (Exod. 34:6–7a). Again, beyond having a loving heart as our heavenly Father, God defines love as an essential quality of his very being. We have a difficult time understanding divine love because the English language uses this one word in so many different ways. We love our favorite sports team. We love our warm coat in the winter. We love our work. We love our mate. Each of these statements uses the same word in different ways, and God's love is on a completely different level than any of these meanings.

The Old Testament uses several different words for God's love. The word *hesed* occurs frequently, with more than 250 references. It has no direct translation into English, so descriptions serve as the best way to understand it. God's *hesed* love is unconditional. God loves his children with no strings attached. "Steadfast" further describes this love. He loved and worked with his people through the thick and thin of life, such as the wilderness wanderings of the Hebrew nation and the successes and failures of King David. This love assured God's people that they could always depend on him, no matter what. "Kindness" or "loving kindness" are other English words that describe the way God expresses love for humanity. He always has our best interests in mind.

The New Testament word used for divine love is *agape*. Essentially different from brotherly or romantic affection, *agape* refers to God's self-sacrificing, unconditional, covenantal love for humanity. It is also the love he gifts us with, through the power of his Holy Spirit to love him in return. "We love because he first loved us" (1 John 4:19).

4. God is just.

The Bible often pairs love and justice when speaking of God's work in our world. Love without justice can be too soft, or even hypocritical. Justice without love can be too harsh. True love and true justice require balancing the two. Loving their children requires parents to exercise discipline when necessary. God's holiness includes justice while his love offers redemption freely. "But the LORD Almighty will be exalted by his justice, and the holy God will be proved holy by his righteous acts" (Isa. 5:16). "For he has set a day when he will judge the world with justice by the man he has appointed" (Acts 17:31). God exhibits the perfect balance to his justice with his love for the whole world, which he demonstrated by sending his Son, who died for the sins of all humanity (see John 3:16).

5. God is ever living.

"God also said to Moses, 'Say to the Israelites, "The LORD, the God of your fathers—the God of Abraham, the God of Isaac and the God of Jacob—has sent me to you." This is my name forever, the name you shall call me from generation to generation'" (Exod. 3:15). God does not have a birth date like we do. There never was a time, even before earthly time, when God was not. God is ever living; hence, he is eternal.[11] Our lives depend on air, water, food, shelter, and other necessities. God requires nothing to sustain life.[12]

6. God is spirit.

Jesus is the only human on earth to have ever "seen" God the Father in his full heavenly splendor, so his words provide us with an eyewitness account. He said, "God is spirit, and his worshipers must worship in the Spirit and in truth" (John 4:24). He does not need a body to exist as we do. He inhabits all of creation at once.[13]

> Where can I go from your Spirit? Where can I flee from your presence? If I go up to the heavens, you are there; if I make my bed in the depths, you are there. If I rise on the wings of the dawn, if I settle on the far side of the sea, even there your hand will guide me, your right hand will hold me fast. If I say, "Surely the darkness will hide me and the light become night around me," even the

---

11. See Gen. 21:33; 15:18; Deut. 32:40; 33:27.
12. See Deut. 5:26; Josh. 3:10; 1 Sam. 17:26; 2 Sam. 22:47; Pss. 18:46; 42:2.
13. See Exod. 33:20; Deut. 4:12, 15; 1 Kings 8:27; Isa. 45:15; 66:1–2.

We cannot adequately portray God in human language, but we can know him personally because he draws near to every person on earth across the centuries.

darkness will not be dark to you; the night will shine like the day, for darkness is as light to you.
(Ps. 139:7–12)

7. God is personal.

Many scholars shy away from saying God is a "person." Humans are created persons, so identifying God as a person might lead us to mistakenly think that God's personhood is just like ours. A biblical understanding of God far exceeds anything we will ever attain as created persons. However, God does choose to bend down to our level of understanding in order to relate to us. Therefore, we can truthfully say that God is *personal*. He created us in his image, which includes our ability to reason, feel emotions, and exercise our free will to make independent decisions. We refer to God's bending down to our level as anthropomorphism, visualizing him assuming physical or emotional characteristics. For example, the Bible says God has eyes (Ps. 11:4); ears (Ps. 31:2); hands (Ps. 95:4); feet (Isa. 66:1); joy (Isa. 65:19); and love (1 John 4:16). Imagining God with human characteristics allows us to relate to God in a personal way rather than imagining him as a removed, disconnected, inanimate object or spirit who does not care for us.

8. God is eternal light.

"For with you is the fountain of life; in your light we see light" (Ps. 36:9). We depend on the sun to provide light for our world. God created the sun and is responsible for all light that shines in creation; God does not *need* these sources of light the way we do; rather, he *is* light. "God is light; in him there is no darkness at all" (1 John 1:5). The Psalms often refer to God providing us light. "The LORD is my light and my salvation" (Ps. 27:1a). "For the LORD God is a sun and shield" (Ps. 84:11a). Isaiah and John both looked forward to the day when God will provide us with eternal light: "Your sun will never set again, and your moon will wane no more; the LORD will be your everlasting light, and your days of sorrow will end" (Isa. 60:20). "There will be no more night. They will not need the light of a lamp or the light of the sun, for the Lord God will give them light. And they will reign for ever and ever" (Rev 22:5).[14]

9. God is righteous.

"I will give thanks to the Lord because of his righteousness; I will sing the praises of the name of the Lord Most High" (Ps. 7:17). God has a perfect moral compass, perfect judgment, all necessary information, and therefore always does the right—or righteous—thing. "The Lord is righteous in all his ways and faithful in all he does" (Ps. 145:17).[15] Implied along with his righteousness, Scripture also says that he is good. "'Why do you ask me about what is good?' Jesus replied. 'There is only One who is good. If you want to enter life, keep the commandments'" (Matt. 19:17).[16]

10. God is truthful.

God's character as truthful follows logically from God's holiness and righteousness. Because he is divine, he could not/would not lie. "God is not human, that he should lie" (Num. 23:19). "The one who comes from heaven is above all. He testifies to what he has seen and heard, but no one accepts his testimony. Whoever has accepted it has certified that God is truthful" (John 3:31b–33). Neither does God mislead us with just enough information to allow us to draw untruthful conclusions. God not only speaks truthfully, but he *is* truth: "Jesus answered, 'I am the way and the truth and the life. No one comes to the Father except through me'" (John 14:6).

11. God created with wisdom and rules over his creation with wisdom.

Along with God's righteousness goes the companion quality of having all wisdom and knowledge. "By wisdom the Lord laid the earth's foundations, by understanding he set the heavens in place" (Prov. 3:19). "His wisdom is profound, his power is vast" (Job 9:4a). Isaiah asks, "Who can fathom the

---

14. See also 2 Sam. 22:29; Job 29:3; Ps. 118:27; Isa. 2:5; Dan. 2:22; Mic. 7:8.
15. See also Exod. 9:27; 1 Sam. 12:7; 2 Chron. 12:6; 19:7; Pss. 5:8; 9:8.
16. See also Exod. 18:9; 33:19; 34:6; Pss. 23:6; 25:8; 31:19; 33:5; 34:8; 86:5.

spirit of the Lᴏʀᴅ, or instruct the Lᴏʀᴅ as his counselor?" (Isa. 40:13). He also declares that the Lᴏʀᴅ Almighty is wonderful in counsel and magnificent in wisdom (Isa. 28:29b).[17]

12. God is great.

The Bible often describes many of God's qualities by simply saying, in all things, that God is great. "Sovereign Lᴏʀᴅ, you have begun to show to your servant your greatness and your strong hand. For what god is there in heaven or on earth who can do the deeds and mighty works you do?" (Deut. 3:24).[18] Scripture often refers to God's greatness by referencing three omnis. God is omnipresent—ever present in creation on the surface of the earth, under the sea, across the heavens, and throughout outer space.[19] God is omnipotent—having all power consistent with his nature.[20] God is omniscient—knows everything.[21]

13. God is powerful.

"The Mighty One, God, the Lᴏʀᴅ, speaks and summons the earth from the rising of the sun to where it sets" (Ps. 50:1). To say a bit more about God's omnipotence, God's sovereignty over creation carries with it the realization that God has all the power necessary to carry out his will in our world. Scripture abounds with references to his great power, of which we will share only a few.[22]

14. God is sovereign over all of creation.

"All the ends of the earth will remember and turn to the Lᴏʀᴅ, and all the families of the nations will bow down before him, for dominion belongs to the Lᴏʀᴅ and he rules over the nations" (Ps. 22:27–28). At the same time, God grants his

---

17. See also Gen. 1:31; Job 12:13; 28:23; Jer. 10:7; Dan. 2:20.

18. See also Deut. 5:24; 9:26; 10:17; Pss. 48:1; 77:13; 95:3; 104:1; 135:5; 145:6.

19. See Gen. 28:16; Deut. 4:39; 1 Kings 8:27; 19:9; 2 Chron. 2:6; 6:18; Ps. 139:8.

20. See Gen. 1:3; 17:1; 18:14; 1 Kings 19:11; 2 Kings 20:11; 2 Chron. 20:6.

21. See Job 31:4; 34:21; Pss. 139:4; 147:5; Isa. 40:26; Ezek. 37:3; Amos 4:13.

22. See Exod. 4:11; 9:16; 10:19; 1 Chron. 29:12; 2 Chron. 14:11; 16:9; 20:6; 25:8; Pss. 24:8; 29:4; 33:6, 9.

children, who are created in his image, a free will and respects our decisions. I have observed in business, family, and life that, when someone has control and power over others while at the same time exercising love and compassion, they have no problem allowing freedom. A loving parent allows children freedom within safe boundaries. A manager allows employees freedom to innovate within budgets and safe procedures. In the same way, our loving God does not dictate every event or decision in our lives as we grow and learn to trust him more completely.

Some Christians believe in divine determinism—every event in life occurs at the command of God. Planes crash, violent weather destroys property and lives, children contract deadly diseases—all from the sovereign finger of God. Other Christians have moved in the opposite direction. They say bad things happen to good people because God is powerless to do anything about it. Much like Deists, they say God created our world, set it in motion, and now watches it operate autonomously without intervening himself. Neither of these extreme viewpoints represents a biblical view of God's sovereignty. God maintains ultimate sovereignty over creation to bring his will to pass while at the same time allowing human free will.[23]

15. God is unchanging in nature.

"I the LORD do not change. So you, the descendants of Jacob, are not destroyed" (Mal. 3:6). The Greek and Roman mythological gods and goddesses had many character flaws. Perhaps one of their greatest flaws was their fickle nature. Worshipers never knew which qualities they were going to see on a given day. Some days they were loving, kind, and helpful; other days, not so much. The same is true of humanistic gods today. Fame is fickle; fortunes come and are spent quickly; power is given and taken away on a whim. Material possessions break, wear out, or get stolen. Even philanthropy and good works can lose their honored status over time. In con-

23. See Gen. 50:20; Num. 22:18; 2 Sam. 17:14; Pss. 22:28; 47:8; 83:18; 93:1; 135:6; Isa. 7:7; 37:16.

trast, our God's character, love, mercy, and grace are the same yesterday, today, and forever.[24]

How to Describe God

Looking back over this short list of ways the Bible describes God, we realize that both the list and these brief discussions fall far short of the surpassing magnitude of God. Other biblical concepts of God's character include faithful, patient, long-suffering, compassionate, kind, merciful, and more. Dig deeper into all of these, and others you find in Scripture. You will be amazed at the way God reveals himself to you more and more as you continue to live in his presence.

Numerous verses of Scripture begin with the simple phrase "The Lord is. . ." These verses add depth and texture to some of the traits and attributes we've already discussed. Here are just a few of the verses containing that simple phrase.

- "The Lord is my strength and my defense" (Exod. 15:2).
- "The Lord is slow to anger" (Num. 14:18).
- "The Lord our God, the Lord is one" (Deut. 6:4).
- "The Lord is powerful" (Josh. 4:24).
- "The Lord Is Peace" (Judg. 6:24).
- "The Lord is a God who knows" (1 Sam. 2:3).
- "The Lord is my rock, my fortress and my deliverer" (2 Sam. 22:2).
- "The Lord is good" (Ps. 34:8).
- "The Lord is against those who do evil" (Ps. 34:16).
- "The Lord is a God who avenges" (Ps. 94:1).
- "The Lord is good and his love endures forever" (Ps. 100:5).
- "The Lord is compassionate and gracious, slow to anger, abounding in love" (Ps. 103:8).
- "The Lord is a God of justice" (Isa. 30:18).
- "The Lord is a jealous and avenging God; the Lord takes vengeance and is filled with wrath. The Lord

---

24. See Deut. 7:9; Job 23:13; Pss. 90:2; 102:12, 27; 103:17.

takes vengeance on his foes and vents his wrath against his enemies. The LORD is slow to anger but great in power; the LORD will not leave the guilty unpunished. His way is in the whirlwind and the storm, and clouds are the dust of his feet" (Nah. 1:2–3).

- "The Lord is faithful" (2 Thess. 3:3).
- "The Lord is full of compassion and mercy" (James 5:11).
- "The Lord is not slow in keeping his promise, as some understand slowness. Instead he is patient with you, not wanting anyone to perish, but everyone to come to repentance" (2 Pet. 3:9).

As you read through this list, stop and meditate on what each one means in your life. Think about how these concepts might change or deepen your concept of God. We challenge you to memorize one each week and listen to hear what God tells you about himself.

Conclusion

One of my favorite memories with my son took place during his junior year in high school. My wife and I were invited to teach at a college in western Europe. We packed our bags and flew to Europe for six weeks. My mother gave us a new camera so we could take pictures to share when we returned home. We visited Switzerland, Germany, France, and Austria on our days off from teaching. I especially enjoyed visiting the Swiss and Austrian Alps. The views were breathtaking! As you can imagine, I took dozens of pictures of the incredible, snow-covered mountain ranges.

I could hardly wait to see the pictures when we returned home. I cannot express my disappointment as I filed through my photos of the Swiss and Austrian Alps. Unfortunately, even a high-quality camera cannot capture the wonder and amazement of such beautiful scenery. I apologized to the family back home that my attempt to show them the Alpine ranges failed. You just have to see it for yourself.

That is how I feel as I read back through this chapter about God. Language cannot capture a full-color picture. The best we can do is offer some guidance on how to begin or continue your personal discovery of him. Hopefully, the words and concepts presented in this chapter at least point you in the right direction.

Our dilemma in falling short of a better picture of God reminds us of Paul's imagery of our understanding of heavenly matters: "For now we see only a reflection as in a mirror; then we shall see face to face. Now I know in part; then I shall know fully, even as I am fully known" (1 Cor. 13:12). We find encouragement from Paul's ministry in Athens. While "preaching the good news about Jesus and the resurrection" (Acts 17:18) to local philosophers, Paul proclaimed to them and us, "God did this [placed humanity on the earth] so that they would seek him and perhaps reach out for him and find him, though he is not far from any one of us. 'For in him we live and move and have our being.' As some of your own poets have said, 'We are his offspring'" (Acts 17:27–28). A favorite phrase in Paul's testimony reminds us that God "is not far from any one of us." In other words, we cannot adequately portray God in human language, but we can know him personally because he draws near to every person on earth across the centuries. God always finds ways to make himself known to every searching heart. Now, that is really a good picture of our heavenly Father!

Reflection Questions

1. What new information did you learn in this chapter about God?

2. How would you approach a skeptical friend who doubts God's existence?

3. How might it take more faith to be an atheist than a Christian?

4. What are the top five names for God in the Old Testament that have encouraged your faith in him?

5. Which attributes or characteristics of God make you hungry to know him more completely?

6. Why is God's holiness so central to our understanding of him?

7. How does God's love differ from the ways we commonly use the words that describe him?

8. Why does God offer himself so completely to live in relationship with us?

9. How does God's righteousness differ from the ways many people live their lives in this world?

10. When in your life have you found God to be especially close to you?

THREE
Why God Created

Chapter 2 focused on the first four words of Genesis 1:1, "In the beginning God." Now we look at the remainder of the creation narrative in Genesis 1–2. Genesis 1 offers a general description of God's creative work; Genesis 2 narrows attention to God's creation of humanity and our place in the world.

The Natural World

We learn a great deal about God from studying his creativity in the natural world. Notice God's self-revelation in Genesis 1:1–25:

- God directly involved himself in every step of his creative work. He did not sit idly by and watch the elements of our universe fall into place by themselves.
- God the Father, Son, and Holy Spirit participated in all of creation (see Gen. 1:2; John 1:1–5).
- God planned ahead. Each step in creation shows order, logic, and direction.
- God created the entire universe *ex nihilo*—that is, out of nothing (see Gen. 1:1–26). Imagine his awesome ability and the power of his words as he spoke reality into existence. "He spreads out the northern skies over empty space; he suspends the earth over nothing" (Job 26:7).
- God's creativity shows that he loves variety, beauty, complexity, diversity, and abundance. Just look at the endless possibilities of everything from celestial structures to geology, microorganisms, plants, animals, birds, sea life, and especially humanity.

- God defined boundaries. He separated the light from the darkness (Gen. 1:4b, 14); water in the atmosphere from water on the earth (vv. 6–7); the sea from the land (v. 9). He only allowed each plant and animal to reproduce its own kind (vv. 11–12, 20–22, 24–25).
- God defined a hierarchy within creation (vv. 28–30). Each created being serves a purpose; each has its place in the natural order. Each fulfills God's purpose and plan.[1]
- God designed and built with intelligence far beyond our comprehension. "Where were you when I laid the earth's foundation? Tell me, if you understand" (Job 38:4). "Who has measured the waters in the hollow of his hand, or with the breadth of his hand marked off the heavens? Who has held the dust of the earth in a basket, or weighed the mountains on the scales and the hills in a balance?" (Isa. 40:12).
- All creation belongs to God. "The heavens are yours, and yours also the earth; you founded the world and all that is in it" (Ps. 89:11).

Divine Complexity

Natural scientists often use their limited understanding of the natural world to explain the realities of creation in ways that deny the existence of God. However, their simplistic explanations do not even begin to take divine complexity into account. Consider these three examples.

First, matter (made up of atoms) and energy are the two basic components of the universe. Second, chemistry offers a periodic table containing the known chemical elements organized by atomic number (which indicates the number of protons in the nucleus). Third, biology explores cells as the basic unit of life, which is defined by DNA. The complexity and diversity of each of these parts of the universe has only recently begun to be understood at a superficial level by ex-

---

1. The one exception is humanity, who have the ability to ignore God's purpose and plan.

perts in the field who have devoted their entire lives to their respective studies. When reading about any of these structures in scientific research, especially regarding new discoveries, authorities present information on what they believe is true (which often changes over time), along with what they still do not understand.

Science and technology have claimed for many years that they have answers for every problem known to humanity. Science and technology routinely make big promises but have failed to deliver on many of them. Rather than supplementing biblical truths, they ignore or contradict them. Some go so far as to deny God's existence and place *their* answers above God, in an idolatrous position. Many spokespersons for these answers attempt to lead us to believe they have unlocked the mysteries of the universe. In reality, they have only scratched the surface of the depth of complexity of these fields of study. Human experts are not experts in God's eyes!

The Creation of Humanity

Our study thus far has taken us through Genesis 1:1–25 with the creation of the natural world. Beginning with Genesis 1:26, we gain an entirely different perspective on God's creative ability and heart. Not only do we learn about God's quintessential creative act in giving life to humanity but also perhaps an important reason for God's entire creative enterprise. "Then God said, 'Let us make mankind in our image, in our likeness, so that they may rule over the fish in the sea and the birds in the sky, over the livestock and all the wild animals, and over all the creatures that move along the ground.' So God created mankind in his own image, in the image of God he created them; male and female he created them" (vv. 26–27). "When I consider your heavens, the work of your fingers, the moon and the stars, which you have set in place, what is mankind that you are mindful of them, human beings that you care for them?" (Ps 8:3–4).

Notice first that God created humanity unique from all the other creatures on land, in the air, and in the sea. Then God pronounced a special blessing on humanity, gave them stewardship for all earthly creation, and provided for their every need in a perfect environment (Gen. 1:28–30). The Genesis narrative reaffirms this truth later: "When God created mankind, he made them in the likeness of God" (5:1b). The biblical narrative wants to be absolutely sure that readers remember this essential truth: God created us in God's image and likeness.

Second, God created humanity with unique qualities and abilities not found in members of the animal kingdom. God's declaration, "Let us make mankind in our image, in our likeness" (v. 26) and the follow-through, "So God created mankind in his own image, in the image of God he created them" (v. 27) reminds us of the superior position of humanity in our world. "You have made them a little lower than the angels and crowned them with glory and honor" (Ps. 8:5). Entire books explore the myriad ways that humans differ from animals as a result of being created in God's image. A few of those ways include:

- An internal awareness of a higher power (i.e., God)
- Self-realization about who we are, our place in the world, our character, and our potential
- Higher-level reasoning ability
- Higher-level communication skills for sharing complex thoughts (i.e., language, writing, and mathematical and scientific information)
- Knowledge of good and evil along with the awareness of moral standards
- A conscience to approve or disapprove of moral choices
- A free will to make moral choices
- The capacity for planning
- The ability to improve ourselves and a desire to learn
- Responsibility to steward creation
- Eternal life

But Why?

We have reached a point in the discussion where we must address the all-important *why* question. Parents and grandparents share the experience of being bombarded with, "But why?" after statements, instructions, or suggestions to children of all ages. It's common to the human experience; we want to know why things are the way they are, so we must explore possible reasons for God creating humanity in his image and likeness and placing us in the world.

We begin an answer to that all-important question by disqualifying a few incorrect reasons. First, God did not create humanity because he was lonely. Poets and philosophers down through the ages of time have promoted the "lonely God" theory. The holy Trinity of Father, Son, and Spirit fellowship in ways that far surpass our ability to relate to one another. God has never been lonely.

Second, God did not create humanity because he was incomplete. Parents sometimes say they decided to bring children into their home because their lives seemed incomplete in their current state. God did not create us to meet an unfulfilled need.

Third, God did not create humanity because of some higher law in the universe that required it. Such a view obligates God to a law that would be higher than he is. No such law exists; what source greater than God could have created such a law? God has no obligation to universal laws outside of his being.

Fourth, God did not create humanity simply to prove he could. We have watched reporters on the evening news interview athletes who accomplish great achievements. "Why did you climb the mountain?" "Why did you run the hundred-mile race?" "Why did you swim from Cuba to the United States?" The answer often is the same: *Because I wanted to prove that I could do it.* That response does not explain why God created humanity. He did not need to prove to us or anyone else that he could do it.

In God's self-revelation through Scripture and especially his direct interactions with humanity, no evidence supports any of the concepts listed above. These are simply humanity's attempts to reduce God to the level of human intelligence.

Genesis 1–2 describe our God lovingly creating us as his children and placing us in a perfect environment that had the potential of meeting all our physical needs. What does it say about God that he placed Adam in the garden to work and care for it? He knows we need to be productive. He understands that we need work in order to thrive. He gave us one another to meet our social needs. From the very beginning God was involved with humanity and spent time with us, along with putting effort into providing for us. He planned regular conversations with us to meet our spiritual needs. God desires fellowship with his special creation. This all means, then, that the previous list of ways that humans differ from animals as a result of being created in God's image left out a couple of essentials:

- the ability to live in daily relationship with God (see Gen. 3:8).
- the capacity to give and receive unconditional love among ourselves and between ourselves and God (see 1 John 4:19).

We now need to explore these two concepts further to gain new insight into the question, "Why did the Father create the world and place us in it?" A very important element of our answer to this question comes from a seldom-used word: *effulgence*. Imagine a bright light exploding forth, overpowering the darkness in every direction for as far as the eye can see. Effulgence is light in brilliant radiance. Hebrews 1:3 describes Jesus Christ as the *effulgence* of God's glory. More than merely a flood of light, Jesus embodies the splendor of God's glory (see Exod. 16:10; 24:17; 33:22; Lev. 9:23; 2 Chron. 5:14; Pss. 24:10; 97:6).

Now apply that image of light in its brilliant radiance to God emanating divine love. The fullness of God's love burst forth in creation! He carefully placed the heavenly objects across billions of miles of space. He filled the earth with abundant resources. Trees, plants, and flowers displayed his love of beauty. The incredible variety of animals on land, birds in the sky, and sea life across the vast oceans sprung to life. Then, best of all, he created humanity! Imagine the self-giving love of a parent who does anything and everything to nurture a child. Multiply that by an infinite number, and you begin to catch a glimpse of God's heart breaking forth in love for his world.

The Message captures this thought with the opening words of John 3:16: "This is how much God loved the world."

Commit these words to memory. Hide them in your heart and in the back of your mind. Recall them often as you continue to read this book. That phrase will serve you well as a key to understanding God's motivation in just about everything he has done from the first day of creation until this very moment. "This is how much God loved the world."

Earlier in this chapter we mentioned several ways God reveals himself to us through the natural world. Now let's look at some of the ways God reveals himself to us through our own humanity. A theological concept known as "the analogy of being" offers insight into our understanding of God. The Bible says that God made humanity in his image and likeness. We have offered several examples of that. One of the examples focused on our ability to give and receive love. We love children, parents, other family members, and friends. God loves his children as well, but the difference is that God loves perfectly, and we don't.

Viewing God through Different Lenses

If you have ever visited the eye doctor, you know that the doctor administers an eye test by asking you to read a chart on the far wall with several rows of letters. The letters get smaller as you read down the chart. I have no idea what letters are on the last row; I've never been able to read them. I doubt if anyone but the Lord could read them! Then the doctor places an instrument in front of your eyes with a variety of lenses in it, and your job is to tell the doctor if lens 1 or 2 is clearer, then if lens 3 or 4 is clearer, then if lens 5 or 6 is clearer. At that point I'm usually so confused I can't tell anymore which one is clearer!

We are going to look at Genesis 1–2 through different lenses in much the same way that eye doctors force us to look through different lenses in order to gain clarity. It is amazing the different ways that God can come into focus as we view him through different lenses.

The Transactional Lens

First, let's look at Genesis 1–2 through the transactional lens. We are already familiar with this one. When we go to the

The emotion that God demonstrates over and over throughout Scripture is self-sacrificing, unconditional love.

grocery store, we take our selected items up to the checkout counter. At this point, everything we have selected and put into our cart belongs to the store. The cashier scans each item then announces the total cost of the purchase. We pay the stated amount, and the transaction is complete. Now, the grocery items belong to us. We make transactions like this in person or online nearly every day.

I hesitate to admit it, but in the hundreds of times I have read Genesis 1–2 throughout my life, I have often viewed the events of creation through the transactional lens. God spoke the word, and the universe appeared. God Almighty spoke again, and all living creation appeared. God looked at everything he created and evaluated it. I visualized something like a quality control inspector with a clipboard, perhaps containing three options with check boxes: Needs more work, Satisfactory, and Good. God checked the last box. Then God crafted his special creation: humanity. When he evaluated this addition to all he had made, he added a new box to the evaluation sheet: Very Good!

Unfortunately, that's the only way I used to read the text: God acted, and creation appeared. It was a transaction, and nothing more. I now realize there are two additional lenses through which we should view God's handiwork. We must move from seeing the hand of God at work to considering the heart of our loving God.

The Emotional Lens

Parenting experts fill books and websites with advice about the emotions that expectant parents will experience as they prepare to welcome a new child into their lives. If you are a parent, you know the flood of emotions that pour over you as each stage of parenting unfolds in your life. First, you dream of becoming a parent with anticipation and eagerness and perhaps fear and doubt as you contemplate the possibilities that the future holds for your family. In the next phase of the process, you learn that a baby is on the way. Now a whole new set of emotions floods over you as you prepare for everything that the next nine months will bring. Finally, you welcome a new member of the family into your life and home.

Parents often say they immediately felt overwhelming love for their child when they took them into their arms for the first time. Words cannot adequately express the full spectrum of emotions that fill every fiber of a new parent's being.

With all of that in mind, imagine the emotions our heavenly Father might have experienced as he prepared to bring us, his children, into his life and the world that he created for us. Remember the analogy of being: God made us like himself, which means that God, no doubt, experienced many of the emotions he gave to us: anticipation, joy, expectation, excitement, and of course love come to mind. Think of other emotions you could add to the list. I can almost see the Father, Son, and Holy Spirit talking together about every single detail and every emotion they shared as they prepared for our arrival. Then, when the time was right, they looked at one another, smiled, and said, "Let's do this!"

Think of the wave of emotions God might have experienced as he bent down, carefully formed the human body from the dust of the ground, and slowly, lovingly breathed his breath of life into it, making it a living being (see Gen. 2:7). In that high and holy moment, God entered the world of parenting human beings. We can only begin to imagine the wave of parental emotion that flooded the heart of God as Adam's body came to life. The emotion that God demonstrates over and over throughout Scripture is self-sacrificing, unconditional love. Parents can easily relate to this emotion when they remember what they felt as they held their children for the first time. Is it possible that God experiences this same emotion every time he welcomes a new creation into the kingdom of God?

Jesus told a parable of a woman who searched diligently for a silver coin she had lost, and rejoiced when she found it. He concluded the parable by saying, "In the same way, I tell you, there is rejoicing in the presence of the angels of God over one sinner who repents" (Luke 15:10).

The Relational Lens

Now, let's go back and look at Genesis 1–2 through the relational lens. Think about what we know to be qualities necessary to be a good parent. God is a perfect parent. He now relates to us as his children. What qualities of good earthly parents do you imagine God exhibits in parenting us? The list, of course, is endless. Here are a few that come to mind as we study Scripture. See how many other qualities you can add to this list. A good parent shows:

- Compassion
- Consistency
- Discipline
- Encouragement
- Fairness
- Faithfulness
- Generosity
- Guidance
- Honesty
- Kindness
- Love
- Nurture
- Patience
- Persistence
- Protection
- Support
- Understanding

Scripture offers us numerous examples of God's parenting skills. First, God created a perfect world and placed the first human being in it. He gave his new creature, made in his image and likeness, responsibility for all living creatures and the garden of Eden itself. God had one more amazing creation to complete his masterpiece: "The LORD God said, 'It is not good for the man to be alone. I will make a helper suitable for him'" (Gen. 2:18).

Second, like any good parent, God loved to spend time with his children. His daily walks with them in the cool of the evening illustrate his desire for close connection with them (see Gen. 3:8). Later, God chose his servant Abram, whom God later renamed Abraham, and his wife, Sarai, whom God later renamed Sarah, to be the parents of a great nation. God would bless that nation so that they could pass the blessing on to all the nations of the world. Then God guided Abraham and Sarah through a lifetime of both wonderful and difficult situations. Through it all, they drew closer to God in their relationship and grew in their faith. In fact, God called Abraham his friend (Isa. 41:8).

Third, God exercised parental instruction by forbidding Adam and Eve to eat from the tree of life in the garden of Eden. Again in the New Testament, God reminds us that he sometimes must say no, as all parents must sometimes do. The apostle Paul lived with a physical or spiritual hindrance; Scripture does not name it other than to call it a thorn in Paul's flesh (see 2 Cor. 12:7). Paul pleaded with God three times to remove it from his life. Rather than removing the hindrance, Paul reports that the Lord responded, "My grace is sufficient for you, for my power is made perfect in weakness" (2 Cor. 12:9).

Now look back over the list of parental qualities and also consider the items you added to it. Remember the times when our good God parented you in these ways. Recall every detail. Then take time to thank him for being such a good parent to you.

Why Three Lenses?

Why do we need to take the time to review Genesis 1–2 from different lenses? Some may have a problem with viewing God through the emotional and relational lenses. Those characteristics may sound more like Jesus in the New Testament. Yes, Jesus did exemplify them. One of the objectives of this book is to show how God the Father, God the Son, and God the Holy Spirit have the same characteristics (see chapter 6). When we see Jesus treating people with love and kindness, we know that God the Father also treats people in these same ways. Jesus told us that God the Holy Spirit is our comforter; God the Father also comforts us in the same way.

If we are not careful, we can unwittingly de-personalize God as we pray to him and live with him. We can begin to think of God as an impersonal entity like the electric company that provides power for our homes, or the bank that provides financial resources when we need them. We can categorize God as only the celestial entity who answers our prayers when we find ourselves in difficult circumstances. If we pray the right words in the right way and say them enough times, we imagine in some transactional way that God will find himself duty-bound to answer our prayer. Far too many believers have fallen by the wayside and given up on their faith because they prayed with this mindset. When God did not answer their prayer in the way they wanted, they gave up on their relationship with him and struck out to live life on their own terms.

Nothing could be further from God's plan for us. He hovers over us like any good protective parent and looks after us with love, nurture, and attention to our every need. "He will cover you with his feathers, and under his wings you will find refuge; his faithfulness will be your shield and rampart" (Ps. 91:4). God spoke powerful words through a prophet: "It was I who taught Ephraim to walk, taking them by the arms; but they did not realize it was I who healed them. I led them with cords of human kindness, with ties of love. To them I was like one who lifts a little child to the cheek, and I bent down to feed them" (Hosea 11:3–4). The prophet Zephaniah echoed this same message from God with a reminder: "The LORD your God is with you, the Mighty Warrior who saves. He will take great delight in you; in his love he will no longer rebuke you, but will rejoice over you with singing" (Zeph. 3:17).

Does God respond to our every request on our timetable? Of course not. Do parents grant their children every request that they have? We are sure you have witnessed at least one complete meltdown in the candy aisle of the grocery store because of parents not meeting a child's demand. Do these parents love their children and want the best for them? You know they do. Likewise, our heavenly Father has our best interests in mind, and parents us in nourishing ways that go far beyond our ability to understand. How do we know? The Bible tells us so.

Why Take the Risk?

Scripture clearly teaches us that our heavenly Father is the most perfect parent our minds can imagine. We affirm that as

Christians. However, we must consider one of the most difficult questions asked of pastors and church leaders: If God knew that humanity might use our free will to disobey him, why did he give us such a dangerous ability? Why take the risk?

Perhaps part of the answer lies in a personal question: If you are a parent, why did you decide to bring children into your home, knowing they could make life-altering choices that might break your heart? I have asked that question many times across the years of my ministry. Answers include: *I knew children could bring great joy and satisfaction to my heart. I wanted to invest all of my love and care in my children with the possibility that they might grow up to be outstanding individuals. My heart of love compelled me to pour myself into my child with the hope that they would thrive in life.*

Notice how these responses flow from hearts of love with hope in the possibilities that children will flourish as they grow and develop into adults. Perhaps God thought some of those same sentiments. One thing remains certain. God did not want robots that respond in pre-programmed ways. Computer programmers and engineers can produce such beings. Robot responses are no better than my little sister's doll that "talked" to her whenever she pulled the string on the doll's back. God wanted children who love him willingly. He wants us, of our own free will, to choose to love him and one another in much the same way that he loves us. "We love because he first loved us" (1 John 4:19).

Taking a Deeper Dive

The eighth bullet point after "The Natural World" heading at the beginning of the chapter stated, "God designed and built with intelligence far beyond our comprehension." Scientists in a variety of fields have studied the mysteries of our natural world for centuries. Here is just one example of how God's intricate design mystifies us even today. One of the disciplines I learned about and used during my time working with information technology was database design and queries. Some database applications are very simple and have limited interactions between elements (a single piece of data). Others have a wide variety of data types and relationships that can be complex and dynamic. The recent publicity regarding artificial intelligence (AI) has made the broader public more aware of these structures and the level of complexity they can contain, along with the difficulty of cross-referencing and assimilating information that can be obscure and cryptic from diverse sources. This level of difficulty even requires special computer processing chips and software to train and then run the database query software referred to as AI.

However, if we look at what God created, just the aspects that we can see and understand—physics, chemistry, biology, etc.—the level of complexity, adaptability, and diversity is many magnitudes beyond anything humanity has conceived, much less built. One example of the unbelievable intelligence of God is DNA. Using just four building blocks—nucleotides: adenine (A), thymine (T), guanine (G), cytosine (C)—God created a standard database format that is used to define everything about the construction and operation of all living things, plant or animal. The DNA structure is estimated to hold up to three billion units of information that could each contain multiple different values. The simplicity of this design yet the ability for this database to contain complex, interrelated data that can be dynamic is truly amazing. Finally, this design and operating information is simply and easily passed on to the next created being through God's plan for propagation. The concept that any part of the creation process happened by accident is, statistically, extremely improbable (having a probability too low to inspire belief) and, logically, completely absurd.

Conclusion

This chapter has attempted to answer the all-important *why* question. Why did God create the world and place humanity in it? It's a complex question that has interested philosophers and theologians for millennia. We trust the concepts and mental exercises presented have given you food for thought and ignited your imagination for further exploration of Scripture into the incredible mysteries of our heavenly Father.

Reflection Questions

1. What new information did you learn in this chapter about God?

2. What do you learn about God when you consider his amazing creativity in bringing our world into existence?

3. Give an example of the divine complexity God built into creation.

4. Why, after thousands of years of research, are scientists only now beginning to understand some of the complexities of God's creation?

5. Why do those who doubt God's existence place so much blind confidence in their own theories about creation?

6. How would you describe to a friend some of the many ways humanity differs from all other created beings?

7. Why do you think God created humanity and placed us in the world?

8. What are some of the ways God's emotional and relational interactions with Adam and Eve resemble earthly parents welcoming a new child into their home?

9. Why do you think God gave humanity free will?

10. What are some of the ways Christian parents nurture their children to foster in them a desire to live in intimate relationship with God?

FOUR

What God Desires for Us

My wife and I often watch television together at the end of a busy day. I especially like a whodunit program. Most mystery shows fall into one of two categories. Either the plot introduces clues to who committed a crime, then reveals the culprit in the last five minutes of the program. Or the program begins with the camera showing us immediately who committed the crime, and the rest of the show offers clues as to the motive for the criminal act. Regardless of which plot method we watch, I usually turn to my wife at the end and say, "I didn't see that coming."

In this chapter, we will explore five things God desired to see happen when he created humanity. Rather than making you wait until the end of the chapter to reveal God's desires, we are going to identify them first, then offer biblical evidence to explain them. Once you see the entire list, you will recognize that just about everything you read in the Bible, from Genesis to Revelation, refers to God's desires for us in one way or another.

1. God Desires to Live in Intimate Relationship with Us

To have an intimate relationship with someone means knowing each other completely on a two-way street. God the Father knows each of us perfectly because he created us. His desire is for us to know him as well. "For I desire mercy, not sacrifice, and acknowledgment of God rather than burnt offerings" (Hosea 6:6). Clues to God's first desire appear early in Genesis 3. Here are a few examples.

God created the most perfect living arrangement anyone on earth could ever imagine.

The garden of Eden contained every creature comfort Adam and Eve could want. Afterward, did God intend to sit on his heavenly throne in isolation and watch his children live their earthly lives? Absolutely not! Like any loving parent he longed to spend time with his creation daily. Adam and Eve "heard the sound of the LORD God as he was walking in the garden in the cool of the day" (Gen. 3:8).

The Bible does not say exactly what sort of sound the couple heard as God approached them, but they obviously recognized it and were familiar with it. The Hebrew word *halakh*, which is translated as "walking," has both theological and relational implications. The word implies that God took walks with his children both repeatedly and habitually. God made a regular habit of meeting with his children in the garden. It appears he loved to simply spend time with them. The Bible says he came in the afternoon as the cool breezes began to blow through the garden.

Can you imagine what God and his children must have felt as they engaged together in fellowship and daily conversation? We will say much more about this story in the next chapter. For now, let's move to the next example of God's desire to live in vital relationship with his children.

Enoch had a close relationship with God.

Some believers who read about our heavenly Father's self-revelation in the Old Testament assume that people in the early days of civilization did not yet know enough about God to have a meaningful relationship with him. They assume early worshipers acknowledged a distant and impersonal deity like those of their pagan neighbors. Nothing could be further from the truth, nor is this what God intended!

Enoch was a descendant of Seth, who was the third son of Adam and Eve. Like Adam and Eve, Enoch too walked with his heavenly Father. The same Hebrew word from Genesis 3:8 appears in Genesis 5:24: "Enoch walked faithfully with God; then he was no more, because God took him away." The word for "walked" in this verse implies a vital daily relationship between God and one of his children. Joseph Coleson summarizes it well: "One may say Enoch 'walked' with God each moment of each day, though he lived in a sinful world that had alienated itself from God."[1] The second half of Genesis 5:24 alludes to the unique place that Enoch occupies in Scripture. He and the prophet Elijah are the only two Bible characters to be described as transitioning directly from this life to the next without passing through the grave. He and God were obviously really close! My pastor imagined it perhaps occurring like this: One afternoon God said at the conclusion of their daily walk, "Enoch, we're closer to my house than yours. Why don't you just come on home with me?"

Noah also had a very personal relationship with God.

The Bible identifies three characteristics of Noah's life that separated him from his sinful environment: "Noah was a righteous man, blameless among the people of his time, and he walked faithfully with God" (Gen. 6:9b). The same word for "walked" that was said of Adam, Eve, and Enoch is also used for Noah. He too lived close to God. As a result of his vital connection to his heavenly Father, Noah lived a life of integrity with his family and his neighbors. The Bible says he lived without blame. He also was a righteous man, which means he had honest and right relations with others and served God faithfully.

Perhaps we find the best example of just how closely Noah lived to the Lord by looking at the precise construction directions he received from God for the ark. It is one thing to have faith in a general sort of way that God has heard our prayers. It is quite another to listen to the voice of the Lord in your heart then draw detailed plans for something no one has ever seen before. No doubt, Noah developed highly tuned ears for the voice of God.

---

1. Joseph Coleson, *Genesis 1–11: A Commentary in the Wesleyan Tradition*, New Beacon Bible Commentary (Kansas City, MO: Beacon Hill Press of Kansas City, 2012), 186.

In addition to naming specific individuals who walked with God the Father, Genesis 3–11 offers a few bright spots in God's interactions with his children. Corruption and violence seemed to control the lives of the majority of people. God's reset of life on earth with the flood did not cure humanity's pride and bent toward self-preference. God could have easily given up on the entire humanity-with-free-will project, but he absolutely did not. God's persistence in continually reaching out to humanity is another example of God's incredible, long-suffering love for his children, along with his desire to restore us to the relationship humanity had with him before the fall from grace in the garden.

2. God Desires to Enter into a Contract with Us

The first contract that God entered into with human beings was with Adam in the garden of Eden: "And the LORD God commanded the man, 'You are free to eat from any tree in the garden; but you must not eat from the tree of the knowledge of good and evil, for when you eat from it you will certainly die'" (Gen. 2:16–17). God had not yet created Eve when he established this contract with Adam. However, Adam must have informed her of both the contract terms and the consequences of disobedience because she repeated the contractual language to the serpent (see Gen. 3:2–3). Notice that she added a phrase not found in God's conversation with Adam: "and you must not touch it" (v. 3).

God later entered into a contract with Noah as he and his family reestablished life on earth following the flood. In that contract, which extends to this day, God promised never to send another flood of global magnitude to the earth. This was a general contract with humanity and all creation.

Next, God chose Abram for a special contract.[2] What an unthinkable proposal! The Almighty God of the universe signing his name to a contract with a mere man. This would take

---

2. The word "covenant" in many Bible translations also means "contract." We use the latter here since it is more readily understood today.

God's persistence in continually reaching out to humanity is another example of God's incredible, long-suffering love for his children.

God's relationship with his children to a much more personal level. The contract God made with Abram had a much deeper meaning. First, the contract would bless Abram and, through him, bless the world. The contract also included God's redemptive plan for the spiritual salvation of all who would accept his offer, as we will see later. Here again, God reveals the unending, unconditional love of a Father who wants only the best for his children.

God went beyond a single contract with Abram; they entered into several contractual agreements over the course of many years.

Contract #1 between God and Abram

Notice a few of the many interesting aspects of the first contract between God and Abram, found in Genesis 12:1–3. Take time to read it for yourself, and then consider the following observations.

- God came to Abram with the idea of a contract, not the other way around: "The LORD had said to Abram" (v. 1). Can you even imagine the humility God displayed as he committed himself to a contract with a mere man? No other god in any religion of the pagan nations would have made such a contract with a human. God shows his tender heart toward his children in ways we could never have imagined.

- God required Abram to give up everything in order to obey him: his country, his people, and his father's household (see v. 1). God required total commitment from Abram, just as he does today from us.

- Abram had no idea where God was leading him when he set out on his divinely ordered journey with his family. God did not specify a destination beyond "the land I will show you" (v. 1). Can you imagine how Abram might have explained the situation to Sarai, his wife, and their traveling companions? God only told Abram to go. In hindsight, we know God was directing them to the land of Canaan, later known as the promised land (see Gen. 12:6–9; 15:17–21; 17:8). God expected Abram to trust him completely without having a detailed plan. Scripture tells us that God has a plan for our lives as well, but few if any of us are given a detailed roadmap. God continually builds our trust in him throughout our journey of faith.

- God apparently did give Abram specific traveling directions during his journey. Abram had no modern-day atlas, map, or GPS. He lived intimately enough with God both to understand and follow God's traveling instructions.

- God filled his contract with Abram with promises and blessings. After promising to show Abram where to go, God promised more blessings than Abram could have ever envisioned at the time. We tend to think of strengthening our relationship with God through worship and praise. In this case, God begins the conversation with all the great things he is going to do for Abram and his family: "I will make you into a great nation, and I will bless you; I will make your name great, and you will be a blessing. I will bless those who bless you, and whoever curses you I will curse; and all peoples on earth will be blessed through you" (12:2–3).

- In the case of Abram, God exemplified a proud Father delighting in a man who lived close to God, recognized his voice, paid attention to specific details, and obeyed him. Later, the Israelites proclaimed God's love and faithfulness as they returned to Jerusalem from exile: "You are the LORD God, who chose Abram and brought him out of Ur of the Chaldeans and named him Abraham. You found his heart faithful to you, and you made a covenant with him to give to his descendants the land of the Canaanites, Hittites, Amorites, Perizzites, Jebusites and Girgashites. You have kept your promise because you are righteous" (Neh. 9:7–8). Jesus made a similar observation in Matthew 7:11: "If you, then, though you are evil, know how to give good gifts to your children, how much more will your Father in heaven give good gifts to those who ask him!"

- God's contract with Abram included blessings for more than just himself and his family. God committed to using Abram to bless all the peoples on earth (see Gen. 12:3). This promise was fulfilled with the birth, life, death, and resurrection of Jesus Christ, the Savior of the world, and it continues to be fulfilled through Christ's disciples as we share the gospel and minister to all nations.

- Abram exercised blind faith in his heavenly Father, took him at his word, and hit the road without asking a single question: "So Abram went, as the LORD had told him" (Gen. 12:4a). God and Abram were now in business together! God has the same expectation of us as we journey with him.

Contract #2 between God and Abram

More than a decade passed between the first and second contractual agreement between God and Abram. Let us look at a few of the interesting features of the second contract, found in Genesis 15:1–21. Take time to read it for yourself, and then consider the following observations. The features of this new contract offer us further insights into the good parental practices of God.

- The Lord initiated the second contract with Abram just as he had the first one: "After this, the word of the LORD came to Abram in a vision" (v. 1a).

- God began the conversation with words of encouragement: "Do not be afraid, Abram" (v. 1b). We find this phrase often in Scripture when the presence of the Lord or angels appear to people. Heavenly visitors usually frightened those to whom they appeared. In Abram's case, he lived in close enough relationship with the Lord that he would've welcomed the heavenly visit. His fear in this encounter was more likely about something else. First, he might have feared having to fight additional enemies like the ones he dealt with in Genesis 14 while rescuing Lot. Additionally, he might have feared reaching the end of his earthly life without having produced a son to carry on the family heritage.

- Like parents often do, the Father continued the conversation with further encouragement in the form of a promise that God himself would be his shield and great reward (v. 1c).

- Abram reminds us to approach God with humility (see v. 2). He addressed God as "Sovereign Lord," a title that reflects the servant-master relationship they had.

- God welcomed Abram's concerns, which even approached complaints (see vv. 2–3). God always invites two-way communication with us. He wants us to share everything that is going through our hearts and minds, even when we are discouraged or experiencing doubt.

- God and Abram participated together in a covenant-making ritual patterned after treaty rituals of the Ancient Near East (see vv. 9–21). Abram brought and prepared animals for the ceremony; in a vision, God appeared in the form of a smoking firepot with a blazing torch and passed between the animal pieces. God and Abram finalized the terms of the contract in that special moment.[3] God performed a ritual that was probably familiar to Abram as a confirmation and assurance of their agreement.

The most significant verse of Scripture in this contract opens a window into our understanding of New Testament faith in Jesus Christ. Genesis 15:6 boldly declares for Abram and all of his spiritual descendants, "Abram believed the Lord, and he credited it to him as righteousness."

Paul explained the new contract in Christ as justification by grace through faith alone: "What then shall we say that Abraham, our forefather according to the flesh, discovered in this matter? If, in fact, Abraham was justified by works, he had something to boast about—but not before God. What does Scripture say? 'Abraham believed God, and it was credited to him as righteousness'" (Rom. 4:1–3). This passage explains Paul's earlier statement, "For in the gospel the righteousness of God is revealed—a righteousness that is by faith from first

---

3. Alex Varughese and Christina Bohn, *Genesis 12–50: A Commentary in the Wesleyan Tradition*, New Beacon Bible Commentary (Kansas City, MO: Beacon Hill Press of Kansas City, 2019), 69.

to last, just as it is written: 'The righteous will live by faith'"
(Rom. 1:17).

These Old and New Testament passages became the
theological centerpiece of the Protestant Reformation, the
effects of which we enjoy today as we live out our Christian
faith. God consistently demonstrates his plan for the salvation
of humanity based on our faith in what he promises. These
promises remain true for all time. Numbers 23:19 indicates
that God does not change his mind.

Contract #3 between God and Abraham

God the Father approached Abram again with a third
contract when Abram was ninety-nine years old (see Gen.
17:1–22). Take time now to read it for yourself. God offered
Abram a different contract this time. The first two were what's
known as "suzerain-vassal covenants," which means they
were between a powerful party, the suzerain (God) and a
weaker party, the vassal (Abram). They were unconditional,
one-sided contracts where God offered blessings that Abram
simply received. This third contract is known as a "promisso-
ry covenant," which means it has if-then clauses throughout.
God's promises in the contract are conditional based on the
obedience of Abram and the Hebrew people who will follow
in his lineage.[4]

The following are some of the most significant features
and terms of this contract. We will explore the features and
terms separately.

Contract Features

- God identifies himself only once in this chapter as
  God Almighty (*El Shaddai*); Abram knows him well
  from their personal relationship and needs no further
  descriptions (see v. 1).
- This contract changed Abram and Sarai so dramatically that God changed their names; they were no longer the same people (see vv. 5, 15). Abraham means
  "father of a multitude," while Sarah means "princess."

---

4. Varughese and Bohn, *Genesis 12–50*, 93–94.

Only a loving God would give careful attention to such seemingly insignificant details. That's how much he cares for his children.

- Finally, God lovingly allowed for Abraham's inner doubts and the proposal of an alternate solution, as he did in the second contract (see vv. 17–19).

Contract Terms

- God names the first command and condition of the contract: "Walk before me faithfully and be blameless" (v. 1). The invitation to walk faithfully with God uses the same word for "walked" as was used to describe the relationships that Adam, Eve, Enoch, and Noah had with God. To be blameless does not mean to be without flaws but to be faultless in relationship with God and others.

- In return for Abraham's walking faithfully and being blameless, God repeated his promise to bless Abraham and Sarah with a child and then more descendants than they can count (see v. 2; 15:4–5). The promises of land and of relationship are reaffirmed too (see 17:7–8). These three aspects (descendants, land, and relationship with God) constitute the fundamental elements in God's covenant with Abraham, which are repeated throughout the Pentateuch. "Descendants" is about the future and continuity of relationship with God. "Land" is about sacred space in which to live out a relationship with God. And "relationship with God" is about a personal, trusting interconnection between God and his people. This is the ultimate goal of covenant with God.

- Most contracts with which we are familiar have a termination or expiration date but not this one. God calls it an "everlasting covenant" (vv. 7, 13, 19) that is for "generations to come" (vv. 7, 9, 12), and God also refers to the land as an "everlasting possession" (v. 8).

- The previous contract required Abram to cut animals into pieces to ratify it. In this contract, God instructed

Abraham and his descendants to signify total allegiance to the Lord with circumcision (vv. 9–14).

The terms of this third contract remind us of the contract God the Father offers us as we trust in his Son, Jesus Christ, for our salvation, repent of our sins, and pursue holiness. God then promises to care for us and bless us. Our contract with God also has no expiration date as we look forward to eternity. From the days of the exodus, God called his children to "circumcise your hearts, therefore, and do not be stiff-necked any longer" (Deut. 10:16). The prophet Jeremiah echoed this command: "Circumcise yourselves to the LORD, circumcise your hearts, you people of Judah and inhabitants of Jerusalem, or my wrath will flare up and burn like fire because of the evil you have done— burn with no one to quench it" (Jer. 4:4). Finally, the New Testament calls believers to signify total allegiance to the Lord through circumcision of the heart (see Rom. 2:29).

Other Contracts between God and His Children

We have identified contracts that God initiated with Noah and Abraham. God also entered into contracts with Moses (see Exod. 19–20; Deut. 28); David (see 2 Sam. 7; Pss. 72, 89); and some of the kings who followed after David, like Jehoiada (see 2 Kings 11:17) and Josiah (see 2 Kings 23:3). A common thread in these contracts features God's desire to have a people who will love and serve him completely as they live righteously with family, friends, and neighbors.

All of these divinely initiated contracts are interconnected. They build on one another, adding a deeper understanding of God and his desires for our lives as we live in relationship with him. Like links in a chain, they expand God's self-revealed identity in the greatest love story ever told.

3. God Desires That We View Him Not Only as Our Provider But Also as Our Redeemer

God's unusual encounter with Moses in the burning bush is one of the most familiar stories in the Bible. When we look closer, we can see that God identified himself to Moses

As you reflect on the five desires God has for his children, remember that these are not five different desires. They are interconnected.

in a manner that reveals an often overlooked continuation of God's self-revelation to humanity. It's so subtle that we can easily miss it. First, in Exodus 3:6, God clarified his relationship with Moses as the same relationship he had with Abraham, Isaac, and Jacob. Next, Moses and Aaron returned to Egypt, where Pharaoh refused their requests and increased the hardship of the enslaved Hebrews, which made their leaders angry with Moses and Aaron (see Exod. 5:1–21).

Moses wisely turned to the Lord in prayer (see 5:22–23). Read carefully the amazing revelation with which God responded to them: "God also said to Moses, 'I am the LORD. I appeared to Abraham, to Isaac and to Jacob as *God Almighty*, but by my name the LORD *I did not make myself fully known to them*'" (6:2–3, emphasis added). Read that last phrase again "but by my name the LORD I did not make myself fully known to them" (v. 3). You mean the famous biblical patriarchs—Abraham, Isaac, and Jacob—did not have a complete picture of God Almighty? That is correct!

God affirmed with absolute certainty during Moses's encounter at the burning bush that he is the Lord (see 3:6–20). God reaffirmed it in 6:2, 6, and 8 with Moses and Aaron at the business end of Pharaoh's stubbornness and the Hebrew leaders' anger. Abraham, Isaac, and Jacob knew him as *El Shaddai*, God Almighty—that is, God our provider. So, during the early era of salvation history, God did not make himself fully known to his children.

God was now ready for his children to know him by a new name: God our Redeemer, the Redeemer of Israel (see 6:6–8). God promised "with that name: I will bring you out, I will free you, I will redeem you, I will take you as my own, I will be your God, I will bring you to the land, and I will give it to you."[5] Throughout the Old Testament following the exodus, God identifies himself as the God who brought the Israelites out of Egypt. This is an entirely new way of understanding God. Now, the Hebrew people will know their Lord

---

5. H. Junia Pokrifka, *Exodus: A Commentary in the Wesleyan Tradition*, New Beacon Bible Commentary (Kansas City, MO: Beacon Hill Press of Kansas City, 2018), 96.

in a more intimate way; their relationship with him will grow deeper and therefore stronger.

4. God Desires to Establish a Spiritual Kingdom in Our World

The interlinking contracts God made with Abraham and Moses took on a global and eternal perspective as he entered into another contract, this time with King David, the second king of Israel. The Bible chronicles David's incredible exploits. Citizens of his day and historians down through the ages have referred to David's reign as Israel's golden age. Even to this day, souvenir shops in the Holy Land sell memorabilia commemorating David's golden age.

Yet all of King David's royal accomplishments pale in comparison to the greatest blessing God bestowed upon him. Once again, God initiated the conversation that led to a contract between David and his Lord. Like Abraham's first two contracts, God did not require David or his descendants to meet certain conditions in order to maintain the agreement. God committed himself to remaining faithful to the terms of the contract for all earthly time *and* eternity. Note some of the terms:

- "Now I will make your name great, like the names of the greatest men on earth" (2 Sam. 7:9b).
- "I will also give you rest from all your enemies" (7:11b).
- "When your days are over and you rest with your ancestors, I will raise up your offspring to succeed you, your own flesh and blood, and I will establish his kingdom" (v. 12).
- "I will establish the throne of his kingdom forever" (v. 13b).
- "Your house and your kingdom will endure forever before me; your throne will be established forever" (v. 16).[6]

6. See also 1 Chron. 17:11–14 and 2 Chron. 6:16–17.

A quick perusal of the terms of this contract sounds like God is promising David and his descendants a permanent earthly kingdom, but based on biblical history, we know that not to be the case. Someone will come from the house of David to establish an everlasting spiritual kingdom, and with the benefit of hindsight, we now know that this Someone is the Messiah, Jesus Christ. Christ sits on the throne, ruling justly over a kingdom that lasts forever and ever.

The Old Testament prophets studied David's contract and saw the day coming when God's desire for a spiritual kingdom in our world would be realized. Here are a few samples from the prophets, followed by the scriptures that show Jesus as the fulfillment of those prophecies:

- "For to us a child is born, to us a son is given, and the government will be on his shoulders. And he will be called Wonderful Counselor, Mighty God, Everlasting Father, Prince of Peace. Of the greatness of his government and peace there will be no end. He will reign on David's throne and over his kingdom, establishing and upholding it with justice and righteousness from that time on and forever. The zeal of the Lord Almighty will accomplish this" (Isa. 9:6–7).

- "A shoot will come up from the stump of Jesse; from his roots a Branch will bear fruit" (Isa. 11:1).

- "'The days are coming,' declares the Lord, 'when I will raise up for David a righteous Branch, a King who will reign wisely and do what is just and right in the land'" (Jer. 23:5).

- "You will conceive and give birth to a son, and you are to call him Jesus. He will be great and will be called the Son of the Most High. The Lord God will give him the throne of his father David, and he will reign over Jacob's descendants forever; his kingdom will never end" (Luke 1:31–33).

- "He has raised up a horn of salvation for us in the house of his servant David (as he said through this holy prophets of long ago)" (Luke 1:69–70).

Looking back over the terms of God's contract with David, New Testament believers quickly recognize that our heavenly Father's desire for us involved him sending the Second Person of the Trinity, his beloved Son, to our world. Approximately two thousand years of time passed between God's first contract with Abraham and the fulfillment of his contract with David in the form of Jesus. God knew even then that his incredible desires for his children would require sending his Son to us on a special, redemptive mission in order to bring that desire to reality.

5. God Desires to Fill Us with His Spirit

Religions in every corner of our world, from the beginning of time until today, have visualized a deity or multiple deities living high on mountains or in other dimensions, far beyond our reach. Even the Lord's chosen people—the Hebrew nation in the Old Testament—imagined God living somewhere far beyond their local, mundane existence. Only occasionally did God's people see manifestations of God's Spirit in the lives of people like Moses, the artisans of the tabernacle, Joshua, Samson, and their prophets. They often felt abandoned by God and alone in many ways, especially as hundreds of years passed following the end of the Old Testament era without hearing a word from him.

As God's covenants with humanity came into clearer view across the centuries of God's self-revelation, the Old Testament prophets began to sense God's voice telling them that he planned to step into human history once more. He would send the Messiah to sit on David's throne to rule his people in holy righteousness. Furthermore, he desired to establish his permanent, constant, and abiding residence in their hearts. They had no idea how God could possibly accomplish it, but they felt compelled to proclaim the divine promise nonetheless. Jeremiah prophesied this way:

> "The days are coming," declares the LORD, "when I will make a new covenant with the people of Israel and with the people of Judah. It will not be like the covenant I made with their ancestors when I took them by the hand to lead them out of Egypt, because they broke my covenant, though I was a husband to them," declares the LORD. "This is the covenant I will make with the people

of Israel after that time," declares the Lord. "I will put my law in their minds and write it on their hearts. I will be their God, and they will be my people."
(Jer. 31:31–33)

David's kingdom divided after his son King Solomon died. Then, to make matters worse, enemy nations surrounded them, destroyed their fractured kingdoms, and carried the majority of the Hebrew citizens to foreign lands to serve foreign empires. The prophet Jeremiah went into captivity with his fellow people, south, to Egypt. He saw lost hope in the eyes of his friends and neighbors; he heard their heart cries and their desires for their lost homeland, which lay in broken pieces. But the prophet of God did not lose hope. He saw a day coming in the future when not only would captives return to their promised land but God would also establish a new contract with them. According to Jeremiah, they could not begin to imagine the plans God had in mind for them!

Ezekiel was another Israelite prophet who, like Jeremiah, went into captivity with his fellow citizens, but he went east, to Babylon. The biblical record therefore gives readers an account of the Hebrew exile in stereo, from both Egypt and Babylon. Ezekiel could have easily surrendered all hope since he, along with everyone he knew, lost everything. However, like Jeremiah, he chose to maintain his hope and trust in God. He heard the promises of God in his spiritual ears and proclaimed them to his fellow captives. God had not given up on them:

I will show the holiness of my great name, which has been profaned among the nations, the name you have profaned among them. Then the nations will know that I am the Lord, declares the Sovereign Lord, when I am proved holy through you before their eyes. . . . I will sprinkle clean water on you, and you will be clean; I will cleanse you from all your impurities and from all your idols. I will give you a new heart and put a new spirit in you; I will remove from you your heart of stone and give you a heart of flesh. And I will put my Spirit in you and move you to follow my decrees and be careful to keep my laws.
(Ezek. 36:23, 25–27)

The prophet Joel also saw the day coming when God's Spirit would fill the hearts of his children:

> And afterward, I will pour out my Spirit on all people. Your sons and daughters will prophesy, your old men will dream dreams, your young men will see visions. Even on my servants, both men and women, I will pour out my Spirit in those days.
> (Joel 2:28–29)

Conclusion

As you reflect on the five desires God has for his children, remember that these are not five different desires. They are interconnected. God desires to live in intimate relationship with his children, just as he walked with Adam and Eve and the patriarchs. Each of the other four desires that God has for us (entering into a contract with us; being our redeemer; establishing a spiritual kingdom; and filling us with his Spirit) are manifestations and iterations of his first desire. He walked with Adam and Eve, Enoch, Noah, and other righteous individuals for many years.

God then revealed a desire to work through a specific individual—Abraham. He worked in the life of his friend Abraham and extended blessings to Abraham's offspring. God desired for the blessings he gave them to spread organically to all people, through Abraham and his descendants. He then became God the Redeemer with Moses and the Hebrew people, leading to the promise of an eternal kingdom through David.

Reflection Questions

1. What new information did you learn in this chapter about God?

2. How has God's desire to live in intimate relationship with you impacted your life?

3. How do you think God made it possible for early citizens of this world, like Enoch, to live in such a close relationship with the Lord when they knew so little about him?

4. How has God's desire to enter into a contract with you impacted your life?

5. How does Abraham and Sarah's lifetime relationship with God encourage your faith in God through the long haul?

6. How does the concept of blameless differ from the concept of flawless?

7. How has God's desire to be your Redeemer impacted your life?

8. How has God's invitation to become part of his spiritual kingdom in our world impacted your life?

9. How has God's desire to fill you with his Spirit impacted your life?

10. In Scripture, why do you think the phrase "walking with God" is such a common reference to individuals living for the Lord?

FIVE

How God Works to Redeem Us

Preparation for bringing a newborn baby home from the hospital can be difficult. Only those who have made such detailed preparations understand the complexity of the task. Clean out a room or space in a multi-use room for a nursery. Purchase and assemble a bassinet and, later, a baby bed. Locate a dresser for clothes and supplies. Hang pictures on the walls. Buy or find clothes to fit a newborn. Stock diapers, wet wipes, lotion, and a dozen other necessary items. Get a baby carrier and, later, a child's car seat. This list does not identify every task, but you get the picture. In this chapter, we will explore the implementation of God's redemptive plan for humanity after humanity exercised free will to disobey God and break his heart. Then we will see how the revelation of his redemptive plan develops from Genesis 3 to Revelation 22.

God's Preparation for Our Redemption

We discussed in chapter 3 the risk the Father took in giving humanity free will. God created humanity with the ability to think and make moral decisions for themselves, unlike a robot programmed to respond to commands in prescribed ways. Genesis 3 details the conversation the serpent had with Eve and Adam.[1] The serpent did not *force* the first couple to yield to temptation; he only dangled the option before them, promising the tantalizing possibilities for a glorious outcome. Satan still can only offer us tempting options; we still have

---

1. John identified Satan or the devil as "that ancient serpent," an obvious reference to Genesis 3:1–6 (see Rev. 20:2).

the *choice* to obey God or satisfy our own selfish desires. Satan cannot *force* us to do anything.

Adam and Eve opted to break the only rule God the Father gave them when he welcomed them into the perfect environment he lovingly prepared for their enjoyment. They hid from their Creator when they realized the result of their moral choice. Some interpret the question in Genesis 3:9—"Where are you?"—to mean that God actually did not know where they were hiding. Actually, God knew their hiding place precisely, just as a parent knows the hiding place of a three-year-old but still calls out with the question, "Where are you?" Listen carefully to these tender words and hear them as a compassionate question from a loving Father. These are the Father's first words aimed toward redemption. He needed them to choose to emerge from hiding and join him. He needed them to consider honestly what their action had done to their relationship with their Father. Why were they hiding from their Father in the first place? God then allowed them to play the blame game and learn that the first step toward redemption required them to recognize their need for it. Then he described the significant changes that would come to their lives as consequences for their sinful choice.

God often tucks clues about himself and his plans for us in seemingly unrelated scriptures. We find an amazing clue about the plan of our triune God for our redemption and the Father's early parental preparation for that redemption in Genesis 3:15. Read carefully and see if you can discern how the Father told the disobedient couple that he would work on their behalf and all their descendants. He wanted to restore them to his original desire for their lives and their relationship with him: "And I will put enmity between you [the serpent] and the woman, and between your offspring and hers; he will crush your head, and you will strike his heel."

A literal interpretation of God's announcement indicates that most people will fear serpents and that serpents may strike anyone who dares to get in their personal space. That is a valid surface-level reading. However, Bible scholars through the ages have also realized a deeper meaning. Notice how the language changes in the second portion of the verse. The first part of the sentence speaks of Eve and all her offspring; the second part focuses on Satan and one person: "*he* will crush your head, and you will strike *his* heel." Joseph Coleson says about this verse, "Throughout Christian history, some interpreters have taken this word as being also a prediction or a declaration of God's redemptive purpose. . . . When we read verse 15 in light of God's redemption fulfilled in the life and work of Jesus the Messiah, we are justified in seeing in this verse God's promise of ultimate victory over the source of temptation."[2] In other words, our loving God offered hope and a redemptive future in the midst of the first couple suffering the consequences of willful sin. That promise means as much to us today as it did to them.

Coleson further explains the spiritual meaning of this verse: "The divine Offspring of the woman, Jesus Christ, would crush the serpent's head, ultimately reversing the effects of sin for any and all who believe. This great work would cost him, though. The serpent would strike at his heel, and venomous serpents can kill. Jesus died, but death could not hold him."[3] For that reason, scholars identify this as the proto-gospel—or first good news—of God's redemption through Christ.

Martin Luther taught an important guide for interpreting Scripture that believers have used ever since. Luther advised to let simple passages interpret the difficult ones. Three simple statements in the New Testament add support for the proto-gospel interpretation of Genesis 3:15. They lend weight to the belief that God brought this verse to reality in the life, ministry, death, and resurrection of Jesus Christ.

1) Paul drew his theological treatise to the Roman church to a close with a reference to Genesis 3:15: "The God of peace will soon crush Satan under your feet. The grace of our Lord Jesus be with you" (Rom. 16:20).

2) John alluded to the timing of God's redemptive plan when he said, "All inhabitants of the earth will

2. Coleson, *Genesis 1–11*, 135–36.

3. Coleson, *Genesis 1–11*, 136.

worship the beast—all whose names have not been written in the Lamb's book of life, the Lamb who was slain from the creation of the world" (Rev. 13:8).

3) John later envisioned God's response to Satan, referring to him as the serpent from Genesis: "He seized the dragon, that ancient serpent, who is the devil, or Satan, and bound him for a thousand years" (Rev. 20:2).

God Offers Options

Most believers know the story of the heartbreak Adam and Eve experienced as one of their sons killed the other one. The biblical account of Cain and Abel confirms that Cain chose to disobey God just as his parents did in the garden (see Gen. 4:1–16). However, this story also subtly offers us new insight into the parental involvement of our God to guide his children toward righteous actions *before* they fall into sin.[4] Never assume that God sat in heaven and merely watched this story unravel. As we explore the way the events unfolded, watch for God's intervention.

We can infer by Cain and Abel's actions at the beginning of the story that Adam and Eve taught their sons to worship God. Their worship included personal sacrifices to reflect their love and commitment to him. Both boys brought a worship sacrifice. God accepted Abel's gift but rejected Cain's (see vv. 1–5). The text does not specify the reason for the rejection. It simply says, "The LORD looked with favor on Abel and his offering, but on Cain and his offering he did not look with favor" (Gen 4:4b–5a). We do not believe God judges capriciously through divine determinism—that is, arbitrarily accepting one offering and rejecting another simply because he is God. We can, however, use worship practices from that culture to speculate possible reasons for God's rejection of Cain's offering.

It appears that Abel brought God a very fat firstborn animal from his flock. Abel selected it as the best offering he could bring to show his total commitment to God. Cain

---

4. This parental behavior occurs repeatedly throughout Scripture, e.g., the Hebrew nation in the desert, the Israelites in the promised land, Christ warning the Pharisees, and the seven churches in Revelation.

brought a grain offering from his field, which we learn that worshipers often brought later in the Old Testament. Why might God have rejected Cain's offering? It's possible that Cain's was not a first-fruits offering like Abel's. Perhaps Cain had forgotten to plan ahead and hastily grabbed some grain on the way to worship. Or perhaps his offering somehow did not show undivided commitment to God. We only know that his offering did not please God.

The most divinely insightful part of the story unfolds in verses 6–7. God allowed Adam and Eve to weigh their decision to disobey him on their own. The loving heart of our heavenly Father took a different approach with Cain. He communicated directly with Cain, attempting to calm his anger and talk him out of doing something he would regret:

> Then the LORD said to Cain, "Why are you angry? Why is your face downcast? If you do what is right, will you not be accepted? But if you do not do what is right, sin is crouching at your door; it desires to have you, but you must rule over it."

These verses clearly demonstrate the prevenient grace of God, intercepting Cain and trying to talk sense into him before he gives in to sinful temptation. The Lord offered a better response that would bring about a restored relationship. The Lord really did care about Cain's spiritual life. He implored Cain to calm down, think through the situation, and reject temptation. We know, of course, that Cain ignored God's advice, but we clearly see the loving heart of a heavenly parent offering redemption and a way to avoid the consequences of sin.

God Foreshadows His Redemptive Sacrifice

Our discussion of God's redemption plan moves forward to Abraham and his family. We will consider God's work with humanity in Genesis 5–11 in chapter 8. Recall from God's contracts with Abraham, discussed in chapter 4, how God repeatedly promised that Abraham and Sarah would have a son. They had to wait for the fulfillment of that promise much longer than anyone would have anticipated, so they sometimes doubted God's timing. In fact, their lengthy wait led them to believe that God might *not* fulfill his promise. Then, when

Abraham was a hundred years old and Sarah was ninety, God brought Isaac into their home (see Gen. 17:17; 18:10; 21:5). Only God Almighty could have fulfilled the long-lost dream of the elderly couple!

The story continued when Abraham heard God calling in Genesis 22. Abraham quickly responded as he had on previous occasions, "Here I am" (v. 1). God knew how much this earthly father loved the son he and his wife had waited on for so long. That is why God began his instruction to Abraham with, "Take your son, your only son, whom you love—Isaac" (v. 2a). Notice God's emphasis on his awareness of just how special Isaac was to Abraham and Sarah. What God said next—instructing Abraham to sacrifice Isaac as a burnt offering—must have shocked Abraham to the core of his being (see v. 2b).

As the story plays out, showing Abraham obeying this inconceivable command, we see the strong relationship Abraham had with God in the way he set out the very next morning. Notice how Abraham's comment to his servant indicated that he trusted God to somehow spare Isaac's life: "We will worship and then *we* will come back to you" (v. 5b, emphasis added). When Isaac questioned the missing lamb, Abraham trustingly answered, "God himself will provide the lamb for the burnt offering, my son" (v. 8). Can you imagine the questions bouncing around in Abraham's head as he and Isaac climbed the mountain of sacrifice? Even so, his lingering questions did not deter Abraham from obeying God's instructions.

At the last possible moment, God rewarded Abraham's trust in him, presenting us with one of the most powerful object lessons on divine redemption in the entire Old Testament. We read Abraham's spiritual takeaway from the day: "So Abraham called that place The LORD Will Provide. And to this day it is said, 'On the mountain of the LORD it will be provided'" (v. 14).

No doubt the heart of every parent recoils when hearing the Father's command for Abraham to offer his son Isaac as a sacrifice. Child sacrifice was a common worship practice of surrounding pagan nations—but not for those who worshiped Abraham's God. Nowhere in the Bible did God condone child sacrifice. We feel Abraham's pain at the thought of losing his long-awaited son. What was God thinking? Why would he take Abraham and Isaac through such a stressful exercise?

Twenty-first-century readers looking back four thousand years offer possible answers. Perhaps God wanted us to feel Abraham's pain so we could feel a small sample of the Father's pain at the thought of offering his only Son on a cross for our spiritual redemption. Perhaps the Father wanted us to recognize that no other sacrifice could take the place of his Son, as the substitute ram did in Abraham's story. Perhaps he wanted us to interpret the two powerful comments of Abraham as prophecies of our coming redemption: "God himself will provide the lamb" (v. 8) and "The LORD Will Provide" (v. 14). God did, indeed, provide the Lamb, but at what personal cost? May we never forget the tremendous cost to God (both Father and Son) for our redemption!

God Redeemed the Hebrew Nation

God revealed himself to Moses as the Redeemer of Israel (see Exod. 6:6–8). We considered Moses's contract with God in chapter 4. Now we will focus attention on God's deliverance of the Hebrew nation from Egyptian slavery. The exodus is the most important event in the Old Testament. The rest of the Old Testament refers back to this divine act again and again as the best illustration of the nature of God.

The God of Abraham, Isaac, and Jacob watched carefully over the developing nation. He saw Jacob's family move to Egypt to avoid starvation during a famine. He watched over his people as a new Egyptian pharaoh came to power who had no regard for the descendants of Joseph. In fact, God told Abraham that his people would be enslaved in "a country not their own" for four hundred years (Gen. 15:13). Although four hundred years is a very long time for a people group to endure so much suffering, God used the heartless actions of the pharaoh as part of the process to build the Hebrew nation. The idea that God would stand idly by and watch what happened to his people is beyond comprehension and not at all supported by his actions throughout Scripture.

God revealed his redemption plan to humanity in stages, just as he gradually revealed his many names and his self-revelation across the generations.

We also see an abundance of divine patience. Moses repeatedly made excuses or raised issues that he thought indicated he was not the right person to lead his people through God's deliverance. God patiently addressed each objection, one after another, while at the same time building faith in Moses so he would eventually trust God for the necessary ability to lead the Israelites. That is who God is. He wants us to do his will, and he also enables us to trust him to provide whatever we need so that we *can* accomplish his will.

Exodus chapters 7 through 12 describe Moses and Aaron performing miracle after miracle through God's enabling power bestowed on them. At the same time, we see Pharaoh's hardened heart continue to be unyielding to God's command to release his people. Why did God go through the process of multiple plagues? Why not simply wipe out the Egyptians as he had the people of Noah's time, or like he did later, when Israel defeated their enemies in the promised land? Perhaps the answer lies in what God, through Moses, told Pharaoh: "But I have raised you up for this very purpose, that I might show you my power and that my name might be proclaimed in all the earth" (Exod. 9:16). God desired that his name be glorified—and it was. Word of God's deliverance of the Hebrew people from Egypt spread to neighboring nations. In subsequent books of the Bible, we find that other nations knew of and even feared the God of the Israelites because of this miraculous event.

We learn much about the Redeemer of Israel through the ritual of Passover (12:1–30). God wanted the Israelites to always remember who he was and what he did in delivering them so that his name would be glorified. What do we learn about God from the Passover celebration?

- God wants our gratitude; he wants us to be grateful for the things he does for us.
- God wants us to live ready to act at a moment's notice. The people were to eat a fast-food meal with their belts on, their cloaks tucked into their belts, their sandals on, and their staffs in hand.

- We must always honor and praise God; he is our teacher who prepares us in advance for what is to come.
- God wanted his children to recognize him as the one who cares the most for them, is always faithful to his promises, and is powerful enough to deal with their greatest foes. Most importantly, God delights in delivering people from bondage.
- God was preparing his people for redemption by the blood of a sacrifice without blemish. Redemption through a blood sacrifice becomes central in the sacrificial system God later establishes for his people. We cannot understand the significance of Christ's death on the cross for our redemption without understanding the spiritual meaning of blood sacrifices in the Old Testament. We will explore that in chapter 6.

From the initial departure from Egypt to the final crossing of the Jordan River, we see God's providence for his people. He guided, provided, protected, and removed enemies and obstacles. A pillar of cloud and fire led them through the wilderness and shielded them from harm. Notice again the patience of God. At times "the people feared the LORD and put their trust in him" (Exod. 14:31). At other times, the people griped and grumbled about their circumstances (see 15:24; 16:3; 17:1–7).

Through it all, God continued to provide for his people as he guided them back to the promised land in spite of their half-hearted obedience. We see here one of the most important lessons of the wilderness experience: God is incredibly gracious! Both the Old and New Testaments place primary focus on the grace of our loving heavenly Father. To this day we continue to sing the most frequently recognized Christian song, "Amazing Grace."

God used the time wisely as he moved the large caravan of as many as two million former slaves from Egypt to the promised land. They did not know it at the time, but he was forming them into a nation—the people of God. All nations of the world have rules by which they live together. God gifted his people with the Ten Commandments (see 20:1–17). A great deal of drama from the new nation surrounded their receiving and accepting these directives from God for spiritual and moral living. We do not have space in this short narrative to recount the drama. Suffice it to say, God proved to be incredibly patient as he brought a new rule of order to them. The first four commandments guided their relationship with God; the remaining six commandments guided their relationships with one another. Jesus summarized the Ten Commandments and, indeed, all the other hundreds of commandments provided for the Israelites in the Old Testament very simply: "'Love the Lord your God with all your heart and with all your soul and with all your mind.' This is the first and greatest commandment. And the second is like it: 'Love your neighbor as yourself.' All the Law and the Prophets hang on these two commandments" (Matt. 22:37–40).

God continued to show patience and restraint as he led his people through the wilderness. In one of the many conversations Moses had with God, the Lord described himself in this way: "The Lord, the Lord, the compassionate and gracious God, slow to anger, abounding in love and faithfulness, maintaining love to thousands, and forgiving wickedness, rebellion and sin" (Exod. 34:6b–7a). In the latter part of verse 7, God concluded by saying that those guilty of unconfessed sin would experience the consequences of their actions and suffer punishment. We will consider that matter in chapter 8.

The Redeemer of Israel remained faithful to the promises he made to Abraham as he returned the Hebrew nation from Egypt to the promised land. Read it for yourself in Exodus, Leviticus, Numbers, and Deuteronomy. From that time onward in salvation history, God's people often referred to their Redeemer as the Lord their God, who brought them out of Egypt. The people retold their redemption story from generation to generation.

We were slaves of Pharaoh in Egypt, but the Lord brought us out of Egypt with a mighty hand.

For you are a people holy to the Lord your God. The Lord your God has chosen you out of all the peoples on the face of the earth to be his people, his treasured possession.

But it was because the LORD loved you and kept the oath he swore to your ancestors that he brought you out with a mighty hand and redeemed you from the land of slavery, from the power of Pharaoh king of Egypt. (Deut. 6:21; 7:6, 8).

God Repeatedly Redeemed the Hebrew Nation

God met Moses on Mount Sinai, where he gave specific and detailed instructions for the civil and spiritual guidance of the Israelites. In these early days of their journey, God challenged Moses with these powerful words for his people: "'Now if you obey me fully and keep my covenant, then out of all nations you will be my treasured possession. Although the whole earth is mine, you will be for me a kingdom of priests and a holy nation.' These are the words you are to speak to the Israelites" (Exod. 19:5–6). They did not live into this promise as God intended, yet still he graciously guided them to the promised land.

The Hebrew nation concluded their wilderness wandering after forty years and settled into the land God had promised to Abraham. It might seem that "a land flowing with milk and honey" (Exod. 3:8) would provide the ideal environment for them to thrive as the people of God. Moses challenged his people during their wilderness wandering and in his final address to them, recorded in Deuteronomy, to remember that they were no longer slaves but had a divinely endowed identity as God's people: "For you are a people holy to the LORD your God. The LORD your God has chosen you out of all the peoples on the face of the earth to be his people, his treasured possession" (Deut. 7:6; see also 14:2; 26:18). This identity became such a powerful image for the Hebrew nation that Peter adopted it for believers in the New Testament: "But you are a chosen people, a royal priesthood, a holy nation, God's special possession, that you may declare the praises of him who called you out of darkness into his wonderful light" (1 Peter 2:9).

However, God's special nation did not live into God's desire for them to be his holy people once they settled into their permanent home. This narrative cannot adequately process all that happened through the ups and downs of nearly one thousand years, the resettlement of the land, and the closing of the Old Testament narrative, but a quick snapshot looks something like this:

- They settled into the promised land (see Joshua).
- They cycled twelve times between forgetting God, falling into sin, crying out for God's help, and experiencing God's deliverance (see Judges).
- God reluctantly granted their request for a king, and they became a political kingdom like surrounding nations (see 1 & 2 Samuel).
- The twelve tribes fractured into the two kingdoms of Israel and Judah while falling spiritually further away from God (see 1 & 2 Kings).
- Babylon and Egypt conquered the two kingdoms, destroyed the temple, ransacked the promised land, and took the vast majority of the Hebrew people back into captivity and exile (see Ezekiel, Jeremiah, Lamentations, & Daniel).
- A remnant of the exiles returned to the promised land, rebuilt the city walls of Jerusalem and the temple, and reestablished a mere shadow of what the once great nation had been under the golden age of King David (see Ezra & Nehemiah).

The exile experience proved to be a turning point for the Hebrew people. Slowly and quietly, without most of the people realizing it at the time, God continued patiently to work with his people, not only redeeming them from their foreign captors but also shaping them into the people of God. "The events of the exile precipitated a major theological crisis for those who survived. The descendants of Abraham remained without the symbols of God's special blessings—their temple, their kingship, and their nationhood."[5] In light of all this loss, how could they still see themselves as God's treasured possession?

This period of time in Israel's history changed everything! They became known as Jews, since many of them descended from the tribe of Judah. They learned the Aramaic language during their Babylonian resettlement. They learned modern business practices from their captors. Without the temple as a centralized worship location, they established synagogues within local communities for corporate worship.[6] Perhaps most importantly, foreign captivity gave the Hebrew nation time to reflect on their relationship with God. They renewed their commitment to Deuteronomy 6:4: "Hear, O Israel: The LORD our God, the LORD is one." In so doing, they renounced their propensity toward idolatry in all of its varied forms. From that time onward, they committed themselves to worship only the Lord their God.

Paul used an interesting phrase to describe God's careful preparation for the next big development in his redemption plan: "But when the set time had fully come, God sent his Son, born of a woman, born under the law" (Gal. 4:4). Hear that concept again: "he [God the Father] made known to us the mystery of his will according to his good pleasure, which he purposed in Christ, to be put into effect when the times reach their fulfillment—to bring unity to all things in heaven and on earth under Christ" (Eph. 1:9–10). God the Father brought everything together in just the right time and just the right way so as to introduce his Son to our world. Then God's redemption plan came into full view!

God Offers Redemption through Christ Jesus

The concept of redemption in the Old Testament primarily involved "deliverance of a person or people group from a

---

5. Alex Varughese, ed., Robert D. Branson, Jim Edlin, and Tim. M. Green, *Discovering the Old Testament: Story and Faith* (Kansas City, MO: Beacon Hill Press of Kansas City, 2003), 205.

6. Varughese, *Discovering the Old Testament*, 206.

dangerous situation to a secure one."[7] The repeated physical deliverances of God's people throughout the Old Testament became examples or illustrations of how God wanted to bring spiritual redemption to everyone on earth. God promised spiritual redemption to Adam and Eve through the proto-gospel, or first good news, in Genesis 3:15. He attempted to reason with Cain and convince him to reject the temptation for revenge in Genesis 4:6–7. God foreshadowed the high price for our spiritual salvation that he was willing to pay by drawing us into the agony Abraham felt as he contemplated the possibility of sacrificing his son in obedience to God (Gen. 22:1–19). The physical journey of the Hebrew nation from Egypt to the promised land illustrates our spiritual journey from sinful bondage to new life in Christ through the new birth and growth in grace, leading us finally to our own promised land, where we will live forever in God's presence.

Conversely, the concept of redemption in the New Testament primarily involved spiritual deliverance, especially through God's work in Christ Jesus. Christ's life and ministry proclaimed God's desire for our spiritual health: "The Word became flesh and made his dwelling among us. We have seen his glory, the glory of the one and only Son, who came from the Father, full of grace and truth" (John 1:14). We will explore the blessing of Christ's incarnation in chapter 6. For now, we focus attention on Christ's death and resurrection as the way to our spiritual redemption.

Paul declared that God offers redemption to us as a free gift of his grace: "This righteousness is given through faith in Jesus Christ to all who believe. There is no difference between Jew and Gentile, for all have sinned and fall short of the glory of God, and all are justified freely by his grace through the redemption that came by Christ Jesus" (Rom. 3:22–24). We will also explain in chapter 6 the fulfillment of the terms of the first covenant as God reveals them to us in the second covenant. For now, hear how the possibility for our redemption came about through Christ's sacrificial death and resurrection: "For this

---

7. Robert D. Branson, ed., *Global Wesleyan Encyclopedia of Biblical Theology* (Kansas City, MO: The Foundry Publishing, 2020), 327–28.

reason Christ is the mediator of a new covenant, that those who are called may receive the promised eternal inheritance—now that he [Jesus] has died as a ransom to set them free from the sins committed under the first covenant" (Heb. 9:15).

God's redemption for humanity through Christ's death on the cross holds many mysteries that exceed our ability to fully understand while we are on this side of eternity. We rejoice in the good news that we do understand and leave with God the mysteries we do not yet understand. However, the years of church history's attempts to explain some of the mysteries have brought us some ideas that do not hold true when compared with orthodox doctrines of the Christian faith. One of these mysteries deals with the relationship between the members of the Trinity surrounding Christ's death.

On the night of his betrayal, Jesus led his disciples to the garden of Gethsemane to pray with him. He went to a quiet location and prayed, "My Father, if it is possible, may this cup be taken from me. Yet not as I will, but as you will" (Matt. 26:39). Some Christian leaders interpret this prayer to mean that the Son's will was not yet fully aligned with the Father's will. They claim that Jesus needed more prayer and reflection to gain the resolve to follow through with the Father's will. The doctrine of the Trinity makes that interpretation impossible. The Father, Son, and Holy Spirit are of the same essence. The plan of salvation for humanity originated from our triune God. Therefore, the will of the Father regarding the cross was also the will of the Son. Jesus himself said well in advance of his crucifixion because he knew what lay ahead for him, "I lay down my life—only to take it up again. No one takes it from me, but I lay it down of my own accord. I have authority to lay it down and authority to take it up again" (John 10:17–18).

Another common misunderstanding comes from Jesus's words on the cross: "My God, my God, why have you forsaken me?" (Matt. 27:46). We know Jesus was quoting Psalm 22:1. Some believe Jesus was reporting that God the Father placed the sins of the world onto him then turned his back on the revolting image of the sinfulness of humanity, now on Jesus. This idea asserts that Jesus died alone, forsaken by his Father in his hour of need. In so doing, Jesus's death appeased the

God's redemption for humanity through Christ's death on the cross holds many mysteries that exceed our ability to fully understand while we are on this side of eternity. We rejoice in the good news that we do understand and leave with God the mysteries we do not yet understand.

Father's wrath against sin, thus mediating the gap between God and humanity.

A different interpretation offers an understanding that is more biblically faithful and theologically sound. Instead of abandonment, "the psalm does not dwell on this motif; it moves from desperation to hope, from suffering to salvation, and from humiliation to vindication."[8] In Psalm 22:23–24, we read, "You who fear the LORD, praise him! All you descendants of Jacob, honor him! Revere him, all you descendants of Israel! For he has not despised or scorned the suffering of the afflicted one; he has not hidden his face from him but has listened to his cry for help." Jesus did not believe his Father had rejected him as he hung on the cross. Rather, he died in full confidence that the Father had heard his cry and would vindicate him in glorious resurrection.

Parents sometimes hold their suffering child's hand through a serious illness or accident. During those long and anguished hours, parents often vicariously identify so closely with the suffering of the one they love unconditionally that they feel the same pain emotionally. God created us in his image and likeness. Therefore, God the Father not only remained in solidarity with his Son as he died on the cross but also felt his pain emotionally and spiritually. The Father's heart broke in ways that go far beyond our ability to comprehend as he watched his Son suffer and die for the sins of the entire world. The doctrine of the Trinity supports this often overlooked mystery of the atonement.[9]

The redemption God brought through Christ's death on the cross was not complete once Christ died. Christ's resurrection from the dead on the third day validated not only his

---

8. Robert S. Snow and Arseny Ermakov, *Matthew: A Commentary in the Wesleyan Tradition*, New Beacon Bible Commentary (Kansas City, MO: Beacon Hill Press of Kansas City, 2019), 399.

9. This theological interpretation is known as "patripassianism" and has both a heretical and orthodox explanation. The heretical version, also known as "modalistic monarchianism," says that God the Father became God the Son; hence, God the Father literally died on the cross. The orthodox explanation sees members of the Trinity living and working together in such a symbiotic way that they share non-physical emotional and spiritual pain.

virgin conception, his earthly ministry, his divine-human nature, his atoning death, and his mediation between God and humanity, but also the glorious reality that he is the Son of God! Peter and other apostles declared to the Sanhedrin, "The God of our ancestors raised Jesus from the dead—whom you killed by hanging him on a cross. God exalted him to his own right hand as Prince and Savior that he might bring Israel to repentance and forgive their sins. We are witnesses of these things, and so is the Holy Spirit, whom God has given to those who obey him" (Acts 5:30–32).

Yes, God the Father miraculously raised his Son from death to life. The disciples and more than five hundred of his followers witnessed this physical resurrection. From that day forward, the gospel message of Christianity proclaimed a resurrected Savior. Christ's movement would not have made it to the second century without his resurrection from the dead. C. S. Lewis spent many years of his academic career attempting to disprove the validity of Christianity. However, his extensive research could not overcome the overwhelming evidence of Jesus's physical resurrection from the dead. He gave his heart to Christ and spent the rest of his life proclaiming the good news of redemption through Jesus Christ. He wrote that "to preach Christianity [in the New Testament] meant to preach the resurrection."[10]

Furthermore, the Father did much more than bring his Son back to life on that first resurrection morning. He also proclaimed to the world that he is the Father in a new way of human understanding. Genesis 1–2 teach that he is Father of all creation. Genesis 12 all the way through to the conclusion of the Old Testament teaches that he is Father and Redeemer of the Hebrew nation, his chosen people. The resurrection of Christ declares to the world that he is the Father of an eschatological redemption that will eventually return all creation back to the purposes God originally intended. All creation is now on that God-ordained trajectory.

---

10. C. S. Lewis, *Miracles* (New York: Macmillan Publishing Co, 1947), 171.

Jesus Christ, the Redeemer of the world, will guide the process of this eschatological redemption to the day of completion. Paul described it in two ways. First: "For God was pleased to have all his fullness dwell in him, and through him to reconcile to himself all things, whether things on earth or things in heaven, by making peace through his blood, shed on the cross" (Col. 1:19–20). Second, Paul wrote, "In him we have redemption through his blood, the forgiveness of sins, in accordance with the riches of God's grace that he lavished on us. With all wisdom and understanding, he made known to us the mystery of his will according to his good pleasure, which he purposed in Christ, to be put into effect when the times reach their fulfillment—to bring unity to all things in heaven and on earth under Christ" (Eph. 1:7–10).

Conclusion

This chapter has attempted to shed new light on God's work to redeem his children. Rather than being an afterthought following the fall in the garden of Eden, God employed plans before the beginning of time to restore lost relationships with his children and return them to live in the desires he had for them at the creation of humanity. God revealed his redemption plan to humanity in stages, just as he gradually revealed his many names and his self-revelation across the generations. Looking back from our twenty-first-century perspective, it makes more sense now. However, believers who only understood bits and pieces of God's grand plan exercised great faith in the One who loved them and called them into intimate relationship with him.

We primarily think of our spiritual redemption in terms of God forgiving our sins and making us righteous by grace through faith alone. However, the New Testament also uses the notion of redemption in declaring that God adopts us into his redeemed family. "The Christian who accepts the salvation of Jesus is released from the world of sin and death to God's household."[11] Paul tells us that the incarnation and work of Je-

---

11. Branson, *Global Wesleyan Encyclopedia of Biblical Theology*, 330.

sus was "to redeem those under the law, that we might receive adoption to sonship" (Gal. 4:5). Elsewhere, Paul explains, "Not only so, but we ourselves, who have the firstfruits of the Spirit, groan inwardly as we wait eagerly for our adoption to sonship, the redemption of our bodies" (Rom. 8:23).

The unfolding of God's redemption in our spiritual lives includes not only our new birth and growth in grace but also our sanctification. We refer to this as full salvation. God's desire for his children to be filled with his Spirit became a reality at Pentecost (see Acts 2:1–4). Not only were Jesus's followers filled with the presence and power of the Holy Spirit on that day, but every believer from then until now can also enjoy that privilege. We will examine this in more detail in chapter 6.

Sometimes we are tempted to think we fully understand God's redemption plan, but we do not. We must exercise faith in what lies ahead for us, for our children, and for our grand-children until God brings all things to completion at the end of time. We will consider this middle position between "the already" and "the not yet" in chapter 10.

Reflection Questions

1. What new information about God did you learn in this chapter?

2. What encouragement do you find for your personal spiritual journey when you read that God offered redemption to Adam and Eve in his first conversation with them following their disobedience?

3. Why do you think Cain refused to listen to God's advice when God tried to discourage him from killing his brother?

4. How does the emotional struggle of Abraham in his willingness to offer Isaac give us insight into the high price our heavenly Father paid in offering his Son for the sins of the world?

5. How do you see the prevenient grace of God at work in Pharaoh's heart as he tried to get him to release the Hebrew nation from slavery?

6. What do you learn about the patience, providence, and love of God as he guided the Hebrew nation through the desert from Egypt to the promised land?

7. Why did the Hebrew people so often in their history point back to God's deliverance from Egyptian bondage?

8. How did God the Father express love for his Son and for lost humanity as he permitted Jesus Christ to submit himself to death on the cross?

9. How did God the Father not abandon his Son when the world's hatred killed him?

10. How is Christ's resurrection the greatest validation that Jesus Christ is Lord of all?

SIX

How God Provides for Us

Imagine you are walking through a store and see a sweep-stakes promotional table where you can sign up for a chance to win an all-expenses-paid trip to the vacation destination of your choice. You write your name, email address, and phone number on the entry form and drop it in the box. Three weeks later, you get notified that you won! You select your destina-tion and make arrangements for the trip of a lifetime. After you land at the airport, pick up your luggage, and meet your limo driver, you are surprised to learn that the driver is not taking you to a resort hotel. Instead, you arrive at a private mansion, reserved just for you, and larger than anything you have ever seen before. When you enter, you are greeted by your own personal butler, chef, housekeeper, and gardener. This really is going to be a trip to remember!

Before you know it, your week of luxurious living comes to a close. You pack your bags and prepare to head back home. When you get to the front door of the mansion, the butler hands you a gift-wrapped box. You quickly open the box and find a set of keys. As it turns out, the sweepstakes you won did not just entitle you to a one-week lavish vacation in this home; it gave you the deed to the mansion and the services of the professional staff for the rest of your life! How could you have possibly imagined when you completed the simple form at the store that your life would change forever?

From Imagination to Reality

Don't disregard this imaginative story too quickly. It is closer to theological reality than you might think. At just the right time, God sent his Son to our world for you and for everyone else who has lived or will ever live on earth. God's simple plan for salvation—justification by faith alone—provides for a changed life and more than we could ever imagine for all eternity. God's Son grew up in a family setting that probably seemed as ordinary as any other home in Nazareth. However, when he visited the temple with his parents at the age of twelve, everyone realized he was anything but an average Jewish child (see Luke 2:41–52). For the next approximately eighteen years, we assume he experienced life on earth much like any other young man of that land. Then something supernatural happened that changed our understanding of God and life on earth forever.

Jesus was baptized in the Jordan River by his cousin John the Baptist. Those watching this religious ritual would not have observed anything out of the ordinary until Jesus began to step out of the river. No one would have anticipated the moment; no one would have imagined that anything like this would ever happen. God's self-revelation to humanity suddenly took a giant step forward. Matthew describes the event this way: "As soon as Jesus was baptized, he went up out of the water. At that moment heaven was opened, and he saw the Spirit of God descending like a dove and alighting on him. And a voice from heaven said, 'This is my Son, whom I love; with him I am well pleased'" (Matt. 3:16–17). What just happened? God the Father—who is holy, holy, holy—introduced the world to Jesus his Son, and then the Spirit of God descended on Jesus in the form of a dove. Think about that for a moment. The God who previewed the gospel to Adam and Eve in the garden, who started the Hebrew nation with Abraham and Sarah, who delivered that Hebrew nation from Egyptian slavery, who foretold the coming of the Messiah through the prophets—that same God just announced to the world that he has a Son and also demonstrated that he has a Spirit. Who is this God with three identities? No doubt, everyone who witnessed this heavenly announcement left with more questions than answers.

Jesus began addressing this confusion of God's self-revelation when he preached the Sermon on the Mount (see Matt.

5–7). Several times throughout his message he referred to God as "Father." For example, "Be perfect, therefore, as your heavenly Father is perfect" (Matt. 5:48). He then taught his listeners how to begin their prayers with the now familiar words, "Our Father in heaven . . ." (Matt. 6:9). Do you see the incredible new insight in these words? Jesus identified God as *our* Father, not just *his* Father. In chapter 2, we listed many of the names of God found in the Old Testament. "Father" was not one of them, except for the prophecy about the coming Messiah in Isaiah 9:6 that included the title "Everlasting Father."

This book is titled *God the Father.* Yet we have hesitated to give many details until Jesus, the Father's Son, revealed him to the world. Now, we see the God of the Old Testament in a new light. God's desires for humanity when he created us and the redemption he promised us throughout salvation history now find their fulfillment in the life, ministry, death, and resurrection of Jesus. Our heavenly Father did not send his Son to earth to make life better *for a season* (like a weeklong vacation at a resort). Rather, he sent his Son to completely revolutionize our lives for time and eternity. Of course, the illustration of the sweepstakes vacation imagined material concepts. God's plan of salvation through Jesus Christ transforms our *spiritual* lives on earth and for eternity through our never-ending relationship with God. Our limited minds cannot begin to conceive the Father's blessings through Jesus Christ and the work of the Holy Spirit transforming us into Christlike disciples.

God the Father Provides for Us

The remainder of this chapter will explore some of the many ways God provides for us. The most important provision the Father gives us is the gift of his Son coming to our world. We must never take for granted the significance of the revelation that Jesus introduced us officially to our heavenly Father and promised the coming of the Holy Spirit to live with and in us until we reach our eternal home.

Once Jesus introduced us to our heavenly Father, we see the revelation of God in the Old Testament more completely. We now realize that the God of the Old Testament is much more than Creator, Protector, and Deliverer. We understand that God works in our lives like a loving parent provides for their children. Jesus made that comparison in his "how much more" examples:

- "Consider the ravens: They do not sow or reap, they have no storeroom or barn; yet God feeds them. And how much more valuable you are than birds!" (Luke 12:24)
- "Consider how the wild flowers grow. They do not labor or spin. Yet I tell you, not even Solomon in all his splendor was dressed like one of these. If that is how God clothes the grass of the field, which is here today, and tomorrow is thrown into the fire, how much more will he clothe you—you of little faith!" (Luke 12:27–28)
- "Which of you, if your son asks for bread, will give him a stone? Or if he asks for a fish, will give him a snake? If you, then, though you are evil, know how to give good gifts to your children, how much more will your Father in heaven give good gifts to those who ask him!" (Matt. 7:9–11).

Following are a few examples of the many ways that God the Father provided for his children throughout the Old Testament.

Presence

Our heavenly Father made his presence known in tangible ways to men and women throughout salvation history before Jesus came to earth. Adam and Eve (Gen. 3:8), Abram (Gen. 12:1–3), Isaac (Gen. 26:24), Jacob (Gen. 28:15), and Joseph (Gen. 39:2, 21, 23) are only a few of the many individuals to whom God made his presence known in the first book of the Bible. God assured Moses of his continued presence as he led the Hebrew people from Egypt to the promised land. "Moses said to the LORD . . . 'If you are pleased with me, teach me your ways so I may know you and continue to find favor with you. Remember that this nation is your people.' The LORD replied, "My Presence will go with you, and I will give you rest'" (Exod. 33:12a, 13–14). This sampling of biblical references reminds us that God revealed himself to various individuals in nearly every book of the Old Testament.

Comfort

The Psalms often acknowledge God's comfort in the lives of those who live in relationship with him:

- "You, LORD, have helped me and comforted me." (Ps. 86:17b)
- "When anxiety was great within me, your consolation brought me joy." (Ps. 94:19)
- "My comfort in my suffering is this: Your promise preserves my life." (Ps. 119:50)
- "May your unfailing love be my comfort, according to your promise to your servant." (Ps 119:76)

God's great prophet Isaiah often testified to divine comfort in his life and the lives of the Hebrew people who serve him: "In that day you will say: 'I will praise you, LORD. Although you were angry with me, your anger has turned away and you have comforted me'" (Isa. 12:1). God especially pays attention to those who suffer affliction: "Shout for joy, you heavens; rejoice, you earth; burst into song, you mountains! For the LORD comforts his people and will have compassion on his afflicted ones" (Isa. 49:13). God also works uniquely in the lives of those whose world seems to be falling apart: "The LORD will surely comfort Zion and will look with compassion on all her ruins; he will make her deserts like Eden, her wastelands like the garden of the LORD. Joy and gladness will be found in her, thanksgiving and the sound of singing. I, even I, am he who comforts you. Who are you that you fear mere mortals, human beings who are but grass" (Isa. 51:3, 12). Isaiah captures God's parental concern for his children with this special message: "As a mother comforts her child, so will I comfort you; and you will be comforted over Jerusalem" (Isa. 66:13).

Other prophets in God's service proclaimed that his comfort would someday come for his children. God said through Jeremiah, "Then young women will dance and be glad, young men and old as well. I will turn their mourning into gladness; I will give them comfort and joy instead of sorrow" (Jer. 31:13). God instructed Zechariah to say, "Proclaim further: This is what the LORD Almighty says: 'My towns will again overflow with prosperity, and the LORD will again comfort Zion and choose Jerusalem'" (Zech. 1:17).

Refuge

God provided Moses with a place of refuge when revealed his presence and glory in a unique way: "When my glory passes by, I will put you in a cleft in the rock and cover you with my hand until I have passed by" (Exod. 33:22). At the conclusion of Moses's leadership of the Hebrew people to the promised land, he reminded his people, "The eternal God is your refuge, and underneath are the everlasting arms" (Deut. 33:27).

The psalmists had confidence that God would provide a refuge for them when they needed it:

- "For in the day of trouble he will keep me safe in his dwelling; he will hide me in the shelter of his sacred tent and set me high upon a rock." (Ps. 27:5)
- "In the shelter of your presence you hide them from all human intrigues; you keep them safe in your dwelling from accusing tongues." (Ps. 31:20)
- "God is our refuge and strength, an ever-present help in trouble." (Ps. 46:1)
- "Be my rock of refuge, to which I can always go; give the command to save me, for you are my rock and my fortress." (Ps. 71:3)

Notice that God's refuge was not defined by a physical location but by his presence.

Listening Ear

Years after God gave the Ten Commandments, Moses gathered the Hebrew people and reminded them that God carefully listened to them and responded to their needs: "The LORD heard you when you spoke to me, and the LORD said to me, 'I have heard what this people said to you. Everything they said was good'" (Deut. 5:28). Moses also testified that while he met with God on the mountain receiving God's commandments, God listened to him personally. "Now I had stayed on the mountain forty days and forty nights, as I did

God's desires for humanity when he created us and the redemption he promised us throughout salvation history find their fulfillment in the life, ministry, death, and resurrection of Jesus.

the first time, and the LORD listened to me at this time also" (Deut. 10:10).

The Hebrew people moved into the promised land after their long trek from Egyptian bondage. Settling into the occupied land brought many challenges from pagan neighbors, as recorded in the book of Judges. The people cried out to God for a deliverer to rid them of their enemies. God heard every prayer. At the end of the judges' era God told Samuel, "About this time tomorrow I will send you a man [Saul] from the land of Benjamin. Anoint him ruler over my people Israel; he will deliver them from the hand of the Philistines. I have looked on my people, for their cry has reached me" (1 Sam. 9:16). While recounting his own divine deliverance from his enemies and from King Saul, David testified, "In my distress I called to the LORD; I called out to my God. From his temple he heard my voice; my cry came to his ears" (2 Sam. 22:7).

The psalmists assure us that God always listens to our prayers:

- "You, LORD, hear the desire of the afflicted; you encourage them, and you listen to their cry." (Ps. 10:17)
- "In my distress I called to the LORD; I cried to my God for help. From his temple he heard my voice; my cry came before him, into his ears." (Ps. 18:6)
- "The eyes of the LORD are on the righteous, and his ears are attentive to their cry." (Ps. 34:15)

Leadership

God led people in the early days of the developing human race in a variety of ways. Some followed his leadership, and others did not (see Gen. 1–11). Beginning in Genesis 12, God decided to focus special attention on one man and his family. He carefully led Abram and Sarai from Ur of the Chaldeans to the promised land (see Gen. 12:7). Abram is a good example for us of following God's leading without knowing exactly where he would end up. God's response to Abram's obedience summarizes our understanding of God's grace that we receive by faith alone: "Abram believed the LORD, and he credited it to him as righteousness" (Gen. 15:6).

One of the greatest examples of God's leadership in the Bible is his daily involvement in delivering the oppressed Hebrew people from Egypt and guiding them to the promised land. He summarized his plan to Moses at the burning bush: "So I have come down to rescue them from the hand of the Egyptians and to bring them up out of that land into a good and spacious land, a land flowing with milk and honey" (Exod. 3:8). Moses had no idea at the time how God would use him in unusual ways to bring his people out of Egypt and resettle them in the land flowing with milk and honey. Several Old Testament books detail the level of God's leadership exhibited in bringing his plans to completion, including Exodus, Leviticus, Numbers, Deuteronomy, Joshua, and Judges. Ezekiel 34 highlights the way that God is our shepherd leader. In chapter 7 we will explore the biblical imagery of God as our shepherd.

Instruction

Throughout Scripture we see God responding quickly when his children seek his instruction. God focused particular attention on his clear instruction to the Hebrew nation when he stopped the exile caravan three months into their journey at Mount Sinai. He taught them everything they needed to know and do to live as his "treasured possession" (Exod. 19:5). We know of the most famous portion of this instruction as the Ten Commandments (see Exod. 20:1–17). The remainder of the book of Exodus details God's instruction for their worship rituals and all they needed to do to live in a way that was pleasing in his sight. God's presence blessed his people in a special way as they worshiped him according to his instruction: "Then the cloud covered the tent of meeting, and the glory of the LORD filled the tabernacle. Moses could not enter the tent of meeting because the cloud had settled on it, and the glory of the LORD filled the tabernacle" (Exod. 40:34–35).

Moses renewed the covenant God made with his people by reminding them of this important truth: "The secret things belong to the LORD our God, but the things revealed belong to us and to our children forever, that we may follow all the words of this law" (Deut. 29:29). This passage clearly tells us that God has made his instructions very clear. There are no riddles to be solved or hidden revelations we must uncover in order to follow God's plan for our lives. Solomon made a request of God as he prayed the prayer of dedication for the temple: "Teach them the right way to live, and send rain on the land you gave your people for an inheritance" (2 Chron. 6:27).

Job's friend Elihu asked a probing question: "God is exalted in his power. Who is a teacher like him?" (Job 36:22). The psalmists offer good insight into the reality that God instructs us:

- "Who, then, are those who fear the LORD? He will instruct them in the ways they should choose." (Ps. 25:12)
- "Since my youth, God, you have taught me, and to this day I declare your marvelous deeds." (Ps. 71:17)
- "I have not departed from your laws, for you yourself have taught me." (Ps. 119:102)

God himself promised us leadership when we seek him: "I will instruct you and teach you in the way you should go; I will counsel you with my loving eye on you" (Ps. 32:8).

We could fill the rest of this chapter, and dozens more, identifying ways God the Father provided for his children in the Old Testament. He still provides for believers today just as he did in the past. He looks after our physical, psychological, and emotional needs in a thousand different ways. However, we need to turn our attention to some of the ways God provides for our spiritual needs. In order to fully understand God's long-range plan across the centuries of salvation history, we must carefully examine the images, practices, and rituals God gave the Hebrew people in the Old Testament in order to gain clarity and understanding about the incarnation of Jesus Christ in the New Testament.

From the Old Covenant to the New

God's provision for our spiritual lives began early in human history. We infer that God instructed Adam and Eve to bring sacrificial offerings as acts of worship because it seems that they in turn instructed their sons, Cain and Abel, to worship with sacrifices (see Gen. 4:1–5). Noah and his family offered sacrifices to God following the flood (see Gen. 8:20–22). Abraham worshiped God with sacrifices (see Gen. 15:9–18). Moses and the Hebrew nation offered a Passover sacrifice on the night of their deliverance from Egyptian slavery (see Exod. 12). These examples illustrate worshipers showing their commitment and gratitude to God by giving their best to him.

One more Old Testament example illustrates God's preparation to give his best to us. In chapter 5, we analyzed the agonizing pain Abraham must have felt as he followed God's instruction to take Isaac to the mountains of Moriah to offer him as a worship sacrifice (see Gen. 22:1–19). Two verses illuminate Abraham's incredible faith in God. Abraham told Isaac, "God himself will provide the lamb for the burnt offering, my son" (Gen. 22:8). After God provided a ram as a substitute for Isaac, Scripture says, "So Abraham called that place The Lord Will Provide" (Gen. 22:14). Some biblical scholars interpret this event as a foreshadowing of the Father's willingness to offer his Son for the sins of the world.

These examples serve as precursors to the highly detailed sacrificial system God gave to Moses at Mount Sinai (see Exod. 20–31). We do not have time to explore every feature of this deeply significant system of worship. Instead, we will consider the system offerings that foreshadow the fulfillment of God's plan in the life and death of Jesus Christ, which will give us a new level of understanding of the incredibly high price God paid for our salvation, and of the benefits we receive both in this life and in the life to come.

Old Testament Covenant Sacrificial System Offerings

Leviticus chapters 1–7 explain the five primary sacrifices of this worship ritual. The following outline summarizes the central features that help us understand the training God gave his people so we can humbly appreciate our salvation through Jesus Christ.[1]

---

1. Material in this outline comes from Thomas J. King, "Sacrificial System" in Robert Branson, ed., *Global Wesleyan Encyclopedia of Biblical Theology* (Kansas City, MO: The Foundry Publishing, 2020), 358–62.

I. Voluntary Offerings

A. Burnt Offerings (Lev. 1)

    a. These were also called whole burnt offerings because fire completely consumed them.

    b. The central purpose of these offerings included welcoming God's presence, fully surrendering to God, celebrating important milestones in individual or community life, and offering atonement (see Gen. 8:20; Lev. 1:4; 22:18; Num. 15:3; 1 Sam. 6:14; 2 Sam. 6:17).

B. Grain Offerings (Lev. 2)

    a. These rituals offered a gift or tribute to God.

    b. The central purpose of these sacrifices were the same as the burnt offerings.

    c. Worshipers who could not afford an animal or bird sacrifice brought grain offerings.

    d. Priests offered part of the offering to God and ate the rest, representing the relationship God had with his people.

C. Well-being Offerings (Lev. 3)

    a. These sacrifices were also called peace offerings.

    b. Priests offered them in three forms: thanksgiving offering to thank God for blessings (see Lev. 7:12–15); votive offering at the completion of a vow (see Lev. 7:12–15); and free will offering to praise God for no particular reason (see Lev. 7:16–17).

    c. Worshipers participated in eating a portion of these offerings, symbolizing fellowship between God, the priests, and the people.

II. Required Offerings

A. Sin Offering (Lev. 4)

    a. For a sin offering, the priest sacrificed a bull or male goat and sprinkled the blood in various places around the tabernacle or temple.

    b. This sacrifice reminded priests and worshipers that sin breaks God's law and his heart. Sin desecrates the sinner's heart, the lives of those affected, and the place of worship, which represents God's presence.

Sin interrupts relationship between the sinner, others, and God.

    c. The Day of Atonement called worshipers to repent of their sins, acknowledge the damage sin inflicts on themselves and others, and dedicate their lives to God in order to be holy and righteous in daily living.

    d. Thomas King summarizes the sin offering sacrifice in this way: "Ancient Israel's prophets highlighted this understanding through their critique of the sacrificial system. They proclaim that proper fulfillment of the sacrificial system should result in justice, care for the needy, loyalty, knowledge of God, righteousness, kindness, and a humble walk with the Lord (Isa 1:11-19; Hos 6:6, Amos 5:21–24; Mic 6:6–8)."[2]

B. Guilt Offering (Lev. 5)

    a. This sacrifice required individuals who were guilty of sins—against God, against the holy things of God, or against other people created in the image of God—to bring specific sacrifices according to the nature of their sin. Sins included inferior worship practices, which offended God, or the breaking of any of the commandments five through ten, which hurt others.

    b. This offering required not only the proper sacrifice but also a full repayment plus twenty percent.

    c. This sacrifice reminded worshipers of the ultimate importance of maintaining a close relationship with God and with other people and, again, that atonement for sin cost the life of the innocent sacrificial animal.

New Testament Fulfillment of the Old Covenant in Jesus Christ

Most believers today know that Jesus died for our sins. They have been taught that Jesus's sacrifice on the cross and his shed blood covered their sins. Many sing songs in worship

---

2. King, "Sacrificial System," *Global Wesleyan Encyclopedia*, 361.

regularly about the sacrificial blood of Christ. However, many of these same believers cannot explain the reason Christians believe this, or why it makes sense in the twenty-first century. The letter to the Hebrews offers us the best analysis of the fulfillment of the old covenant God made with Moses and the Hebrew people in the life, death, and resurrection of Jesus Christ.

We have an easier experience understanding the book of Hebrews when we realize it is one interconnected narrative. Imagine the writer proclaiming this message to you in one long sentence without taking a breath. The writer wants us to realize that the new covenant God initiated with us through the incarnation of his Son fulfills the Old Testament sacrificial system. God gave the Sinai covenant to Moses; Aaron served as the priest who led the people in worship using the directives for the various rituals. Jesus is above the angels, Moses, and Aaron (see Heb. 1–10). Jesus, the Son of God, is our great high priest who now intercedes for us in heaven (see Heb. 4:14–16).

God gave Moses detailed instructions for building and furnishing the tabernacle of worship in the wilderness. Solomon followed those detailed instructions carefully as he constructed the physical temple. Every feature of the worship places, and every object in them, along with the priestly ceremonial robes, carried important spiritual significance. Everything in one way or another served as an object lesson to draw us into closer relationship with God and other people. Both the tabernacle and the temple were earthly representations of the heavenly worship center where Christ, our high priest, now lives (see Heb. 8:1–9:10). The heavenly temple is far superior to earthly ones.

Jesus Christ not only serves as our high priest in the new covenant but he also willingly offered himself as the perfect, sinless sacrifice for our sins. The sacrificial blood of animals in the old system reminded worshipers of the seriousness of sin and their need for forgiveness. However, that blood failed in an important way: "the gifts and sacrifices being offered were not able to clear the conscience of the worshiper. They are only a matter of food and drink and various ceremonial washings—external regulations applying until the time of the new order" (Heb. 9:9b–10). Christ's sacrifice far exceeded the sacrifices of the old covenant:

> How much more, then, will the blood of Christ, who through the eternal Spirit offered himself unblemished to God, cleanse our consciences from acts that lead to death, so that we may serve the living God! For this reason Christ is the mediator of a new covenant, that those who are called may receive the promised eternal inheritance—now that he has died as a ransom to set them free from the sins committed under the first covenant. (Heb. 9:14–15)

Hebrews 9:22 summarizes the spiritual significance of blood in both the old and new covenants: "In fact, the law requires that nearly everything be cleansed with blood, and without the shedding of blood there is no forgiveness." Hebrews 9 ends with this sobering reminder: "Just as people are destined to die once, and after that to face judgment, so Christ was sacrificed once to take away the sins of many; and he will appear a second time, not to bear sin, but to bring salvation to those who are waiting for him" (vv. 27–28).

Hebrews offers many more comparisons between the old and new covenants. It places particular significance on how each feature of the new covenant far exceeds everything about the old one. "Under the first covenant God could not be directly approached because of sin. Through the second, free access to him has been provided. The graciousness of this new covenant makes our obedience all the more important."[3] Take time to read carefully the letter to the Hebrews and study the many spiritual insights related to our salvation in Jesus Christ. God truly did provide full salvation both for this life and eternal life with him.

Another Promise Fulfilled

We briefly mentioned God's gift of the Holy Spirit at Pentecost (Acts 2:1–4) near the end of chapter 5. God's work

---

3. Albert F. Harper, ed., *The Wesley Bible: A Personal Study Bible for Holy Living* (Nashville: Thomas Nelson Publishers, 1990), 1,842.

Our heavenly Father made his presence known in tangible ways to men and women throughout salvation history before Jesus came to earth.

to redeem us includes not only the blood of Christ sacrificed on the cross for our sins but also a new relationship with God through the infilling of God's Spirit. Jeremiah and Ezekiel both prophesied that someday God's desire to fill us with his Spirit would be a reality. We explored those prophecies in chapter 4. Jeremiah spoke of a new covenant between God and humanity. That new covenant would make it possible for God to inscribe his law on human minds and hearts, enriching their relationship with God (see Jer. 31:31–33). Ezekiel spoke of God sprinkling clean water on his children to make them spiritually clean. He saw the day when God would give them a new heart and spirit and dwell within them with his Holy Spirit (see Ezek. 36:25–27).

Jesus spent his last night before surrendering to death on the cross sharing the final words of his earthly ministry with his disciples. He saved the best for last! He spoke of his temporary separation from them, of a home in heaven with him someday, and of being with them until that day. He promised, "I will not leave you as orphans; I will come to you" (John 14:18). The disciples could not understand these strange words. Jesus actually told them his words would eventually make sense with the coming of the Holy Spirit. Take time to read the full account of that discussion in John chapters 14–16. The disciples did not realize it that night, but the promised Holy Spirit fulfilled the prophecies of Jeremiah and Ezekiel.

Following his death and resurrection, Jesus gave his disciples an important assignment: "Do not leave Jerusalem, but wait for the gift my Father promised, which you have heard me speak about. For John baptized with water, but in a few days you will be baptized with the Holy Spirit'" (Acts 1:4–5). The disciples followed Jesus's direction and gathered in a room to pray and wait ten days for the promised gift from the Father. The Father brought the promise to reality on the day of Pentecost: "When the day of Pentecost came, they were all together in one place. Suddenly a sound like the blowing of a violent wind came from heaven and filled the whole house where they were sitting. They saw what seemed to be tongues of fire that separated and came to rest on each of them. All of them were filled with the Holy Spirit" (2:1–4).

The rest of the book of Acts describes the incredible spiritual impact the Holy Spirit had throughout the world as he empowered Christ's disciples. Some Bibles refer to this book as the Acts of the Apostles; a better name might be the Acts of the Holy Spirit. The Spirit not only gave the disciples power to proclaim the gospel message of salvation through Jesus Christ but also cleansed their hearts from all that was un-Christlike. Many years later, Peter testified to God sending his Holy Spirit to a group of gentile believers. Peter reported to the Jerusalem elders, "God, who knows the heart, showed that he accepted them by giving the Holy Spirit to them, just as he did to us. He did not discriminate between us and them, for *he purified their hearts by faith*" (15:8–9, emphasis added). Another promise fulfilled.

Conclusion

In this chapter, we have looked at a few of the many ways God provides for our physical, psychological, and emotional needs. More importantly, God established a new covenant with humanity to meet all of our spiritual needs. When we refer to full salvation, we mean two important gifts of God. First, we trust in Jesus Christ alone for our salvation by identifying with him in his death on the cross for the forgiveness of our sins. We are born again to eternal life through his shed blood. All of this comes by faith alone as a free gift from God. Second, we fully consecrate ourselves to God as living sacrifices (see Rom. 12:1–2). Again, by faith alone as a free gift from God, we receive the fullness of the Holy Spirit. He lives within our hearts and works to transform us into Christlike disciples. God has truly provided us with everything we need today and forever. "His divine power has given us everything we need for a godly life through our knowledge of him who called us by his own glory and goodness" (2 Peter 1:3).

Reflection Questions

1. What new information did you learn in this chapter about God?

2. How was the conclusion of Jesus's baptism by John the Baptist the greatest breakthrough in God's self-revelation to humanity?

3. How do Jesus's teachings in the Sermon on the Mount about God the Father revolutionize our understanding of God's work with humanity throughout the Old Testament?

4. How have you sensed God's presence in your life as he has provided for your needs?

5. Why did God give the Hebrew nation such a detailed sacrificial system of worship as they traveled from Egypt to the promised land?

6. What features of the Old Testament sacrificial system help you better understand God's will for your life?

7. How does the sacrificial system help you understand Jesus's death on the cross for the sins of humanity?

8. How is God's new covenant with humanity better than the old one?

9. How did the Holy Spirit make such a radical change in Christ's disciples following the day of Pentecost?

10. How do the stories in the book of Acts help you understand why it could be called the Acts of the Holy Spirit instead of the Acts of the Apostles?

SEVEN | How God Relates to Us

One of my responsibilities at a previous ministry required the services of a printing company. We had a great relationship with the firm we used. Our team once toured the facility and found the printing presses, sorters, and binding equipment amazing. However, we were equally impressed with the warehouse of printed materials waiting to be mailed. The largest warehouse in the facility housed greeting cards—hundreds of thousands of them filling the entire building. We asked if these cards served all of next year's holidays. The tour guide said, "No. These cards are for the next three months!" At the time of this book's writing, U.S. Americans buy 6.5 billion greeting cards per year.

Greeting cards are obviously big business. People want to connect with one another at important life events. Birthdays, graduations, holidays, illnesses, births, deaths, weddings, anniversaries, relocations, and times of remembering one another identify a few of the many reasons people connect using greeting cards. Maintaining meaningful relationships with others adds significant value to our lives. God created us for relationship with him and with one another. The most meaningful relationship you will ever have in this life is with your heavenly Father. This chapter will explore some of the many ways God involves himself in our lives and relates to us. We will first review some the most common misconceptions about God; then we will turn our attention to the kind of relationship God wants to have with us.

Distorted Perceptions of our Heavenly Father

Some people perceive God as a stern judge sitting behind a large courtroom desk. Every time you come into contact with him, he stares you down with his judgmental eyes, drops his gavel, and declares, "Guilty as charged!" Those who buy into this misconception of who God is often do not even try to establish a relationship with God, viewing his authority as unreasonable and unloving or believing they are too far gone for divine love, help, or mercy.

Some people imagine God as a heavenly grandfather who sees no wrong in anything people do because his grandfatherly love blinds him to their lifestyle choices. He wants them to enjoy their lives in any way they see fit. He has no interest in disciplining people and is content to sit back and let people do whatever they want.

Some people picture the popular Christmas personality, Santa Claus, as their perception of God. He hands out gifts, answers prayers, and laughs along his merry way. He does not even have a naughty list. Everyone makes his nice list. People can pray to him when they find themselves in a crisis or difficult circumstance. Otherwise, they can ignore him, just as we pack images of Santa away until his special season of the year.

Some people visualize God as a weights-and-measures official, sitting at a desk with a balance scale. He watches the choices we make in life and places them on the scale. Our good deeds go on one side; our bad deeds go on the other. At the end of our time on earth, God measures our good deeds against our bad ones. If our good deeds outweigh our bad ones, he grants us a heavenly reward. This misperception of God seems to be the most popular by far.

Some people surmise that God created the vast universe, placing plants, animals, birds, sea life, and humanity on the earth, then sat back on his celestial throne. He worked much like a clockmaker building an old-fashioned mechanical clock—winding it up and watching it tick. According to this view, God has no direct involvement with our earthly lives; we are on our own. He gains satisfaction just watching the movement of the universe and our lives. When we die, we vanish from reality as though we never lived.

One last misperception of God visualizes him sitting by the prayer phone waiting for us to make the first move to reach out to him. He has no intention of involving himself in our lives until we come to him for help. We have to initiate the relationship if there is to be one. This misperception leaves the impression that God is distant and aloof, detached from our earthly concerns. Relationship is a one-way street.

Our Heavenly Father Reaches Out to Us First

The Christian tradition distinguishes itself from other religions of the world by this astounding truth: God has always reached out to us first. Recall how you felt when a friend you had not connected with in a long time sent you a greeting card, email, text, or reached out on social media. This person made the effort. Suddenly, you felt noticed. Your friend cared enough to make a connection. That experience gives us a tiny glimpse into God reaching out to us for the first time, the hundredth time, or the thousandth time. We are always on his mind. He is always seeking ways to intersect with us. He has a relentless pursuit.

We call those initial divine contacts "prevenient grace." This grace reaches out to us with loving arms before we know God in a personal way. God takes an interest in us long before we have any interest in him. "But God demonstrates his own love for us in this: While we were still sinners, Christ died for us" (Rom. 5:8). Jesus told us, "No one can come to me unless the Father who sent me draws them" (John 6:44). The Father does not limit his drawing to a select few; he invites everyone into this blessed relationship. He urges us to join the "whoever believes in him" of John 3:16. Thomas Langford calls this grace "God's active and continuous presence."[1] Allen Coppedge says it is the "general grace given to all people that restores in them the ability to accept God's offer of redemption."[2] John Wesley described the efforts of the Trinity in

---

1. Thomas A. Langford, *Theology in the Wesleyan Tradition*, Practical Divinity, Vol. 1, Rev. Ed. (Nashville: Abingdon Press, 1998), 20. Quoted in J. Gregory Crofford, "Prevenient Grace" in Al Truesdale, ed., *Global Wesleyan Dictionary of Theology* (Kansas City, MO: Beacon Hill Press of Kansas City, 2013), 430.

2. Allen Coppedge, *Shaping the Wesleyan Message* (Nappanee, IN: Evangel Publishing House, 2003), 111. Quoted in Crofford, "Prevenient Grace," *Global Wesleyan Dictionary of Theology*, 430.

reaching out to us as, "the drawings of the Father, the enlightening of the Son, and the convictions of the Holy Spirit."[3]

Therein lies the key: no one earns or deserves this grace that goes before. That is what makes it so amazing. God offers it to everyone, reaches out in love to everyone, and remains doggedly persistent in urging everyone to join in relationship with him. Those who accept this free gift of salvation through Jesus Christ by faith through divine grace alone soon realize they have entered into a spiritual mystery that enlivens every moment of every day, not just for an earthly lifetime but also for eternal life with him. This new reality far exceeds our wildest expectations. Paul referenced Isaiah 64:4 when he reminded us, "However, as it is written: 'What no eye has seen, what no ear has heard, and what no human mind has conceived'— the things God has prepared for those who love him" (1 Cor. 2:9). Until then, we should participate in all the ways our triune God reaches out for relationship with us.

Our Heavenly Father Is Our Helper

Television and social media advertisers constantly remind us that many of us need jobs done for which we ourselves have little to no expertise. Of course, advertisers are quick to let us know we can text or email one of their many professionals who will come and do the job for us for a reasonable price. Help is on the way. In like manner, believers have a divine helper ready to assist at a moment's notice.

Moses reminded the Hebrew people, "There is no one like the God of Jeshurun, who rides across the heavens to help you and on the clouds in his majesty" (Deut. 33:26). Again, Moses said, "Blessed are you, Israel! Who is like you, a people saved by the LORD? He is your shield and helper and your glorious sword" (Deut. 33:29). Samuel testified to God's helping hand this way, "Then Samuel took a stone and set it up between Mizpah and Shen. He named it Ebenezer, saying, 'Thus far the LORD has helped us'" (1 Sam. 7:12).[4] The psalm-

---

3. Crofford, "Prevenient Grace," *Global Wesleyan Dictionary of Theology*, 430.
4. Ebenezer means "stone of help."

From the creation of humanity through all of human history and into eternity, it is plain to see that God desires to be in intimate relationship with us.

ist described God's help in this way: "who saves me from my enemies. You exalted me above my foes; from a violent man you rescued me" (Ps. 18:48). Again we hear the psalmist's prayer: "But you, LORD, do not be far from me. You are my strength; come quickly to help me" (Ps. 22:19). "The LORD is my strength and my shield; my heart trusts in him, and he helps me. My heart leaps for joy, and with my song I praise him" (Ps. 28:7). Literally dozens of references throughout the Old Testament speak of God's help in time of need.

Our Heavenly Father Is our Keeper

An intimate personal relationship with God affords us the assurance that he safely keeps us in his hand. Children often run to their parents when a rainstorm brings the frightening sounds and sights of thunder and lightning. They know their parents will keep them safe. God comforted Jacob as he moved away from home: "I am with you and will watch over you wherever you go, and I will bring you back to this land. I will not leave you until I have done what I have promised you" (Gen. 28:15).

The heavenly Father promised the Hebrew people his help as they traveled from Egypt to the promised land: "See, I am sending an angel ahead of you to guard you along the way and to bring you to the place I have prepared" (Exod. 23:20). The Lord gave Aaron and his sons a blessing for the Hebrew people that is now famous: "The LORD bless you and keep you; the LORD make his face shine on you and be gracious to you; the LORD turn his face toward you and give you peace" (Num. 6:24–26). In verse 27, God told Moses that when Aaron and his sons blessed the people, "So they will put my name on the Israelites, and I will bless them." God not only gave comfort to his children by giving them an audible blessing by the priests, but he also promised to bless them himself.

The psalmists constantly reminded God's people that God was their keeper:

- "You, LORD, will keep the needy safe and will protect us forever from the wicked." (Ps. 12:7)
- "Keep me as the apple of your eye; hide me in the shadow of your wings." (Ps. 17:8)

- "In the shelter of your presence you hide them from all human intrigues; you keep them safe in your dwelling from accusing tongues." (Ps. 31:20)
- "Indeed, he who watches over Israel will neither slumber nor sleep." (Ps. 121:4)

The prophet Isaiah testified that relationship with God brings peace of heart and mind, a blessing in short supply in our troubled world today. "You will keep in perfect peace those whose minds are steadfast, because they trust in you" (Isa. 26:3). God delivered a powerful message not only to the Hebrew nation in exile but also to all who live in relationship with him: "I, the LORD, have called you in righteousness; I will take hold of your hand. I will keep you and will make you to be a covenant for the people and a light for the Gentiles" (Isa. 42:6).

Our Heavenly Father Is Our Protector

We have recounted in several contexts the incredible way God protected the Hebrew nation as they escaped from Egyptian bondage. The angel of God used a cloud to guide the people through the desert. At night the cloud shifted to the rear of the traveling caravan to provide a protective wall between them and the Egyptian army (see Exod. 14:20). We often fail to visualize the protecting hand of God. However, God sometimes grants us spiritual eyes to realize that he is as close as we need him to be. Elisha's assistant realized that in a moment of doubt: "And Elisha prayed, 'Open his eyes, LORD, so that he may see.' Then the LORD opened the servant's eyes, and he looked and saw the hills full of horses and chariots of fire all around Elisha" (2 Kings 6:17).

The Lord reminded King Asa of Judah, "For the eyes of the LORD range throughout the earth to strengthen those whose hearts are fully committed to him" (2 Chron 16:9a). The psalmists reaffirmed God's protection multiple times. "The angel of the LORD encamps around those who fear him, and he delivers them" (Ps. 34:7). "He will cover you with his feathers, and under his wings you will find refuge; his faithfulness will be your shield and rampart" (Ps. 91:4). "As the mountains surround Jerusalem, so the LORD surrounds his people both now and forevermore" (Ps. 125:2).

Every Bible student, young and old, recalls the incredible way God protected Daniel as he remained faithful to his Lord while in exile. God especially proved himself faithful to Daniel when the king threw him into the lions' den. Here is his testimony to God's protection: "My God sent his angel, and he shut the mouths of the lions. They have not hurt me, because I was found innocent in his sight. Nor have I ever done any wrong before you, Your Majesty" (Dan. 6:22).

Another biblical word often used in the Bible for God's protection is "shield." We do not often think of needing a soldier's shield. However, think of the many ways we see or hear about the need for a shield in everyday life. Insurance companies shield policyholders from disaster. Politicians are often protected by bulletproof glass during open-air events. Doctor tell us we need a shield of protection from all manner of diseases through inoculations, proper diet, and regular exercise. Without thinking about it, we depend on all sorts of shields in our daily lives. Most importantly, we need a divine shield to protect us spiritually in ways that only God can provide.

God appeared to Abram in a vision and reminded him, "Do not be afraid, Abram. I am your shield, your very great reward" (Gen. 15:1). At the conclusion of the wilderness wandering of the Hebrew nation, Moses proclaimed, "Blessed are you, Israel! Who is like you, a people saved by the LORD? He is your shield and helper and your glorious sword" (Deut. 33:29). The psalmist testified, "We wait in hope for the LORD; he is our help and our shield" (Ps. 33:20). The book of Proverbs also promises the Father will be our shield. "He holds success in store for the upright, he is a shield to those whose walk is blameless" (Prov. 2:7). "Every word of God is flawless; he is a shield to those who take refuge in him" (Prov. 30:5).

Each of these passages of Scripture reminds us of an important truth. God does not build some sort of protective bubble around us as a shield; rather, he himself is our shield. How unbelievable is that?

Our Heavenly Father Is Our Friend

God spoke to his prophet Isaiah about the ways he had cared for the Hebrew people from the days of the patriarchs until his time. God pointed to the close relationship he had with Abraham by calling him his friend: "But you, Israel, my servant, Jacob, whom I have chosen, you descendants of Abraham my friend" (Isa. 41:8). What better status in life than to have God call you friend! God had a similar relationship with Moses: "The LORD would speak to Moses face to face, as one speaks to a friend" (Exod. 33:11). When the circumstances of life turned against Job, he recalled his former life: "Oh, for the days when I was in my prime, when God's intimate friendship blessed my house" (Job 29:4).

The ultimate expression of God's desire to be our friend came in Jesus's ministry to his disciples, when he said, "I no longer call you servants, because a servant does not know his master's business. Instead, I have called you friends, for everything that I learned from my Father I have made known to you" (John 15:15). Jesus taught only what the Father taught him. "I do nothing on my own but speak just what the Father has taught me" (John 8:28). Therefore, we can be sure the Father desires our friendship.

Our Heavenly Father Is Our Counselor

Believers sometimes seek spiritual counsel from professionals who can help bring clarity and understanding to troubling situations or circumstances. They can also help point individuals toward righteous paths. The psalmists remind us that our heavenly Father also offers us spiritual counsel:

- "I will praise the LORD, who counsels me; even at night my heart instructs me." (Ps. 16:7)
- "You guide me with your counsel, and afterward you will take me into glory." (Ps. 73:24)
- "I will instruct you and teach you in the way you should go; I will counsel you with my loving eye on you." (Ps 32:8)

Old Testament references to God counseling his children seem to create images of an individual sitting together with a wise counselor who gives helpful direction. Jesus expanded our understanding of divine counsel when he promised his disciples that the day was soon coming when our divine counselor would shift from being with us in time of need to *living* with us and being *in* us. "If you love me, keep my commands. And I will ask the Father, and he will give you another advocate to help you and be with you forever—the Spirit of truth. The world cannot accept him, because it neither sees him nor knows him. But you know him, for he lives with you and will be in you" (John 14:15–17). We have the opportunity to enjoy the daily privilege of having the Holy Spirit living in our hearts and offering us divine counsel.

Our Heavenly Father Is Our Benefactor

A benefactor is someone who looks after us and provides for our needs. Sometimes we know the name of the person and the reason they are helping us; sometimes they remain anonymous. The benefactor may support someone for a limited period of time, like paying university expenses for a degree. Or a benefactor may look after a person's daily needs for a lifetime.

We live in a world filled with so-called self-made individuals. According to them, they owe nothing to anyone; they pulled themselves up by their own bootstraps and fulfilled their dreams all on their own. Christ followers know that this attitude and perception have no place in their lives. We depend on the providential hand of God to provide for us on a daily basis. We realize that God not only created the world but also looks after it, provides for the needs of creation, and guides it to his purposes. On a global level, God superintends the entire universe. On a personal level, God listens carefully to the prayers and petitions of his children and provides for their needs. Like many earthly benefactors, God continues to work quietly in the shadows without recognition. We must never fail to recognize all that he does for us on a daily basis.

The Bible offers more examples than we can mention, but here are a few. Our loving heavenly Father cared deeply for Adam and Eve following the garden fall and provided for them as they adjusted to life outside the perfect environment they left behind. God carefully guided Abram and Sarai as they left their native land and headed by faith to a land God promised them. God also promised them a son and descendants more numerous than all the grains of sand on the seashore, a promise that God fulfilled. God looked after and provided for Joseph as his brothers sold him into enslavement. God carefully cared for the two million slaves he delivered from Egyptian bondage and led back to the promised land. On and on the story goes, right up to the present day. We are just as blessed and resourced by our heavenly Father as the individuals highlighted in Scripture.

Psalm 71 offers us one of the clearest testimonies in Scripture of the providential care of our heavenly Father. The psalmist penned these words not as a young person asking God to be a refuge and deliverer in the days ahead but rather as an old person testifying to God's past faithfulness. Some of the language in Psalm 71 echoes the language of Psalm 22, which Jesus quoted from the cross. Jesus affirmed that he knew the Father would not abandon him but would deliver him (see Ps. 22:19–24).

Read Psalm 71 for yourself slowly and carefully. Then apply each verse to your life and see how you can think in these ways as you live your life each day. The psalmist challenges us with these spiritual truths that have carried him from birth to old age. They will carry us as well.

- God himself is our place of refuge (v. 1).
- God rescues, delivers, saves, and listens to us (v. 2).
- God is our rock of refuge and our fortress where we are always welcome (v. 3).
- "For you have been my hope, Sovereign Lord, my confidence since my youth" (v. 5).
- "From birth I have relied on you; you brought me forth from my mother's womb. I will ever praise you" (v. 6).
- "I have become a sign to many; you are my strong refuge" (v. 7).
- God alone is worthy of our praise as we declare his splendor all day long (v. 8).
- "My mouth will tell of your righteous deeds, of your saving acts all day long—though I know not how to relate them all" (v. 15).
- "Since my youth, God, you have taught me, and to this day I declare your marvelous deeds" (v. 17).

- We can count on God to care for us in old age as we testify of his faithfulness to our children and grandchildren (v. 18).
- "Your righteousness, God, reaches to the heavens, you who have done great things. Who is like you, God?" (v. 19).
- "I will praise you with the harp for your faithfulness, my God; I will sing praise to you with the lyre, Holy One of Israel. My lips will shout for joy when I sing praise to you—I whom you have delivered" (vv. 22–23).

Perhaps the clearest illustration of our heavenly Father as our benefactor appears in the book of Ruth, where Boaz came to the aid of Ruth and her mother-in-law, Naomi. He became Ruth's *go'el*—that is, her redeemer who rescued her from financial plight and disenfranchisement (see Ruth 2–4). In Ruth's case, as with our heavenly Father in our lives, the benefactor continues to rescue and care for those who need him over the long haul of life.

Our Heavenly Father Leads Us Like a Shepherd

We find the imagery of God leading his children like a shepherd throughout both the Old and New Testaments. Sheep cannot be herded or driven like cattle. Sheep are especially prone to wandering if they are not constantly led in the right direction. They both welcome and follow a caring shepherd who gains their trust and provides the pasture and water they need. This metaphor of God as a shepherd, not as a slave driver, should tell us how our God thinks and feels about his special creation.

Perhaps the most famous passage of Scripture, given by God through King David, describes our divine shepherd in Psalm 23. The psalm begins with "The Lord is my shepherd" (v. 1). The psalmist then describes the many ways God guides and provides for his children. He offers a place to rest and leads to quiet waters (v. 2). He restores weary souls and guides in paths of righteousness (v. 3). He supports broken hearts in the dark night of the soul and provides comfort (v. 4). He prepares a table of plenty and anoints the heads of his children with oil (v. 5). He surrounds his children with goodness and mercy and leads them to his eternal dwelling place (v. 6).

At the end of his life, Jacob testified that God had been his shepherd: "Then he blessed Joseph and said, 'May the God before whom my fathers Abraham and Isaac walked faithfully, the God who has been my shepherd all my life to this day. . ." (Gen. 48:15). Isaiah portrayed God in an incredibly inviting way as he described him shepherding his children: "He tends his flock like a shepherd: He gathers the lambs in his arms and carries them close to his heart; he gently leads those that have young" (Isa. 40:11). What more could a child of God ask for than to be gathered into God's strong arms and clutched close to his heart? Notice how he leads: gently. Notice the extra care he takes, like a mother sheep nurturing her lamb. Could you imagine a more winsome image of our loving heavenly Father?

The prophet Jeremiah ministered during the period of exile of the Hebrew people. He looked into the future, to the day when the captives would be released from their bondage and return home to their promised land: "Hear the word of the LORD, you nations; proclaim it in distant coastlands: 'He who scattered Israel will gather them and will watch over his flock like a shepherd'" (Jer. 31:10). Following the exile, the prophet Zechariah also proclaimed this message of God's continued leadership and direction of his children: "The LORD their God will save his people on that day as a shepherd saves his flock. They will sparkle in his land like jewels in a crown" (Zech. 9:16). God, through the prophets, promised to gather his children to himself. He promised to watch over them, save them from whatever harm they may encounter, and glorify his children, making them shine brightly. How much more could any father do for his children?

During his earthly ministry, Jesus used the imagery of sheep and shepherds to describe his relationship with his followers in John 10. Those who heard his message did not understand it at the time, but they later realized Jesus was offering them new insight into God's plan of salvation. He began by referring to himself as a shepherd who enters the

The Christian tradition distinguishes itself from other religions of the world by this astounding truth: God has always reached out to us first.

gate to the sheepfold and calls his sheep by name. His sheep recognize his familiar voice and listen carefully to him. Jesus's disciples did not understand the meaning of these images, so Jesus explained, "I am the gate for the sheep," "I am the good shepherd," and, "I lay down my life for the sheep" (vv. 7, 11, 15). Jesus slipped in a powerful proclamation of the gospel message in this imagery: "I have come that they may have life, and have it to the full" (v. 10). Fulfilling the prophecies of old, Jesus said he was watching over his sheep and keeping them from harm, even to the extent of giving his life for them. Then he said his desire is for us to have not only *eternal* life but also a glorious life *now*. We who follow Christ can rest comfortably in the awareness that we are being led daily by a heavenly Shepherd who loves us very much!

Second Best

When we first began to talk about writing this book, we discussed which resources and references were the best and most important. We decided that the best information about God the Father would come from what God said about himself and what names he used when referring to himself. Then we decided that the second-best information about God the Father would be what Jesus said about him.

Jesus tells us that he is the only one who has actually seen God the Father: "No one has seen the Father except the one who is from God; only he has seen the Father" (John 6:46). We have taken time to list references from the Gospels where Jesus tells us about who the Father is, how he thinks, and what he does in specific situations. Space does not allow for a detailed analysis of each reference, but a few observations include: God the Father is a generous, loving benefactor but also executes justice. God provided Jesus with everything he needed while on earth and gave him all power and a kingdom. Most importantly for our study is what Jesus says in John 14:9: "Anyone who has seen me has seen the Father." The last point is one we have attempted to emphasize. All of the characteristics we see in Jesus also describe the Father.

Take some time and read in context each of these excerpts where Jesus talks about the Father, and meditate on what they tell you about our Father.

Matthew

- 5:48: Perfect
- 6:4: Sees what is done in secret
- 6:8: Knows what you need before you ask him
- 6:14: Will forgive you if you forgive others
- 6:26: Feeds the birds of the air
- 7:11: Gives good gifts to those who ask him
- 11:25: Lord of heaven and earth
- 16:17: Reveals things to us
- 18:35: Wants us to forgive from the heart
- 24:36: The only one who knows about the day when heaven and earth will pass away
- 28:18: Has given all authority to Jesus

Mark

- 10:18: Good
- 10:40: Determines who sits at the right and left hands of Jesus
- 14:36: *Abba*, Father, for whom everything is possible

Luke

- 6:36: Merciful
- 10:21: Has hidden things from the wise and revealed them to children
- 10:22: Committed all things to Jesus
- 11:13: Gives the Holy Spirit to those who ask him
- 12:32: Pleased to give us the kingdom
- 13:23–30: Will make a final judgment
- 22:29: Conferred a kingdom on Jesus

John

- 3:16: Loved the world
- 3:17: Sent the Son into the world to save the world
- 5:17: At his work to this very day

- 5:21: Raises the dead and gives them life
- 5:26: Has life within himself
- 6:32: Provides the true bread from heaven
- 6:44: Draws people to him
- 7:16: Provides Christ's teachings
- 8:28: Taught Jesus
- 8:29: Sent Jesus; has not abandoned Jesus
- 8:42: Sent Jesus
- 12:26: Honors those who serve Jesus
- 12:49–50: Commanded Jesus what to say
- 13:3: Put all things under Jesus's power
- 14:9: Reveals himself through Jesus
- 14:16: Gives a Counselor
- 14:23: Loves
- 15:15: Taught Jesus
- 16:23: Gives whatever is asked in Jesus's name
- 19:11: Gave the power that allowed Jesus to be crucified
- 20:17: Is our Father as well as Jesus's Father

Conclusion

Many cultures in our modern world celebrate individualism and the virtue of self-reliance. "If you can dream it, you can do it" serves as a lofty goal in life. However, being a self-reliant individualist is not God's intent for his children. From the creation of humanity through all of human history and into eternity, it is plain to see that God desires to be in intimate relationship with us. First, he initiates the relationship. Then he demonstrates through the ages that he has all the character traits and attributes anyone would ever want in someone with whom they wish to relate. Finally, as we will see in chapter 10, our heavenly Father intends that this relationship will endure throughout eternity.

Reflection Questions

1. What new information did you learn in this chapter about God?

2. What distorted perceptions of God have you heard from others?

3. Why is it important for Christians to affirm the truth that God reaches out to us first with a desire to live in relationship with us?

4. How would you explain prevenient grace to someone unfamiliar with the concept?

5. In what ways has God helped you in life?

6. How has God been your keeper or protector in time of need?

7. How can you develop a stronger friendship with God?

8. How does the Holy Spirit's presence in your life enrich you?

9. How has God been like a shepherd to you?

10. How can you deepen your relationship with God on a daily basis?

EIGHT

How God Corrects Us

Parents experience one of the greatest God-given joys in life when they welcome a child into their home. Whether through birth or adoption, parents often comment on the flood of emotions that roll over them as they hold their children in their arms for the first time. Everything—from schedules to priorities—changes when parents bring a new child into the home. A newborn requires constant care and attention for the first several months of life. Once children develop increased mobility, parents must establish physical boundaries with things like closed doors, gates, and cabinet door locks to protect the young, curious explorers. All of this is only the beginning of parental boundary-setting for a child.

Both parents and children know well the many rules, guidelines, and boundaries required to guide a child from early childhood to adulthood. Since children do not come with instruction manuals, parents must figure out child rearing as they reach each stage of the process. Bookstores abound with parental resources, and the internet offers a wealth of information. Every parent knows the complex balance between a child's autonomous freedom and parental restrictions that are required at each stage of childhood development.

God's Parental Care and Correction

In chapter 3 we discussed the parental analogy between God and humanity. The emotions, concern, and care that earthly parents have for their children can be said to parallel God's emotions, concern, and care for his children, except that God does it perfectly while earthly parents do not. The

Old Testament offers many examples of God's parental care and correction.

Adam and Eve

Genesis 2 demonstrates that God is a loving and kind provider and protector, not wanting his children to know the difference between good and evil (see vv. 15–17). This restriction was not a limit on what God had provided but something that would keep them from hardship and, ultimately, death. However, God is also a God of perfect justice. His desire was for his creation to love and appreciate him enough that they would be satisfied with what he provided and follow his one and only command. His holiness demanded that, if humanity chose not to follow divine commands, then clearly defined and communicated consequences would follow.

Genesis 3 summarizes the moral failure of the first couple. What do we learn about God from his response? He dealt with each one individually. He ignored their excuses without further discussion. He condemned the serpent, who represented Satan, for the deceptive interaction with Eve. The forewarned consequences followed. These consequences applied not only to Adam and Eve but also to all of their offspring forever. Men still experience the hardships of working for a living. Women still experience pain in childbearing (see vv. 14–19). God understood the significance of these long-term consequences and showed compassion for the couple by making garments of skin to cover their nakedness and provide protection. He limited their suffering by limiting their life span since they would no longer have access to the tree of eternal life.

Cain

Most parents, especially in the early stages of child rearing, do not stand idly by and allow their children to flounder when they are facing moral decisions. Parents often help their children explore their options and attempt to guide them toward a good choice. The severity of consequences usually increases with a child's moral development. In other words, a youngster swiping a cookie from the jar before a meal does not invoke the same consequence as a teenager consuming illegal street drugs. Parents want their children to make righteous choices, and many parents attempt to guide their children appropriately in that direction.

God intervened as a loving parent in the life of Cain in an incredible way. This amazing intervention unfolds in Genesis 4:6–7. Review the story in more detail in our analysis in chapter 5 under the subtitle "God Offers Options." Cain's brother Abel worshiped God with an acceptable sacrifice; Cain failed with his worship offering. God did not immediately punish Cain for his failure. Rather than being angry at himself for not bringing an acceptable sacrifice, Cain focused the anger from his failure onto his brother.

God allowed Cain time to process his situation and his misplaced anger, then intervened directly with him. God attempted to get Cain to see the error of his thinking. He reminded Cain that deep in his heart he knew how to do what was right. He rehearsed the negative consequences of choosing a sinful path. He urged Cain to resist the carnal pull to seek revenge against his brother. God did all that a loving parent can do with a child who is at a moral crossroads. Ultimately, we all decide for ourselves, just as Cain did, but only because a loving God has given us free will.

Noah

Genesis 5 gives us a bird's-eye view of several generations of humanity following the garden fall. Generation after generation followed Cain's lead, ignoring God's directives toward righteous living. We have considered God's capacity for having emotions just like humans. We feel God's deep grief over the state of his fallen children, whom he created in his image and likeness (Gen. 1:27). One of the saddest images of God's emotional disappointment comes at the end of Genesis 6:6: "his heart was deeply troubled." God ultimately will not tolerate people who choose to live corrupt and violent lives (see Gen. 6:11–13).

Then another biblical bright spot appears in the narrative: "But Noah found favor in the eyes of the Lord . . . . Noah was a righteous man, blameless among the people of his time,

God balances love and justice perfectly.

and he walked faithfully with God" (Gen 6:8, 9b). What do we learn about God through Noah's story? Consider these observations.

God takes notice of those who choose to pursue a relationship with him (Gen. 6:9). God communicated directly and personally with a man who served him faithfully. God provided protection for Noah, his family, and many animals with a divinely designed boat. The dimensions of the ark were so perfect that they have been used by cargo ship builders for thousands of years, including up to today. God has perfect knowledge of his creation; he selected the ideal mix of animals needed to reestablish the earth's animal kingdom after the flood.

Following the flood, we see God's loving parental involvement with humanity as he made a promise along with a covenant that he would not curse the ground or destroy all living creatures again. He gave the world a rainbow as a sign of his promise. God followed this promise by communicating his expectations for humanity and indicating that consequences would follow if these expectations were not met (see Gen. 9:3–7). Notice that God communicated a clear set of directives for righteous living long before he gave Moses the Ten Commandments in Exodus.

The Patriarchs

Both the Old and New Testaments refer frequently to God's parental faithfulness in the lives and families of Abraham, Isaac, and Jacob. Genesis extends this family story through the lifetime of Jacob's son Joseph. Abraham lived a life of exemplary righteousness, but he and his family did not always exhibit perfect conduct. They learned firsthand how their decisions affected not only themselves but others as well. He and Sarah lied to the Egyptian pharaoh about their marriage (see Gen. 12:11–13), which lie brought serious consequences to Pharaoh when he acted on their misinformation (see Gen. 12:17). Yet God in his grace delivered Abraham from the full consequences of his lie. He then motivated Pharaoh to take Abraham out of this awkward situation.

Years later, Abraham and Sarah got ahead of God's timing and devised a selfish plan to bring a child into their home (see Gen. 16:1–2). The rest of Genesis 16 and Genesis 21:8–21 recount the dysfunctional family dynamic this decision created not only in Abraham's immediate family but also for the broader Middle East and the world. Even in this situation, God lovingly cared for those who were injured by others' poor decisions. He saw Hagar's misery and blessed and comforted her. The descendants of Isaac and Ishmael have warred against one another from time to time across the past four thousand years.

God's promises to Abraham continued in the story of his son Isaac. We see God's parental faithfulness as he appeared to Isaac and reassured him that he would honor the contract he made with Abraham. God directed Isaac to stay in the promised land through a famine, and to allow God to provide for Isaac's needs. God further promised to make Isaac's descendants as numerous as the stars in the sky, to continue to give him the promised land for his settlement, and to bless the nations of the world through him (see Gen. 26:1–6).

God's patience and long-suffering care encircled Isaac and his wife, Rebekah, even through their many mistakes. Most notably, once their twin sons, Esau and Jacob, were born, the parents created domestic disharmony because Isaac openly favored Esau, and Rebekah openly favored Jacob. Esau traded his birthright as the firstborn (a double inheritance and God's special blessing) for a bowl of Jacob's stew (see Gen. 25:29–34). Rebekah sealed the deal by deceiving her husband into giving the birthright blessing to Jacob rather than Esau (see Gen. 27:1-40). Jacob fled his brother's wrath and escaped to a foreign land.

The saga of God's parental faithfulness continued with Jacob and his complex relationships with his brother, his two wives, his father-in-law, and his twelve sons. Take time to read the family drama in Genesis 27–50. As you read, look for all the ways God worked, both directly and behind the scenes to protect, nurture, and bless his chosen family. Joseph summarized well God's parental care when he said to his betraying brothers, "You intended to harm me, but God intended it for good to accomplish what is now being done, the saving of many lives" (Gen. 50:20).

The stories of the patriarchs remind us that God works intimately in the lives of all who love and serve him. Their lives were as messy and complex as ours can be. God never gave up on them, and he will never give up on us. Did they always make wise decisions? Of course not. Did they sometimes make bad situations worse? Of course they did. God worked within the context in which he found them and redeemed matters in such a way as to foster good for his children. The stories of the patriarchs prove Paul's observation, "And we know that in all things God works for the good of those who love him, who have been called according to his purpose" (Rom. 8:28).

Common Misperceptions

We turn now from examples of God's parental care and correction for individuals in the book of Genesis to current common misperceptions of our loving heavenly Father today. I taught students at Christian universities for thirty years and sometimes asked my students how they perceived members of the divine Trinity. The most common answer I received to that question was, "I love Jesus with all my heart and seek to live daily for him. I am sort of afraid of the Holy Spirit because he is, well you know, a disembodied spirit. I don't know the Father because he is distant and aloof in the Bible, demanding obedience to a lot of rules, orchestrating wars, and harshly punishing disobedience." Students broke my heart every time I heard some variation of that answer. I did my best through readings and classroom instruction to correct their misperception of God the Father.

The following quote from the famous atheist Richard Dawkins is one of the most common evaluations of God the Father: "The God of the Old Testament is arguably the most unpleasant character in all fiction: jealous and proud of it; a petty, unjust, unforgiving control freak; a vindictive, bloodthirsty ethnic cleanser; a misogynistic, homophobic, racist, infanticidal, genocidal, filicidal, pestilential, megalomaniacal, sadomasochistic, capriciously malevolent bully."[1] We read similar charges against God the Father all over the place, for example: he commits crimes against humanity, he is a moral monster, or he promotes ethnic cleansing. Believers know from personal experience that nothing could be further from biblical truth. How, then, should we respond to such hateful charges against our loving heavenly Father? You may never encounter people who think this way. We want to address these charges, however, in case you find yourself trying to defend God and your faith to those who think otherwise.

Like Father, Like Son

Jesus surprised his disciples when he explained to them, "If you really know me, you will know my Father as well. From now on, you do know him and have seen him. . . . Anyone who has seen me has seen the Father" (John 14:7, 9b). How could that be? As hard as it may be for us to process, our Lord and Savior, Jesus Christ, is a full-color, high-definition picture of God the Father! Jesus's disciples were just as amazed when Jesus said this to them as my students were every time I read these verses to them after they confessed their radical misconceptions of the Trinity. The letter to the Hebrews says it well: "The Son is the radiance of God's glory and the exact representation of his being" (Heb. 1:3).

Surprising as it may sound, the words of Jesus in the New Testament Gospels reveal not only the loving, self-giving heart of our Christ but also the heart of our heavenly Father. What we say about Jesus, we must say about the Father, and we can also experience these life-giving qualities from the ministry of the Holy Spirit. God the Father, God the Son, and God the Holy Spirit are of the same essence and substance. What we know about one, we know about all.

With that in mind, let's briefly review the summary statements we made about God in chapter 2.

- God is holy.
- God is love.

---

1. Richard Dawkins, *The God Delusion* (London: Bantam Press, 2006), 50.

- God is just.
- God is the source of all being.
- God is ever living.
- God is personal.
- God is eternal light.
- God is righteous.
- God is truthful.
- God created with wisdom and rules over his creation with wisdom.
- God is all powerful.
- God is sovereign over all creation.
- God is unchanging in nature.

Look over this list and affirm each of these statements about the Father, Son, and Holy Spirit. Sometimes we find it easy to think about one concept or another in isolation. But what happens when we expand our thinking about how these attributes or qualities all work together in one unified, divine person?

This process can be especially tricky as we explore how God corrects behavior. Think, for example, about how God's holiness, love, and justice work in harmony. Many Christians today focus primary attention on God's love to the exclusion of his holiness and justice. The Bible clearly tells us that God is a loving heavenly Father. He loved the world so much that he sent his Son into the world to save humanity and not to condemn the world (see John 3:16–17). Jesus said of our loving heavenly Father, "He causes his sun to rise on the evil and the good, and sends rain on the righteous and the unrighteous" (Matt. 5:45). His love allows him to be long suffering (see 2 Peter 3:9).

That is not the entire picture, however. Our heavenly Father must also execute justice because his basic character of holiness demands it. Holiness takes precedence; it is the only attribute that is repeated three times, for emphasis, when describing him. He cannot violate his basic character. Therefore, when someone resists the conviction of the Holy Spirit and willfully chooses to sin against God, as defined by God throughout Scripture, and remains unrepentant, God must execute justice (see Mal. 1:2–3; Jude 1:4, 7–8, 13–14, 22–23; Rev. 2:6). Amazingly, as with all that God is and does, he balances love and justice perfectly. His love offers forgiveness through his Son. At the same time, he cannot forever tolerate sin or those who choose to live in sin. Unfortunately, we are not like God in this way; we rarely find a way to balance love and justice appropriately the way God does.

Critics sometimes accuse God the Father of inconsistency, for judging individuals who have not heard or had an opportunity to respond to the gospel. Paul reminds us that even if an individual has not been directly exposed to the gospel, God has made himself plain to all through natural creation:

> The wrath of God is being revealed from heaven against all the godlessness and wickedness of people, who suppress the truth by their wickedness, since what may be known about God is plain to them, because God has made it plain to them. For since the creation of the world God's invisible qualities—his eternal power and divine nature—have been clearly seen, being understood from what has been made, so that people are without excuse. (Rom. 1:18–20)[2]

God balances love and justice even in this situation, judging individuals based on the measure of spiritual light they have been given.

Additional Divine Attributes

Before we address current common misconceptions of the God of the Old Testament, we need to add additional divine attributes to the list from the last section of material.

Impartiality

We live in a world where judges can be influenced to favor one person over another. This reality has existed throughout recorded history. God challenged the Israelites as they prepared to enter the promised land, "Do not pervert justice or show partiality. Do not accept a bribe, for a bribe blinds the

---

2. See also Rom. 1:20; 2:15; Ps. 19:1–4; 97:6; Acts 14:17.

eyes of the wise and twists the words of the innocent" (Deut. 16:19). Isaiah warned judges in his day, "Woe to those who make unjust laws, to those who issue oppressive decrees, to deprive the poor of their rights and withhold justice from the oppressed of my people, making widows their prey and robbing the fatherless" (Isa. 10:1–2).

For God to have perfect judgment means he judges impartially. Moses reminded his people of this in his final address to them: "For the Lord your God is God of gods and Lord of lords, the great God, mighty and awesome, who shows no partiality and accepts no bribes" (Deut. 10:17). King Jehoshaphat appointed judges in his kingdom and gave them this challenge: "Now let the fear of the Lord be on you. Judge carefully, for with the Lord our God there is no injustice or partiality or bribery" (2 Chron. 19:7). The apostle Peter also reminded his readers of God's impartiality: "Since you call on a Father who judges each person's work impartially, live out your time as foreigners here in reverent fear" (1 Peter 1:17).

Jealousy

Many parents teach their children not to be jealous of others. Cultures throughout history have condemned jealousy as a vice. However, the Bible teaches us that God is a jealous God. The second of the Ten Commandments says, "You shall not bow down to them or worship them; for I, the Lord your God, am a jealous God" (Exod. 20:5). God offered further instruction to Moses: "Be careful to do everything I have said to you. Do not invoke the names of other gods; do not let them be heard on your lips" (Exod. 23:13). Moses reminded his people in his last address to them, "Be careful not to forget the covenant of the Lord your God that he made with you; do not make for yourselves an idol in the form of anything the Lord your God has forbidden. For the Lord your God is a consuming fire, a jealous God" (Deut. 4:23–24).[3]

Scripture offers a stark contrast between human jealousy and divine jealousy. Children as well as adults can become jealous of friends or family members who have something

---

3. See also Exod. 34:14; Lev. 26:1; 1 Kings 14:22; Ps. 78:58.

Our heavenly Father has never been a war-mongering conqueror for the sake of political conquest. God prefers peace over war whenever possible and welcomes all the nations of the world to love and serve him.

they do not possess. Such a reaction stems from selfishness, covetousness, or greed. They cannot be happy with what they have because they are obsessed with what others have. Divine jealousy, on the other hand, has our best interest in mind. The Hebrew term for "jealous" (*qanna'*) can also be translated "zealous." It conveys passionate concern. The NET Bible translation note reads, "The word 'jealous' is the same word often translated 'zeal' or 'zealous.' The word describes a passionate intensity to protect or defend something that is jeopardized." God jealously guards his children and is jealous of what holds their affection. God alone is worthy of our worship, praise, honor, devotion, and total commitment because he is the one, true, ever-living God.

Closer

The host of a popular television game show often asks a haunting question following a contestant's answer to a game question: "Is that your final answer?" The rules of the game state that contestants cannot replace their answer after they declare their final answer. Scripture tells us that God expects a final answer. Moses challenged his people to finally choose the God/god they would serve: "See, I set before you today life and prosperity, death and destruction" (Deut. 30:15). Joshua, the Israelite leader who followed Moses, challenged the people this way: "But if serving the LORD seems undesirable to you, then choose for yourselves this day whom you will serve, whether the gods your ancestors served beyond the Euphrates, or the gods of the Amorites, in whose land you are living. But as for me and my household, we will serve the LORD" (Josh. 24:15). The prophet Elijah challenged the people with this: "How long will you waver between two opinions? If the LORD is God, follow him; but if Baal is God, follow him" (1 Kings 18:21). God instructed the prophet Jeremiah to tell his people: "See, I am setting before you the way of life and the way of death" (Jer. 21:8; see also Jer. 38:20–23).

We serve a God of grace and mercy. He often gave second chances to individuals from Genesis to Revelation, and he continues to do the same today. Never forget, however, that the time will arrive in every person's life when God calls for a final decision. He will then close the window to further responses and judge accordingly.

Response to Culture's Misperceptions of God

God's contracts with Abraham in Genesis 12, 15, and 17 promised a homeland for him and his descendants. Those who read the Bible for the first time might think Abraham and his family arrived at their destination to find the real estate vacant. Not so. Abraham found other groups of people living in the land; Joshua discovered similar inhabitants when he led the Hebrew nation back from Egyptian slavery. The inhabitants did not comprise great nations as we may imagine. Rather, they lived in villages and city-states, which were urban centers for several local villages, farmers, and herdsmen. These had walls and rulers with more organization than tribal villages. Places like Hazor and Lachish were of this type. These people groups were separated by mountain ranges and distinguished by culture, custom, and religion. The battles God directed the Israelites to fight with these various cities were never ethnically motivated. Their motivation for these actions lay primarily with the practices of their pagan religions.

We hear reports every day from various news sources about violent crimes committed around the world, often in our own hometowns. Violent gangs rain down terror on citizens as they rob, rape, and murder innocent victims. Friends and family members cry passionately into the news camera, "Where is justice for our child?" "Say her name!" "We demand that the guilty person be punished for this crime." We compassionately identify with these victims and their families in their time of grief and loss. We understand their demands for justice and for an end to despicable crimes. Throughout Scripture, we learn that God listens compassionately to the outcries of suffering from innocent victims. In the days of Abraham, we read, "Then the LORD said, 'The outcry against Sodom and Gomorrah is so great and their sin so grievous that I will go down and see if what they have done is as bad as the outcry that has reached me. If not, I will know'" (Gen. 18:20–21). God sent two heavenly representatives on a reconnaissance mission to the sinful cities. They told Lot, "The outcry to the LORD against its people is so great that he has sent us to destroy it" (Gen. 19:13). The pervasive sin of the citizens brought God's total destruction to the entire area. The Bible offers frequent reminders of this event in Deuteronomy, Amos, Isaiah, Jeremiah, Ezekiel, Zephaniah, and Lamentations in the Old Testament and by Peter, Paul, Jude, and John in the New Testament.

Consider the cultural and pagan religious practices of the Canaanites who occupied the promised land when the Hebrew people returned from Egyptian slavery. Deviant sexual practices dominated the culture, including bestiality and incest. Vulgar sexual symbols of their pagan religion stood boldly in front of their homes. Worshipers even practiced sorcery, idolatry, deviant behavior of their gods and goddesses, and worst of all, child sacrifice.[4] God clearly condemned these pagan practices (Exod. 22:19; Lev. 18:6–18; 20:2–5; Jer. 32:35). "Do not give any of your children to be sacrificed to Molek, for you must not profane the name of your God. I am the LORD" (Lev. 18:21). Examples abound in Scripture of kings and prophets violently opposing child sacrifice.[5] Our loving heavenly Father could no longer allow these pagan reprobates to harm the women and children in these ways. Their godlessness had to be purged from the land. Justice had to be served.

God did not want the Hebrew people to blend in with pagan culture, make treaties with their neighbors, intermarry with them, or adopt their religious practices.[6] God commanded, "Break down their altars, smash their sacred stones, cut down their Asherah poles and burn their idols in the fire. For you are a people holy to the LORD your God. The LORD your God has chosen you out of all the peoples on the face of the earth to be his people, his treasured possession" (Deut. 7:5–6). Later God instructed, "Destroy completely all the places on the high

---

4. This book highlighted an example of this global practice in chapter 1 when describing the Peruvian burial site containing the skeletons of more than 140 children and 200 llamas offered to the rain gods during a period of drought. Such hideous practices of victimizing children breaks God's heart according to Deuteronomy 7 and 12.

5. See, for example, 2 Kings 3:27; 23:10; Isa. 30:33; Jer. 7:31.

6. This command had nothing to do with ethnicity but with the influence a marriage partner would have leading to idol worship as with Solomon.

mountains, on the hills and under every spreading tree, where the nations you are dispossessing worship their gods. Break down their altars, smash their sacred stones and burn their Asherah poles in the fire; cut down the idols of their gods and wipe out their names from those places. You must not worship the LORD your God in their way" (Deut. 12:2–4).

Stephen Green summarized God's reasoning for his commands to the Hebrew people:

> The command to destroy the Canaanite sacred places includes objects used in worship by the Canaanites: altars, sacred stone, Asherah poles, and idols. The underlying rationale is that these objects and the places associated with them would influence and shape Israel's religious life if they were left in the land as Israel took possession of the land. People become habituated through their practices and value systems. Therefore, the elimination of these places and objects would also eliminate the practices associated with these places. The act of destruction not only removed the temptation for Israel to lapse into Canaanite forms of worship, but it eradicated the name of the gods from that place. Only one name can be associated with the land, and it is the name of the God who fulfilled his promises to the people. The name of Yahweh is to be glorified in the whole of the land.[7]

God did not hate the Canaanite people. Before the conquest of Jericho, the Canaanites saw God's power at work with his chosen people but refused to accept him (see Josh. 2:10–11). Rahab witnessed to the Hebrew spies, "When we heard of it [Hebrew conquests], our hearts melted in fear and everyone's courage failed because of you, for the LORD your God is God in heaven above and on the earth below" (Josh. 2:11). She alone among the citizens of Jericho sought to serve the Hebrew God. The Israelites saved Rahab and welcomed her into their faith community (see Josh. 2:1–24; 6:17). Our heavenly Father honored Rahab in a special way by including her in the genealogy

---

7. Stephen Green, *Deuteronomy: A Commentary in the Wesleyan Tradition,* New Beacon Bible Commentary (Kansas City, MO: Beacon Hill Press of Kansas City, 2016), 139.

of his Son, Jesus Christ (see Matt. 1:5). Imagine that. One of Jesus's great-grandmothers was a Canaanite.

People have fought wars throughout recorded history. The Israelite conquest of the promised land looked in many ways like any other tribal war, with one important difference. They fought a religious war in the name of their holy and righteous God, who called them to be holy just as he is holy. The exclusivity of their faith distinguished them from their pagan neighbors. That same exclusivity continued in the New Testament, where Peter declared, "Salvation is found in no one else, for there is no other name under heaven given to mankind by which we must be saved" (Acts 4:12). Peter, of course, spoke of our Lord and Savior Jesus Christ, the one true and living God, who alone is worthy of worship, praise, honor, and glory.

We must consider one additional thought about the Hebrew nation settling in the promised land. They did not war against every tribe and people group they encountered. They lived peacefully as good neighbors with many of them. Language or ethnic and cultural differences did not agitate them to aggression. The Hebrews went to war only with those who practiced detestable pagan religions that harmed women and children and blasphemed their Creator God.

Our heavenly Father has never been a war-mongering conqueror for the sake of political conquest. We know this because of the message he gave King David after his many victories in wars for political conquest. "David said to Solomon: 'My son, I had it in my heart to build a house for the Name of the LORD my God. But this word of the LORD came to me: "You have shed much blood and have fought many wars. You are not to build a house for my Name, because you have shed much blood on the earth in my sight"'" (1 Chron. 22:7–8). God wanted his house to be a house of prayer that welcomed everyone to worship:

> And foreigners who bind themselves to the LORD to minister to him, to love the name of the LORD, and to be his servants, all who keep the Sabbath without desecrating it and who hold fast to my covenant — these I will bring to my holy mountain and give them joy in my house of prayer. Their burnt offerings and sacrifices will be accept-

ed on my altar; for my house will be called a house of
prayer for all nations.
(Isa. 56:6–7)
God prefers peace over war whenever possible and welcomes
all the nations of the world to love and serve him.

Conclusion

The Scripture passages and content of this chapter remind us that our heavenly Father wants the best for our lives.
He seeks to correct us when we need it, just as earthly parents
do for their children. Why? Because he loves us. Moses reminded the Hebrew nation of God's discipline: "Know then in
your heart that as a man disciplines his son, so the LORD your
God disciplines you" (Deut. 8:5).

The writer to the Hebrews spoke extensively on the
importance of divine discipline in Hebrews 12. He quoted
from Proverbs 3:11–12: "My son, do not make light of the
Lord's discipline, and do not lose heart when he rebukes you,
because the Lord disciplines the one he loves, and he chastens
everyone he accepts as his son" (Heb. 12:5–6). The writer concluded this subject with, "They [our fathers] disciplined us for
a little while as they thought best; but God disciplines us for
our good, in order that we may share in his holiness. No discipline seems pleasant at the time, but painful. Later on, however, it produces a harvest of righteousness and peace for those
who have been trained by it" (Heb. 12:10–11). We must always
remember that our heavenly Father corrects and disciplines us
because he loves us so much.

Reflection Questions

1. What new information did you learn in this chapter about God?

2. How was God's parental correction of individuals in the book of Genesis similar to the way parents correct their children today?

3. Why do you think Christians who read their Bibles and attend church regularly continue to have misconceptions of God the Father?

4. Why do you think the world has such terrible misperceptions of God the Father?

5. How does a biblical understanding of the heart of Jesus as evidenced through his life and ministry help us better understand God the Father?

6. Why do many people prefer to focus attention on God's love to the exclusion of his holiness and justice?

7. How is God's jealousy intended for our best interest?

8. How is God's justice a response to the outcry of suffering and innocent victims?

9. How would you explain God's command to destroy the Canaanite culture to someone who does not understand?

10. How would you compare God's reasons for parental discipline to the reasons parents discipline their children?

NINE

How God's Plans Come Together

Grandparents enjoy a double blessing in life. They watch their children grow and mature into adulthood, and then they watch their children raise children. It is especially rewarding for grandparents to hear their grandchildren say or do things they taught their own children to say or do. Grandchildren sometimes even quote their parents with familiar words that grandparents taught to their parents. Family sayings or traits often carry from one generation to the next in remarkable ways. The same generational transfer is often true in families of faith who place a high priority on passing their faith in Jesus Christ on to their children. Local communities of faith occasionally honor a couple on a special wedding anniversary with several generations of family members who all know Christ as their personal Savior.

From Generation to Generation

Abraham and Sarah lived lives of righteousness, faith, and obedience to God despite their occasional missteps. The Bible greatly honors their examples of spiritual resolve through the ups and downs of life (see Heb. 11:8–12). Our loving heavenly Father revealed to them his plan to bless not only them but also their ancestors for a thousand generations. And not just their family, but the Lord also promised that their ancestors would bless all the nations of the world. The remainder of the Bible from Genesis to Revelation details God's faithfulness to this promise.

Abraham could not possibly comprehend God's promise as he looked into the night sky and saw more stars than he could ever count (see Gen. 15:5; 22:17). But he believed God in spite of the magnitude of the promise! His unswerving faith in the God he loved led to God crediting "it to him as righteousness" (Gen. 15:6). The prophet Habakkuk echoed this reminder centuries later: "but the righteous person will live by his faithfulness" (Hab. 2:4). Abraham and Sarah remind us that we must always trust in the God we love and serve in spite of situations that might give us reason to doubt him—because our God faithfully fulfills his promises.

Despite repeated failures by many if not most of the descendants of Abraham and Sarah, God continued to work with the few who remained faithful. Our God consistently shows his persistence in pursuing his chosen people, the Israelites. Christ expanded the family during his earthly ministry to include whoever believes in him. Once again, our God has faithfully guided and blessed those who chose to put their faith in him from generation to generation. God offered specific directions for effectively passing the faith on to the next generation: "These commandments that I give you today are to be on your hearts. Impress them on your children. Talk about them when you sit at home and when you walk along the road, when you lie down and when you get up. Tie them as symbols on your hands and bind them on your foreheads. Write them on the doorframes of your houses and on your gates" (Deut. 6:6–9).

As the Lord guided this generational process and fulfilled his promise to Abraham and Sarah, he also enabled all who lived a life of faith and trust in him to experience his original desires for his children, which we explored in chapter 4. You might want to review God's five desires discussed in that chapter. As you review God's desires, reflect on the ways God has fulfilled those desires in your own life. You might be amazed at how much he has done for you in the past and what he is accomplishing in your life right now.

God's Desires for Humanity Realized

As documented in previous chapters, the entire Bible clearly communicates God's desire to live in intimate relationship with his children. We now have more than four thousand years of salvation history where we see God's desires realized in the lives of men, women, youth, and children. Believers have faithfully lived out and then passed on their witness of a personal relationship with God to their children, other relatives, and friends. God's desire for a personal relationship with all who come to him has continued to live and grow as the progressive self-revelation of God has increased through the ages of time. We are so blessed not only to have the "great cloud of witnesses" (Heb. 12:1) who have blazed a trail for us but especially also the presence of the Holy Spirit within our hearts guiding us into a deeper relationship with him.

Next, God initiated the idea of entering into a covenant or contract with individuals. He always started the conversation, he clearly set the terms of the contract, and he committed himself to remain faithful to his end of the contract. Sometimes his faithfulness depended on individuals also remaining faithful; sometimes he indicated he would continue his faithfulness regardless of how individuals responded. Some of the individuals who entered into contracts with God in the Old Testament include Adam, Eve, Noah, Abraham, Moses, and David. We see God's faithfulness to these contracts bestowed upon the Hebrew nation, also known as the Israelites, later referred to as the Jewish people. His faithfulness to his chosen people continues to this day.

In the New Testament and the age of the church, we see God expanding his contractual faithfulness to all believers in the church of Jesus Christ. Peter, writing to Christians of all ethnic backgrounds, described it this way: "But you are a chosen people, a royal priesthood, a holy nation, God's special possession" (1 Peter 2:9). By comparing this verse to Deuteronomy 7:6, we realize God has extended to the believers in the Christian church all of the spiritual promises he made to the Israelites. God's contractual relationship with his children gives us all the assurance we need that he will continue his faithfulness to believers to the end of the age. The assurance in your life and daily walk affirms that he will never leave you nor forsake you (see Deut. 31:6, 8; Heb. 13:5).

Then God desired to be our redeemer. He talked to Moses at the burning bush about being a redeemer of the enslaved Hebrews in Egypt. God proved himself as a redeemer when he miraculously delivered his chosen people, cared for them during their desert journey, and brought them safely to the promised land. Leaders of the Hebrew people down through the ages of the Old Testament worshiped and praised God for his physical deliverance from slavery. More than eighty times throughout the Bible we read a variation of this powerful testimony: "With a powerful hand the Lord brought us out of Egypt, from the house of slavery" (Exod. 13:14). Later in Hebrew history, the prophets spoke of God's redemption being not only physical but also spiritual. Zechariah indicated that God will send the Messiah (9:9), bring peace and salvation (9:10, 16), destroy Jerusalem's enemies (12:1–14), and establish God's kingdom (14:9).

The New Testament expressed God's desire to be our redeemer as he offered redemption from sin to the entire world. The Father sent his Son, Jesus Christ, into our world not to condemn people but to save all who accept his offer (see John 1:14; 3:16–17). Paul said, "In him we have redemption through his blood, the forgiveness of sins, in accordance with the riches of God's grace" (Eph. 1:7). Paul explained that we must confess our sins and admit that we "fall short of the glory of God" (Rom. 3:23). However, God does not leave us in the sinful mess we have made of our lives. We can personally call upon God and seek his offer of redemption from sin. Then "all are justified freely by his grace through the redemption that came by Christ Jesus" (Rom. 3:24). These are not just religious words about an abstract theological concept. They are words of hope offered to you personally that God is ready to forgive you of your sins when you confess them, come to live in your heart, bring peace, adopt you into his family, and make you into the person you really want to be, with his help.

Beyond that, God desired a spiritual kingdom in our world. He worked with Abraham's descendants to form the Hebrew nation. However, except for the golden age of King David and King Solomon, God's people never became the spiritual kingdom God intended. His desire, from the beginning of time, came to fruition with those who believed in his Son, Jesus Christ. God established his earthly spiritual kingdom with the inauguration of his church on the day of Pentecost (see Acts 2).

Some members of the early church had a difficult time understanding that God wanted to include gentiles in his spiritual kingdom. God revealed his will plainly to Peter when God sent him to believers gathered at Cornelius's house. Peter said, "I now realize how true it is that God does not show favoritism but accepts from every nation the one who fears him and does what is right" (Acts 10:34–35). That is very good news for us today because most Christians around the world are gentiles (non-Jews). We the authors of this book are gentiles; you may be too. God welcomes everyone into his spiritual kingdom that continues for all eternity.

Finally, God desired to fill believers with his Spirit. Old Testament prophets were made aware of God's desire long before it happened. Jeremiah quoted the Lord: "I will put my law in their minds and write it on their hearts. I will be their God, and they will be my people" (31:33). Ezekiel proclaimed God's plan: "I will give you a new heart and put a new spirit in you; I will remove from you your heart of stone and give you a heart of flesh. And I will put my Spirit in you and move you to follow my decrees and be careful to keep my laws" (36:26–27). Joel also recognized God's voice when he spoke of that day: "I will pour out my Spirit on all people" (2:28).

We can now look back to the day of Pentecost when God fulfilled this long-awaited promise of filling believers with his Holy Spirit (see Acts 2:1–4). God also filled the gentile believers with his Holy Spirit (see Acts 10:44; 19:6). Paul offered a new insight when he revealed that the Holy Spirit not only brings us the presence of the ever-living Christ but also, like a down payment on a purchase, God "has given us the Spirit as a deposit, guaranteeing what is to come" (2 Cor. 5:5). The last phrase of this verse, "what is to come," refers to our heavenly home with the triune God.

The Mission of God

This book has focused primary attention on scriptural insights into God the Father. The saints of God throughout the Old Testament did not fully grasp the concept of a heavenly Father until he sent his Son to live among us. Jesus Christ preached and taught clearly about his, and our, Father. When Jesus returned to the Father following his resurrection, they sent the Holy Spirit to live within our hearts. Now, we know that our one Lord (Deut. 6:4) is Father, Son, and Spirit.

However, God's self-revelation did not reach its culmination with the coming of the Holy Spirit on the day of Pentecost. Rather, the high point of God's self-revelation came at the inauguration of the Christian church. The Father commissioned everyone who trusted in his Son as Lord and Savior to become an ambassador of the gospel message through the power of the Holy Spirit to the entire world. Jesus challenged his disciples with the Great Commission at the conclusion of his earthly ministry: "All authority in heaven and on earth has been given to me. Therefore go and make disciples of all nations, baptizing them in the name of the Father and of the Son and of the Holy Spirit, and teaching them to obey everything I have commanded you. And surely I am with you always, to the very end of the age" (Matt. 28:18–20).

That means that God—Father, Son, and Spirit—invites believers to join him in his mission to the world. This mission of God to live in intimate relationship with every man, woman, teenager, and child in the world has been God's desire since the day he created humanity. Church leaders sometimes refer to this when they say, "The church has a mission." The opposite is actually closer to reality: God's mission has a church. As members of his spiritual kingdom, we have the opportunity to cooperate with God through the Holy Spirit's empowerment in all he is doing in our world to proclaim the good news of John 3:16–17: "For God so loved the world that he gave his one and only Son, that whoever believes in him shall not perish but have eternal life. For God did not send his Son into the world to condemn the world, but to save the world through him."

Our heavenly Father sent his Son to us to preach and teach the new covenant (contract) he was entering into with humanity. The New Testament explains that new covenant in detail. The Sermon on the Mount (Matt. 5–7) illustrates an entirely new understanding of God's will for our lives. At the conclusion of his earthly ministry, Jesus offered himself as a sacrifice on the cross for our sins. We find forgiveness and new birth as we enter an intimate relationship with God. Jesus's incarnation in our world also gave us an example to follow. Everything our heavenly Father desires for believers can be summarized in one word: Christlikeness.

The mission of God informs the mission of the church: to make Christlike disciples in the nations. As his commissioned ambassadors, we want everyone in the world to hear the good news of redemption in Jesus Christ. We want them to accept Christ as their Lord and Savior so God can transform them into his disciples. Phineas F. Bresee, the first general superintendent in the Church of the Nazarene and widely recognized as that denomination's founder, summarized it this way: "The church of God, in its highest forms on earth and in heaven, has its gatherings, teachings, and united worship, but it is all to help the individual into the likeness of his Son."[1]

The mission of God has served as a backdrop to every chapter of this book. God declared everything he made at creation as "good." He proclaimed his greatest creation, humanity, as "very good." He enjoyed the relationship he had with Adam and Eve during their walks together in the cool of the evening (see Gen. 3:8). All was well in paradise until the fall of the first couple. God has consistently worked from then until now to restore his relationship with all who want to know him. He has a unique plan for doing that. Peter summarized God's desire well:

> His divine power has given us everything we need for a godly life through our knowledge of him who called us by his own glory and goodness. Through these he has given us his very great and precious promises, so that through them you may *participate in the divine nature*, having escaped the corruption in the world caused by evil desires.
> (2 Peter 1:3–4, emphasis added).

---

1. "Nazarene Essentials: Who We Are—What We Believe," *Holiness Today* (March/April 2015, Vol. 17, No. 2): 5, https://www.nazarene.org/nazarene-essentials-documents.

What an incredible thought: God welcomes us to participate in his divine nature. God hinted at his desire for our lives throughout Scripture. Genesis 1:26 reminds us that God originally created us in his own image and likeness. We are unique from every other living being in this world. The psalmist summarized it well: "You have made them a little lower than the angels and crowned them with glory and honor. You made them rulers over the works of your hands; you put everything under their feet: all flocks and herds, and the animals of the wild, the birds in the sky, and the fish in the sea, all that swim the paths of the seas" (Ps. 8:5–8).

Jesus himself hinted at the Father's goal of Christlikeness for us when he said, "Be perfect, therefore, as your heavenly Father is perfect" (Matt. 5:48). Paul testified to the Spirit's transforming work in his second letter to the Corinthian church: "And we all, who with unveiled faces contemplate the Lord's glory, are being transformed into his image with ever-increasing glory, which comes from the Lord, who is the Spirit" (2 Cor. 3:18). John reminded us that the Holy Spirit's transformation takes place both during the days of our earthly life and on the last day: "See what great love the Father has lavished on us, that we should be called children of God! And that is what we are! . . . Dear friends, now we are children of God, and what we will be has not yet been made known. But we know that when Christ appears, *we shall be like him*, for we shall see him as he is" (1 John 3:1a–b, 2, emphasis added).

The early Christian church understood the Father's desire to make his children like his Son, Jesus Christ. Irenaeus (d. ca. 200), bishop of Lyon, said something like this: "God became what we are so that we may become what God is."[2] Likewise, Athanasius (d. 373), bishop of Alexandria, said, "God was made man that we might be made God."[3] That may sound heretical to some ears; after all, humans can never become equal to the Creator God! Think of it this way: God the Son became human in order to show us the way to become divine (with a lowercase d—indeed, we will never equal the God we worship). In becoming human, Jesus did not cease to be God. Therefore, in becoming Christlike, we will never cease to be human in this earthly life. Jesus exemplified being fully human. As we live fully in Christ, with the mind of Christ (see 1 Cor. 2:16), participating daily in fellowship with him, the Holy Spirit transforms us more and more into Christlikeness. Down through church history, scholars have attempted to describe this work of the Spirit in our lives by concluding that God's aim and work is to make us more like Christ.

God's Two Gifts to Us

The Father never expects us to become like his Son by mere dedicated effort, habitual practice, or even following trendy schemes. He offers us two gifts to fulfill his desire: (1) the means of grace, and (2) the fellowship of other believers within a community of faith. The means of grace include such practices as public and personal prayer, meditation, Scripture reading, participating in the Lord's Supper, personal and corporate worship, fellowship with believers, fasting, discipline, service, and sometimes suffering. God wants us as believers to practice various means of grace in our lives on a daily basis. "As Christians *use* the means of grace, they *participate* in the hope of glory and become *partakers* of the divine nature."[4]

The community of faith provides not only worship and fellowship but also accountability, Christian counsel, emotional support, and an avenue to serve others with the gifts given to believers by the Holy Spirit. God never intends for us to live our Christian lives in isolation; we must not cloister ourselves in a private world. The author of the book of Hebrews challenges us with this important reminder: "Let us consider how we may spur one another on toward love and good deeds, not giving up meeting together, as some are in

---

4. McCormick, "Theosis," 538.

the habit of doing, but encouraging one another—and all the more as you see the Day approaching" (10:24–25).

We have learned a great deal about God in this book. Everything we have discovered tells us he would never hide from us a set of standards or requirements and then surprise us with them on judgment day. The Bible tells us everything we need to know to be prepared for that day. We must remember God always finishes what he starts in us: "being confident of this, that he who began a good work in you will carry it on to completion until the day of Christ Jesus" (Phil. 1:6). Paul says later in this same letter that God will correct our misunderstandings and make clear his will for our lives (see 3:15). Anytime we doubt the value of our participation in the means of grace and the community of believers, we must remember that the Holy Spirit will be faithful to guide us into all truth and seal us for the day of complete redemption (see Eph. 1:13).

More Like Jesus

While ministering as a theology professor at a Christian university, I once had a student in class who entertained me every day in a unique way. He listened carefully to my lecture and classroom discussion. On his way out of the room at the conclusion of every class, he handed me a full-page drawing of a scene that captured the essence of the day's subject. The drawings were amazing. I received my favorite one after our discussion of Christlikeness. When I read it, I laughed out loud. He had drawn a family scene that occurred in Nazareth at the home of Joseph and Mary. The children were arguing with one another about sibling nonsense. Mary reached her limit and asked in frustration, "Why can't you kids be more like Jesus?"

I have pondered that question my entire life. In my student's drawing, the question sounded humorous. But, with careful consideration, it is one of the most important questions the Father wants us to ask as we seek to become like his Son. Pastor Charles M. Sheldon (1857–1946) brought the question into cultural conversations in 1896 with the release of his famous book, *In His Steps: What Would Jesus Do?*. The question received renewed attention a few decades ago when most of my college students and hundreds of thousands of fellow believers wore colorful elastic bracelets with the letters "WWJD" printed on them. Everyone who knew anything about the bracelets knew the letters were supposed to remind them to listen to the still, small voice of God with every decision of the day. The bracelet served as a challenge to seek the mind of Christ not only with every daily decision but also as God's ambassador to the world, inviting everyone into a personal relationship with Christ.

The Father's desire for us to become more like Jesus is possible through the presence of the Holy Spirit (see Col. 1:27). You may be asking what that might look like in your daily routine. The following offers a sampling of the Father's desire for us found in the life and ministry of Jesus.

1. Jesus loved the Father first and foremost; then he loved us as an outgrowth of their love for each other (see Matt. 22:37-40).

2. Jesus had a winsome personality (see John 6:1-2).
3. Jesus lived a life of humility (see Matt. 18:1-5).
4. Jesus lived a balanced life of work, rest, ministry, and leisure (see John 6:22).
5. Jesus had a sense of humor (see Matt. 7:3).
6. Jesus had a heart of compassion and gave his hands to compassionate ministry (see Matt. 8:14-17).
7. Jesus lived a life of fairness (see Matt. 16:13-23).
8. Jesus was courteous (see John 4:4-26).
9. Jesus was thoughtful (see Luke 22:50-51).
10. Jesus paid compliments and showed appreciation (see Luke 7:36-50).
11. Jesus did not attempt to create conflict with his enemies, but when it arose he did not run from it (see John 4:1-3).
12. Jesus did not contemplate his plight in life and feel sorry for himself (see Luke 23:28-31).
13. Jesus was not vindictive and did not retaliate when others treated him wrongly (see Matt. 5:38-46).
14. Jesus did not need to make a name for himself (see Matt. 12:11-16).

15. Jesus expressed strong emotion and indignation when the occasion called for it (see Matt. 21:12–13).
16. Jesus showed great courage throughout his life (see Luke 4:1–13).
17. Jesus had a clear mission and purpose for his life (see John 4:34–38).
18. Jesus lived with eternity's values in view (see Matt. 24–25).
19. Jesus realized and accepted his human limitations (see Matt. 26:36–46).
20. Jesus always sought to do the will of his Father (see John 4:34; 6:38).
21. Jesus lived in constant communion with his Father (see John 11:41–42).
22. Jesus depended on the Holy Spirit for constant spiritual strength and encouragement (see John 17:1–26).
23. Jesus lived a life of service (see John 13:15).
24. Jesus submitted himself to suffering on our behalf (see 1 Peter 2:21).
25. Jesus submitted himself to death on the Cross to accomplish our salvation (see Matt. 27:32–56).[5]

Jesus also exemplified such qualities as patience, sympathy, frankness, cooperation, discernment, non-conformity, reconciliation, and peace. No book could possibly list all of the admirable qualities of Jesus Christ. He did all things well!

Peter offered a good list of godly qualities for believers who want to live into God's desire for them: "For this very reason, make every effort to add to your faith goodness; and to goodness, knowledge; and to knowledge, self-control; and to self-control, perseverance; and to perseverance, godliness; and to godliness, mutual affection; and to mutual affection, love" (2 Peter 1:5–7). Paul also suggested the following advice on this matter: "We also glory in our sufferings, because we know that suffering produces perseverance; perseverance, character; and character, hope. And hope does not put us to shame, be-

5. Frank Moore, *Breaking Free from Sin's Grip: Holiness Defined for a New Generation* (Kansas City, MO: Beacon Hill Press of Kansas City, 2001), 127–32.

God's self-revelation did not reach its culmination with the coming of the Holy Spirit on the day of Pentecost. Rather, the high point of God's self-revelation came at the inauguration of the Christian church.

cause God's love has been poured out into our hearts through the Holy Spirit, who has been given to us" (Rom. 5:3–5).

Paul again emphasizes how the Father makes us more like his Son in Romans 8: "Therefore, there is now no condemnation for those who are in Christ Jesus, because through Christ Jesus the law of the Spirit who gives life has set you free from the law of sin and death" (vv. 1–2). Paul goes on to say that "those who live in accordance with the Spirit have their minds set on what the Spirit desires" (v. 5). He then adds this powerful reminder: "And if the Spirit of him who raised Jesus from the dead is living in you, he who raised Christ from the dead will also give life to your mortal bodies because of his Spirit who lives in you" (v. 11). The Holy Spirit makes you more like Christ by living in your heart. That's the secret for your spiritual victory!

Paul found a great metaphor in horticulture for the way God works in us. Trees that produce good fruit do not strive daily toward a goal of fruit bearing. They draw water and healthy nutrients from fertile soil, aim their leaves toward the sun, and produce good fruit as a byproduct. Fruit grows naturally, as God intended. Likewise, believers display the fruit of the Spirit as a byproduct of an intimate relationship with God the Father, through God the Son, mediated by God the Spirit. Spiritual fruit grows naturally as we live totally committed to God. "But the fruit of the Spirit is love, joy, peace, forbearance, kindness, goodness, faithfulness, gentleness and self-control. Against such things there is no law. Those who belong to Christ Jesus have crucified the flesh with its passions and desires. Since we live by the Spirit, let us keep in step with the Spirit" (Gal. 5:22–25).

The writer of the book of Hebrews summarized a daily plan for us to cooperate with God's desire for our lives. The plan calls for a simple exercise: "fixing our eyes on Jesus, the pioneer and perfecter of our faith. For the joy set before him he endured the cross, scorning its shame, and sat down at the right hand of the throne of God" (Heb. 12:2). We keep our eyes laser-focused on Jesus throughout each day. Social media and a thousand other distractions threaten to draw our attention away from him and onto mundane matters. We live in a world of short attention spans and voracious appetites for the latest viral internet story. New attention getters call for our daily participation. We must resist their beautifully tuned voices as we keep our eyes fixed on Jesus. Only then can the Holy Spirit work unhindered in our lives. That is the Father's greatest desire for us, and the only way we can escape the alluring draw of the world.

Conclusion

Some people regard the Bible as a disjointed conglomeration of sixty-six documents written in a variety of languages by all sorts of authors across 1,500 years of time. The final book of the New Testament was written nearly 2,000 years ago. We live in a fast-paced culture with a level of global connectedness that is unparalleled in human history. The advent of artificial intelligence promises a level of intellectual sophistication that will supercharge the information revolution. Modern prophets see a new golden age of humanity on the horizon. The more we hear about this golden age the more it sounds like a particular Bible verse: "Then they said, 'Come, let us build ourselves a city, with a tower that reaches to the heavens, so that we may make a name for ourselves'" (Gen. 11:4). The tower of Babel represented one more monument by humanity intended to display their self-sufficient idolatry.

God has always desired the best for his children. Everything we have learned about God through the revelation of himself to us across the centuries of human history tells us that he is always working to redeem us, provide for us, correct us, direct us, and—in short—live in intimate relationship with us. Ultimately, he plans to bring us to live with him in his eternal home. Like the person who won the sweepstakes at the beginning of chapter 6, our only requirement is to accept his free gift, surrender ourselves completely to his will, and allow him to fill us with his Spirit. Everyone who does that will see his plan for their life come together for our good and his glory.

Reflection Questions

1. What new information did you learn in this chapter about God?

2. Why did God continue to be so faithful and patient with the descendants of Abraham and Sarah when they failed so frequently to serve him?

3. How has God's work in your life been a realization of his desires for all his children?

4. How would you explain the mission of God to someone who has not heard of it?

5. Why does our all-powerful God invite his children to participate in his mission to the world?

6. How is Christlikeness a byproduct of an intimate relationship with God?

7. How do believers participate in the divine nature according to 2 Peter 1:3–4?

8. Explain in your own words what Irenaeus meant when he said, "God became what we are so that we may become what God is."

9. How does participating in the means of grace make us more Christlike?

10. How does commitment to the community of faith make us more Christlike?

TEN	# With God in Our Eternal Home

Reflect back on a time in your childhood or teen years when your parent or guardian made a promise to you. It might be a promise as small as a candy bar for doing extra chores around the house or as big as a full day of adventure for making good grades. Remember how you felt about your parent or guardian when the promise became reality. Perhaps you felt justified in trusting them to honor their word; perhaps your trust in them grew stronger with the reminder that they keep their promises. You probably filed that memory in the back of your mind and recalled it the next time this person promised you something. Trust in promise keepers grows through the give and take of daily life.

The Divine Promise Keeper

We called attention in the previous chapter to a reminder that appears more than eighty times in the Bible: "With a mighty hand the LORD brought us [Israelites] out of Egypt, from the house of slavery" (Exod. 13:14). Hebrew leaders reminded their people of this miraculous event not to call attention to the deliverance but to focus attention on the One who delivered them, their divine Promise Keeper. Notice that the repetition of this familiar phrase first occurred immediately after their deliverance from slavery. Each time a Hebrew leader recalled God's deliverance, ancestors looked back into their shared history. Leaders were not challenging their people to score well on a history exam. Rather, they wanted the entire Hebrew nation to trust their Promise Keeper to continue looking after them in an immediate crisis as well as into the distant future, just as he had done in the past.

Joseph clearly understood that God had been orchestrating events throughout his entire life (see Gen. 50:20). He also could look back to the faithfulness of God in keeping his promises to Abraham, Isaac, and his father, Jacob. Because of this, he lived in the confidence that God would continue to watch over the Hebrew nation and someday return them from Egypt to the promised land. "Then Joseph said to his brothers, 'I am about to die. But God will surely come to your aid and take you up out of this land to the land he promised on oath to Abraham, Isaac and Jacob'" (Gen. 50:24). God kept his promise of deliverance four hundred years later at a time that was exactly perfect for his purposes.

God made promises to Abraham, Isaac, Jacob, Moses, David, and a host of others down through the history of the Israelites. More importantly, he kept those promises. The reminder of God's past faithfulness supported his people as they looked forward to God's faithfulness in the future. The Israelites knew they could always trust in their divine Promise Keeper.

Thousands of years have passed since God entered into contracts with Abraham and delivered the Hebrew nation from Egyptian slavery. Generations have come and gone. We now live in the twenty-first century. Does this ancient history relate to our daily lives in any meaningful way? It absolutely does. Believers today have received a sacred heritage of all the saints who have gone before us in Old Testament days, New Testament days, and the past two thousand years of church history. Much has changed in the last three millennia. However, the divine Promise Keeper to the saints has not changed; he continues his faithfulness to every generation.

In the chapters of this book, we have learned that God lovingly created humanity and provided for their every need in a perfect environment. He desired only the best for them. He refused to give up on them when they used their free will to break his rule and his heart. From that day until this very day, God has worked in incredible ways to redeem us from sin, provide for our needs, relate to us as a heavenly parent, correct us when we need it, and prepare us for eternity. He gives us every reason to trust him, not only for our present needs but also for every need we will encounter to the end of our earthly lives. Beyond that, God, our divine Promise Keeper, can be trusted to bring us safely to our eternal home with him. Let us now look at what lies ahead in our eternal future.

Glimpses of Heaven

An understanding of the afterlife remained primarily a mystery throughout the Old Testament. Those who worshiped and served the God of the Bible believed he lived in heaven. However, they did not try to imagine a location of God's dwelling or exactly what would happen to them after they died. In spite of their lack of details related to heaven, those who trusted God had full confidence that they would be with him someday. Notice the last verse of one of the most popular psalms: "Surely your goodness and love will follow me all the days of my life, and I will dwell in the house of the LORD forever" (23:6).[1]

The incarnation of Jesus Christ in our world greatly expanded our understanding of heaven. The New Testament writings bring us many new insights. However, even with all we learned from Jesus, we still have many unanswered questions. Jesus told us enough to enable us to make adequate preparation to join him when the time comes but not enough to satisfy our endless curiosity. Paul characterized it well: "For now we see only a reflection as in a mirror; then we shall see face to face. Now I know in part; then I shall know fully, even as I am fully known" (1 Cor. 13:12). Paul echoed the words of Isaiah 64:4 as he spoke of the wisdom we receive from the Holy Spirit in order to understand God's plan of salvation: "However, as it is written: 'What no eye has seen, what no ear has heard, and what no human mind has conceived'—the things God has prepared for those who love him" (1 Cor. 2:9). God has offered the ultimate promise of the incredible

---

1. See also Job 19:25–27; Pss. 16:9–11; 49:15; 73:23–24; Isa. 26:19; and Dan. 12:2.

blessings awaiting those whom God welcomes into his eternal home. We will now consider this promise of being in heaven with God in several places.

God's Dwelling Place

When we are getting to know someone new, it is common to ask about where they live. Depending on the conversation and the person, we might merely be asking about a country, a state, or a city. Or we might be asking about a specific part of town, neighborhood, or particular address. Where someone lives provides us with important information about who they are. Then, when we actually see where they live, and can observe how they care for their property, how they decorate, and how they use the different features of their home, we learn more about who they are. Likewise, when we look at God's home, we learn more about him.

The Bible locates God in heaven as a special dwelling place. "Look down from heaven, your holy dwelling place, and bless your people Israel" (Deut. 26:15). "Hear the supplication of your servant and of your people Israel when they pray toward this place. Hear from heaven, your dwelling place, and when you hear, forgive" (1 Kings 8:30). The psalmists often referred to heaven as God's dwelling place. Here is one example: "The LORD has established his throne in heaven, and his kingdom rules over all" (Ps. 103:19).[2] Isaiah conveyed the following message to his people: "This is what the LORD says: 'Heaven is my throne, and the earth is my footstool'" (Isa. 66:1).

Old Testament references to heaven as God's dwelling place came with few details. Ezekiel offers one of the most spectacular images of God in his heavenly home. The prophet encountered God in an unusual way. He would never have expected to see God in this place. The Babylonians had deported him and most of his fellow citizens nine hundred miles away from home. How could Ezekiel hope to see God in this unclean, pagan land? Yet, in the midst of the disappointment and loss of exile, "the heavens were opened and I saw visions

---

2. See also Pss. 14:2; 20:6; 33:13; 57:3; and 113:5.

of God" (Ezek. 1:1). Read the encounter for yourself in Ezekiel 1. God did not appear in a burning bush or at a worship center; he came in a windstorm. Ezekiel's descriptions of God's dwelling place sound spectacular, maybe even bizarre. That is because heavenly sights cannot be captured in earthly words. Ezekiel's vision clarified the reality that, even if we do not always see God, God always sees us from his heavenly vantage point because he sees everything. He sees, *and* he cares. He reigns over all creation as our high and awesome heavenly Father.

Firsthand information about this otherworldly place came with the incarnation of Jesus Christ. Jesus affirmed that our heavenly Father lives in a place called heaven: "Let your light shine before others, that they may see your good deeds and glorify your Father in heaven" (Matt. 5:16).[3] Jesus went on to say the Father sits on a throne in heaven (see Matt. 5:34). Ten days after Jesus's resurrection, he gave final instructions to his disciples, and then, "While he was blessing them, he left them and was taken up into heaven" (Luke 24:51). Paul tells us that Jesus now sits at the right hand of the Father in heaven (see Eph. 1:20). God gave Stephen a glimpse into this reality as persecutors stoned him to death for his faith: "'Look,' he said, 'I see heaven open and the Son of Man standing at the right hand of God'" (Acts 7:56). In short, the Bible tells us that heaven is the Father's home and that Jesus is currently there with him.

Our Future Home

Jesus comforted his disciples on his last night with them following their Last Supper together. He knew they found his words frightening and mysterious, so he gave them a brief glimpse into not only what he would be doing when he returned to his Father in heaven but also how his work related to them and to us. "Do not let your hearts be troubled. You believe in God; believe also in me. My Father's house has many rooms; if that were not so, would I have told you that I am going there to prepare a place for you? And if I go and pre-

___
3. See also Matt. 10:32; 18:14; and 23:9.

pare a place for you, I will come back and take you to be with me that you also may be where I am" (John 14:1–3).

We now have a promise from Jesus that we will abide eternally in our Father's house, prepared for us by Jesus himself. Jesus only said what the Father commanded him to say, so this promise is from the Father (see John 12:49). God reminded the Corinthian believers through Paul that "we have a building from God, an eternal house in heaven, not built by human hands" (2 Cor. 5:1). Through Peter, God promised that we have "an inheritance that can never perish, spoil or fade. This inheritance is kept in heaven for you" (1 Peter 1:4). So heaven—kept for us by God himself—is now our home as well.

God's Throne in Heaven

Our insight into specific features of heaven remains limited. Believers have sung songs throughout church history about heaven. Some of them visualize streets of gold, city gates of rare gems and pearls, mansions, crowns, and rewards beyond our wildest imaginations. However, these earthly symbols of highly treasured items fall quickly into the background when we remember the most defining reality of heaven. The definition of heaven means simply being in the presence of God. Once we step in his presence, nothing else will matter. We will agree with the psalmist; just let us dwell in his house with him forever (see Ps. 23:6).

The focal point of John's vision of heaven in Revelation 4 was God's throne and the worshipers around it. The throne of God is important in John's vision and is mentioned forty times in Revelation. Much of the imagery in Revelation has symbolic value but is difficult to visualize. Do not get frustrated if you have trouble unpacking the images. We will offer possible explanations for some of them. Take some time to read Revelation 4 yourself. Then let's consider some of these images that tell us more about who God is.

John found it difficult to translate into mere words what God revealed to him in his visions. Imagine standing at the most beautiful place you have ever been in God's natural world, and trying to describe it to a friend who isn't there with you and can't see it. Your words will never adequately capture what you are seeing. John had the same problem. He did his best to describe for his audience the glory of God radiating from his presence.

God's throne symbolizes ultimate and complete authority over all creation. The precious stones and rainbow symbolize the incredible glory of God. The thunder and lightning symbolize God's power, glory, and presence. In the Old Testament, rough seas brought fear and danger to sailors. Smooth water brought peace to their lives. The sea as smooth as a piece of glass and as clear as crystal symbolizes God's greatness and power to dispel fear and bring perfect peace. The four living creatures symbolize all of God's created beings praising him continually. Their praise rings out across heaven: "'Holy, holy, holy is the Lord God Almighty,' who was, and is, and is to come" (Rev. 4:8). They remind us that God's holiness best describes his essence. The repetition of the word "holy" affirms God's transcendence, separateness from creation, and purity from all unrighteousness. Worshipers around the throne affirm that God reigns eternal; all else in creation is subordinate to him; therefore, all bow before him in humility. God alone is worthy of all glory, honor, and power.

We learn much about the God we serve by imagining through the vision of John how incredibly indescribable God's throne is. We must continually remind ourselves that this is not a fairy tale like we read in children's books. This is an on-the-scene reporter offering us a preview of the indescribable glory of God in all his righteousness.

Hymns in Heaven

Think for a moment about the importance of music in our lives. Many of us surround ourselves daily with music. And even if we don't, we often hear it playing in public places when we leave our homes or places of work. We also attend worship services where we listen to and sing songs about our faith in God. Music plays an important role in our lives, both in and away from formal worship. It comes as no surprise, then, that we will hear music as we arrive at our eternal home.

Revelation 7 visualizes how those who have been redeemed by the blood of Christ Jesus respond as they join in heavenly worship: "And they cried out in a loud voice: 'Salvation belongs to our God, who sits on the throne, and to the Lamb'" (v. 10). Then the prophets and martyrs who served God faithfully join in the praise (see Rev. 10:1–11:14). In John's vision, everyone came to attention as the angel sounded the trumpet, and the entire assembly of worshipers joined together in a mighty song of praise: "The kingdom of the world has become the kingdom of our Lord and of his Messiah, and he will reign for ever and ever" (Rev. 11:15). When you think about it, this is not new information. The kingdoms of this world have always belonged to God. This hymn of praise proclaims to everyone that our God is sovereign over all creation and the only one worthy of worship.[4]

Think of all the great kingdoms and empires throughout biblical history: the Philistines, Babylonians, Assyrians, Persians, Egyptians, Romans, and so many more. Citizens were often required to honor their supreme kings, emperors, and pharaohs as gods. All of those kingdoms fell in time, and their supreme leaders died like every other human being. God gave Daniel a vision of the final day of all the kingdoms of this world (see Dan. 7:9–14). The vision began with a magnificent display of the glory and splendor of God's heavenly throne. Then the mighty kingdom of this world was destroyed. The vision concluded with this powerful image: "There before me was one like a son of man, coming with the clouds of heaven. He approached the Ancient of Days and was led into his presence. He was given authority, glory and sovereign power; all nations and peoples of every language worshiped him. His dominion is an everlasting dominion that will not pass away, and his kingdom is one that will never be destroyed" (vv. 13–14).

This heavenly hymn of praise sung in Revelation 11 reminds all creation that the kingdoms of this world are now bowing to the kingdom of our God, who reigns forever! John's vision sounds like Paul's announcement to the Philippian believers: "Therefore God exalted him to the highest place

---

4. See ideas for this hymn in Ps. 145:13; Dan. 2:44; 7:14, 27; Mic. 4:7; Zech. 14:9.

God's holiness best describes
his essence.

and gave him the name that is above every name, that at the name of Jesus every knee should bow, in heaven and on earth and under the earth, and every tongue acknowledge that Jesus Christ is Lord, to the glory of God the Father" (Phil. 2:9–11).

We learn something else about God from a hymn sung in Revelation 12:10–12. The song reminds all creation that God is more powerful than Satan. Satan tempts, torments, and accuses believers for a season, but God limits his days of opposition. Believers must always persevere through the trials and temptations of the evil one because they triumph over him "by the blood of the Lamb and by the word of their testimony" (Rev. 12:11). God always reigns victorious over sin, evil, and schemes to deceive the hearts of all humanity. God brings ultimate salvation for those who accept his offer. He alone has complete power and authority over his creation.

Another hymn fills the heavenly air in Revelation 15. This hymn of God's faithfulness to his children resounds from the voices of all who have chosen him as their Lord and Savior. Listen to the words of praise sung to our God: "Great and marvelous are your deeds, Lord God Almighty. Just and true are your ways, King of the nations. Who will not fear you, Lord, and bring glory to your name? For you alone are holy. All nations will come and worship before you, for your righteous acts have been revealed" (Rev. 15:3–4).[5] This hymn declares how great God is, how involved he is in our world, how just and true he is, and how sovereign he is over the nations. Furthermore, he is holy, righteous, and uniquely worthy of all our praise.

John's visions of music ringing out in heaven from all creatures in praise to our God tells us that someday we will take our place in the heavenly choir singing with the angels, heavenly beings, and redeemed of all the ages. The good news is that we do not have to wait until we arrive in heaven to begin our songs of praise to God. We can sing praises to the One who is worthy of all our worship throughout our daily routine. We ought to surround our minds and ears with music

---

5. See ideas for this hymn in Deut. 32:4; Jer. 10:7; Pss. 86:9; 98:2; and 111:2–3.

that brings glory, honor, and praise to our Lord and Savior. John's vision calls us to lean into our eternal life every day that we remain on earth.

The New Jerusalem

The city of Jerusalem has represented a special place in salvation history since the day King David set up the worship tabernacle within its walls. God gave Moses and the Hebrew people the tabernacle to symbolize his presence with them as they journeyed through the wilderness and then settled into the promised land. King Solomon replaced the tabernacle with a magnificent temple that continued to represent the presence of God in their midst.

The idea of Jerusalem as the city of God takes on new significance as God gives John a preview of things to come at the end of time. Revelation 21 tells us that a day is coming when God will make all things new with a new heaven and a new earth. The most striking revelation in this vision is that we do not travel somewhere in space to reach our heavenly home with God; rather, God will bring the holy city, the new Jerusalem, to earth. A loud voice from the throne proclaimed, "Look! God's dwelling place is now among the people, and he will dwell with them. They will be his people, and God himself will be with them and be their God" (Rev. 21:3). Just like the garden before the fall, God will walk with us. Our awesome, amazing, holy God chooses to be with his redeemed creation.

Revelation 21 and 22 offer specific details about the new Jerusalem where God welcomes us to live in his presence forever. We do not have time to consider each of these details. Take time to read these two chapters and listen for the voice of the Holy Spirit directing you to make all necessary preparations to be present on the day of the holy city's arrival in our world.

Some of the insights about the new Jerusalem further expand our understanding of who God is. First, the Holy City does not have a temple where we go to worship God "because the Lord God Almighty and the Lamb are its temple" (Rev.

21:22). The new earth does not need a sun or moon because light emanates from the glory of God and the Lamb.

Second, God began life on earth for humans in a garden that had a river flowing through it to maintain life; God's eternal city also has a garden and a river. The river of the water of life flows directly from God's throne and provides life-giving water to all living things. This imagery assures God's constant supply of every need for life. The imagery reminded John's original audience of the ancient walled cities in Old Testament days that had water sources, such as a well or a stream, within their walls to assure life-giving water when under siege. God also planted the tree of life from the garden of Eden on the banks of the river of life. The fruit of that tree is no longer forbidden as in the days of Adam and Eve. We may now enjoy its life-giving fruit that grows fresh and ready to be picked. As we have seen over and over, God provides for the needs of his children.

Third, God invites his children to see him face to face. Throughout the Old Testament, the Israelites were not allowed to see the face of God. They understood that looking into his face would result in immediate death (see Exod. 33:20; Judg. 13:22). Only Jesus Christ, the Son of the Father, could see his face (see John 1:18; 1 John 4:12). Now God invites the redeemed to look directly into his face. That means we will experience the presence and power of God to the fullest capacity of our resurrected bodies. That sight alone will make heaven worth it all! This imagery tells us that God invites us into a deeper relationship with him that will be far superior to anything we can experience in this life. God wants us to know him just as we are known by him.

Fourth, God does two things to identify us as completely his. He writes our names in his Lamb's book of life (see Rev. 21:27), and he writes his name on our foreheads (see Rev. 22:4). Those whose names are written in the book of life have eternal life. God's name on the foreheads of the redeemed affirms his special possession and permission to bask in his presence as we honor and worship him in the new Jerusalem. God is a jealous God who guards his own.

Conclusion

Genesis 1–2 paints a beautiful picture of God's grand design for his creation. We have discussed many features of God's desires for creation and our place in it. This chapter has brought us full circle back to chapter 3, where God set his desires in motion as he outlined his plan for the salvation of his creation. We have explored the full sweep of all God has done for humanity in the salvation he offers every generation from Adam and Eve to today.

God has done an incredible job revealing himself to us. Scholars call it a progressive revelation because our understanding has steadily grown throughout time. It was not until the ministry of Jesus Christ that we learned that God is our Father, Jesus is his Son, and the Holy Spirit lives in believers' hearts. That awareness sheds new light on the God of the Old Testament, particularly the knowledge that we love and serve a heavenly Father. Finally, we shared what can be understood regarding how it will be with God—our heavenly Father—throughout eternity. We have attempted to explore who God is, with a focus on God as Father, through the pages of this book. Our hope is that it has expanded, and perhaps even changed, your image of God the Father as he exists within the Trinity.

Reflection Questions

1. What new information did you learn in this chapter about God?

2. Why is it important for believers to review all the promises God has kept throughout the Bible as we walk with him into our unknown future?

3. What excites you the most as you think about the Bible's description of heaven?

4. Why does God's presence provide the clearest understanding of heaven?

5. How does the description of God's heavenly throne encourage your faith?

6. Why are hymns so important to heavenly worship of God?

7. What are the ways that life in the new Jerusalem will differ from life on earth now?

8. How is the New Jerusalem like the garden of Eden, and how does Revelation 21–22 bring the biblical narrative back to Genesis 1–2?

9. Why does God place his name on the foreheads of the redeemed?

10. How does your hope of heaven influence the way you live for God now?

Afterword

A Final Invitation

Jesus Christ said throughout his earthly ministry, "Whoever has ears to hear, let them hear" (Luke 8:8). He speaks to us through the revelation to his servant John with one final invitation. Who is this Jesus? He identifies himself as "the Alpha and the Omega, the First and the Last, the Beginning and the End" (Rev. 22:13). He encompasses all reality from beginning to end and everything in between. He is our Messiah, "the Root and the Offspring of David, and the bright Morning Star" (Rev. 22:16). His invitation comes with an important declaration: "Look, I am coming soon!" (Rev. 22:7, 12). The writer to the Hebrews repeated the urgency of this invitation: "Today, if you hear his voice, do not harden your hearts" (Heb. 3:7–8, 15; 4:7).[1] Why the urgency? Because the days of this earth are limited. Jesus spoke about the end times with this important reminder: "But about that day or hour no one knows" (Matt. 24:36). Besides that, none of us is promised tomorrow or even the rest of today. We must live ready, as in Jesus's parable of the ten virgins (see Matt. 25:1–13).

John echoes Jesus's final invitation with four pleas of his own: "The Spirit and the bride say, 'Come!' And let the one who hears say, 'Come!' Let the one who is thirsty come; and let the one who wishes take the free gift of the water of life" (Rev. 22:17). God loves us more than we may ever know. Therefore, he pleads with us to make the right choice. We

---

1. Psalm 95:7–8 reminds the Hebrew nation of the original source of this invitation during their journey from Egypt to the promised land.

must also urge family members, friends, and everyone to whom God leads us to join us in making the right choice. Revelation 22:20 seems to open a window into the wooing heart of Jesus, who reminds us one last and final time in Scripture, "Yes, I am coming soon." We affirm with John, "Amen. Come, Lord Jesus."

A Final Thought for Those Who Have Accepted Christ as Savior

We live in a unique time in salvation history. We feel the tension between what God has already revealed about himself to us and what we will learn about him when we get to heaven. This time in between what we often call "the already and the not yet" sometimes reminds us of waiting for the delayed arrival of a loved one. Minutes pass like hours as we stare at the clock, hoping that somehow our anxious anticipation will hurry the arrival of our friends or family members. We repeat John's longing: "Come, Lord Jesus." Then we remember that none of God's saints throughout Bible days or church history idly waited for God to fulfill his promises to them.[2] They remained engaged in the tasks God gave them as they lived into the calling he placed on their lives.

Living faithfully today in a loving relationship with God the Father, Son, and Holy Spirit sometimes resembles the struggles the saints of God have experienced throughout history. They encountered difficult circumstances, opposition, and suffering. Yet, in every situation, God's unfailing love sustained them. The writer to the Hebrews said it well: "The world was not worthy of them" (11:38). Then Hebrews draws us into the narrative with an unusual observation. In speaking of the saints of the Bible, the writer says, "These were all commended for their faith, yet none of them received what had been promised, since God had planned something better *for us* so that only together *with us* would they be made perfect" (vv. 39–40, emphasis added).

---

2. Paul spoke about such idleness in 2 Thessalonians 3:6–15.

The unconditional, steadfast love of God draws us into the story. God did not complete his desires for humanity with saints of old. Believers in the twenty-first century continue the tradition and work with God toward the fulfillment of his original desires for creation. The word "perfect" in Hebrews 11:40 refers to God's fulfilling all his promises throughout Scripture and bringing everything together to reach his original goal. On that great day, all of God's children will be safely home with him. Origen, the first theologian in church history, explained it well: "You see, therefore, that Abraham is still waiting to obtain the perfect things. Isaac waits, and Jacob and all the prophets wait for us, that they may lay hold of the perfect blessedness with us."[3] Therein lies our challenge.

We must live in an intimate relationship with God the Father, Son, and Holy Spirit on a daily basis, participate in the means of grace, and remain closely involved in a community of faith. Paul reminded us that time passes more quickly than we sometimes think: "Our salvation is nearer now than when we first believed." (Rom. 13:11). With that ever before us, "let us not become weary in doing good, for at the proper time we will reap a harvest if we do not give up" (Gal. 6:9). May God bless you as you remain faithful to him, share in his mission to the world, and eagerly anticipate the day we all stand together and see him face to face!

---

3. Quoted in Kevin L. Anderson, *Hebrews: A Commentary in the Wesleyan Tradition,* New Beacon Bible Commentary (Kansas City, MO: Beacon Hill Press of Kansas City, 2013), 314.

Bibliography

Anderson, Kevin L. *Hebrews: A Commentary in the Wesleyan Tradition.* New Beacon Bible Commentary. Kansas City, MO: Beacon Hill Press of Kansas City, 2013.

Branson, Robert D., ed. *Global Wesleyan Encyclopedia of Biblical Theology.* Kansas City, MO: The Foundry Publishing, 2020.

Church of the Nazarene. *Manual: 2023.* Kansas City, MO: Nazarene Publishing House, 2023.

Coleson, Joseph. *Genesis 1–11: A Commentary in the Wesleyan Tradition.* New Beacon Bible Commentary. Kansas City, MO: Beacon Hill Press of Kansas City, 2012.

Dawkins, Richard. *The God Delusion.* London: Bantam Press, 2006.

Geisler, Norman L. and Frank Turek. *I Don't Have Enough Faith to Be an Atheist.* Wheaton, IL: Crossway Books, 2004.

Green, Stephen. *Deuteronomy: A Commentary in the Wesleyan Tradition.* New Beacon Bible Commentary. Kansas City, MO: Beacon Hill Press of Kansas City, 2016.

Harper, Albert F., ed. *The Wesley Bible: A Personal Study Bible for Holy Living.* Nashville: Thomas Nelson Publishers, 1990.

Holiness Today. "Nazarene Essentials: Who We Are—What We Believe." March/April 2015. Vol. 17, No. 2.

Holiness Today. "One Lord, One Faith, One Baptism: Essential Teaching for Faith Formation in the Church of the Nazarene." July/August 2017. Vol. 19, No. 4.

Lewis, C. S. *Miracles.* New York: Macmillan Publishing Co, 1947.

Miller, Rachelle. "To Know." *Reflecting God.* April 5, 2024.

Moore, Frank. *Breaking Free from Sin's Grip: Holiness Defined for a New Generation.* Kansas City, MO: Beacon Hill Press of Kansas City, 2001.

Noble, Tom. "God the Father." *Holiness Today.* May/June 2020. Vol. 22, No. 3.

Pokrifka, H. Junia. *Exodus: A Commentary in the Wesleyan Tradition.* New Beacon Bible Commentary. Kansas City, MO: Beacon Hill Press of Kansas City, 2018.

Powell, Samuel M. *The Trinity.* The Wesleyan Theology Series. Kansas City, MO: The Foundry Publishing, 2020.

Romey, Kristin. "Ancient Mass Child Sacrifice May Be World's Largest." *National Geographic.* April 26, 2018.

Snow, Robert S. and Arseny Ermakov. *Matthew: A Commentary in the Wesleyan Tradition.* New Beacon Bible Commentary. Kansas City, MO: Beacon Hill Press of Kansas City, 2019.

Truesdale, Al, ed. *Global Wesleyan Dictionary of Theology.* Kansas City, MO: Beacon Hill Press of Kansas City, 2013.

Varughese, Alex, ed. and Robert D. Branson, Jim Edlin, and Tim Green. *Discovering the Old Testament: Story and Faith.* Kansas City, MO: Beacon Hill Press of Kansas City, 2003.

Varughese, Alex and Christina Bohn. *Genesis 12–50: A Commentary in the Wesleyan Tradition.* New Beacon Bible Commentary. Kansas City, MO: Beacon Hill Press of Kansas City, 2019.

Wiley, H. Orton. *Christian Theology.* Vol. 1. Kansas City, MO: Beacon Hill Press, 1940.

www.ingramcontent.com/pod-product-compliance
Lightning Source LLC
Chambersburg PA
CBHW070038100426
42740CB00013B/2720